T0055947

THE MECHANICAL HORSE

Discovering America

Mark Crispin Miller, Series Editor

This series begins with a startling premise—that even now, more than two hundred years since its founding, America remains a largely undiscovered country with much of its amazing story yet to be told. In these books, some of America's foremost historians and cultural critics bring to light episodes in our nation's history that have never been explored. They offer fresh takes on events and people we thought we knew well and draw unexpected connections that deepen our understanding of our national character.

The Mechanical Horse

HOW THE BICYCLE RESHAPED AMERICAN LIFE

MARGARET GUROFF

University of Texas Press
Austin

Printed in the United States of America
First edition, 2016
First paperback printing, 2018

Requests for permission to reproduce material
from this work should be sent to:
Permissions
University of Texas Press
P.O. Box 7819
Austin, TX 78713-7819
http://utpress.utexas.edu/index.php/rp-form

The paper used in this book meets the minimum requirements of
ANSI/NISO Z39.48-1992 (R1997) (Permanence of Paper). ♾

Design by Lindsay Starr

Library of Congress Cataloging-in-Publication Data

Guroff, Margaret, 1962– author.
The mechanical horse : how the bicycle reshaped American life /
Margaret Guroff. — First edition.
pages cm. — (Discovering America)
Includes bibliographical references and index.
ISBN 978-1-4773-1587-3 (paper : alk. paper) —
ISBN 978-1-4773-0814-1 (library e-book) —
ISBN 978-1-4773-0815-8 (nonlibrary e-book)
1. Bicycles—United States—History. 2. Cycling—Social aspects—
United States. I. Title. II. Series: Discovering America series.
TL410.G78 2016
303.48'320973—dc23
2015033562

doi:10.7560/743625

In memory of my father and my mother

CONTENTS

INTRODUCTION

The Porsche is mad. I am biking down Wisconsin Avenue in Georgetown on my way to work, slipping past stopped cars at every light. Lane splitting like this is legal in DC, but the guy in the pewter-gray sports car apparently doesn't know that. When his light turns green, he honks as he speeds past me to the next red, where he angles his car to the right to block my path. Naturally, and legally, I pass him on the left.

Next light, same deal. And when I pass him the second time, his window is down.

"You're driving like a maniac," he yells at me. Me, a scrawny-ish, bespectacled lady averaging ten miles an hour. *I'm* the maniac?

I'd like to stop and argue, but that would cause a jam, so I just mutter, "*You* are," and slide by.

That was the last time I saw that particular road-rager—bikes are faster than cars at rush hour, as I hope he glumly realized—but I encounter his ilk often enough. Driving an automobile in heavy traffic can be infuriating, and even though the main thing that slows cars down is all the other cars, a few drivers fixate on cyclists as the problem. Roads are for cars, these drivers think (and sometimes holler): the bike is like a pesky little brother who needs to stay on the sidewalk and out of the way.

There are a couple of problems with that perception. For one thing, cyclists are not allowed on many downtown sidewalks. For another, bikes were on the roads first. Though 125 years of technological progress have obscured this fact, it is actually the car that is the baby brother. Not only did bikes precede cars, but it was bikers who successfully agitated to pave the country's dirt roads, at a time when cars were only dreamt of. And during that nineteenth-century "good roads" movement, bike makers pioneered mass-production techniques that later made the US auto industry possible.

When you look into the bicycle's history, you begin to see its impact all over American culture. It changed women's clothing, helping do away with the restrictive corsets to which they had long been sentenced. It changed people's attitudes toward health and fitness, demonstrating that a little sweat wouldn't kill you . . . and might actually save your life. In fact, much of what looks like America to us—our consumer culture, our air travel, our mobility, both physical and social—was strongly influenced by the bike. The idea of a middle-class woman like me traveling alone, in a garment that barely covered her knees, was unthinkable until the bicycle. So, too, was the idea of that cushy Porsche.

Would there be motor vehicles and liberated women if not for the bike? In some way or other, sure, probably. But much of American history cannot be told as it happened without the bicycle leading the way.

Whenever I encounter an aggressive driver who thinks bikes are a nuisance on the road, I fantasize about us pulling over together so that I can drop some knowledge on them—not just about rights-of-way and the value of deep, cleansing breaths, but also about the historical respect due the bicycle, even if not to any particular cyclist. Alas, when these conflicts arise, the driver and I are usually both in a rush, and one of us always gets away.

So I am telling you.

The draisine—named for its inventor, Baron Karl von Drais of Mannheim, Germany—was propelled by the feet pushing off the ground. This copper etching, which appeared in the June 1819 issue of the *Analectic Magazine* in Philadelphia, was based on a color print in the February 1819 issue of the British publication *Ackermann's Repository of Arts*.

THE BIRTH OF THE BIKE

It was nearly 10:30 p.m., and the artificial horse was nowhere in sight. A reporter had heard that the miraculous new machine was coming, though, so he waited expectantly in Philadelphia's Washington Square, among fashionable citizens out for a stroll after a long day of rain. It was May 1819, and the park—planted with trees, laid out with pathways, and surrounded by a white picket fence—was lit by candle-lantern streetlights and a misty half-moon.

Suddenly, the beast appeared, urged forward by a rider making huge, swinging strides with his legs. It went fast, probably about six miles an hour, a typical runner's pace. In the early nineteenth century, no one traveled that fast easily for long without the help of a horse.

The fascinated reporter took off after the rider, but before he could get far, someone in the park shouted, "Here comes another!" and a second rider flashed by him "like lightning," the reporter wrote. "Having a great desire to examine this curious machine, I exerted myself to overtake it, and luckily as I was almost exhausted the rider stopped, but the crowd collected around him, so I could only get a faint idea of its construction."

This amazing vehicle was a draisine, the most direct ancestor of the bicycle. Though American newspapers had been writing about the European invention for months, the first one had appeared in Philadelphia only the previous week. Roughly the same height as a modern bike, the draisine consisted of two in-line, wagon-spoked wheels connected by a curving horizontal bar that acted as a frame. There was a tiller attached to the front wheel for steering, and a saddle in the center, but there were no pedals. Instead, a rider straddled the saddle, gripped the tiller, and propelled the draisine like a scooter. With each step, the rider pushed off against the ground, allowing the draisine to coast until it needed a push with the other leg. Those who first saw the machine in action compared it to ice skating on the road. A typical draisine could weigh fifty pounds or more, twice the weight of an average bicycle today, so there wasn't much coasting uphill. Downhill or on level ground, though, it could move.

The draisine had been invented two years earlier in Germany by its namesake, Karl von Drais, a civil servant whose well-connected father had arranged for his release from the daily duties of his job as a forester. Times were tough in Europe: the 1815 eruption of Mount Tambora in what is now Indonesia had kicked up a persistent dust cover over the Northern Hemisphere that significantly cooled parts of the continent, causing freezes throughout 1816—the so-called year without a summer—and famine beyond that. In 1817, a feed shortage in Germany forced the slaughter of many horses. And it was in this context that Drais invented his man-powered vehicle, a sort of substitute horse. Though it could not haul loads or power machines, as horses could, the draisine could carry a rider.

Drais first demonstrated the wooden machine in Mannheim in the summer of 1817, and before long he was selling plans for the devices, and German mechanics were building and selling knockoffs. In the following year, Drais patented the draisine in France, where it made a splash among the elite under the new name of "velocipede," constructed from the words for "swift" and "foot."

Crossing the channel to England, the draisine was revamped in 1818 by a London coach maker named Denis Johnson. With larger wheels and some iron parts in place of Drais's wooden ones, the machine was renamed a "hobby-horse" or "dandy charger," after the flamboyantly dressed young men who affected them.

In the United States, the draisine made its first public appearance in February 1819, when a musical-instrument maker in Maryland exhibited a specimen he had built based on a European drawing. The maker, James Stewart, advertised the device as "a new mode of travelling, combining the advantages of carriage, horse, and foot" and displayed it in Baltimore's Concert Hall, charging twenty-five cents admission, the equivalent of about $4.60 today. Originally open only during the day, the exhibit eventually added evening hours to accommodate the wives and children of men who had seen it.

One intrigued viewer was Philadelphia's Charles Willson Peale, a nationally famed artist and naturalist. The seventy-seven-year-old Peale, best known for painting portraits of George Washington and other Revolutionary War heroes, was also an avid amateur zoologist and paleontologist. Peale founded a private museum of science and curiosities that showcased a mastodon skeleton he had personally extracted piece by piece from a sloppy bog on a New York farm. (At its unveiling, the skeleton display was only the second fossil reconstruction in the world.)

In early 1819, Peale came out of artistic retirement to visit Washington, DC, and paint President James Monroe and other dignitaries. On the way home afterward, he stayed for several days in Baltimore, where he encountered the amazing mechanical horse. Peale wanted one.

After returning to his estate on the outskirts of Philadelphia, he found a British illustration of the draisine in a local shop and based the design of his own on it, hiring a blacksmith to make the machine from scrap iron taken from an old grain thresher. Peale deposited the machine in his museum, where it earned "a very considerable profit" in admission fees and inspired imitators, as he wrote to his son Rembrandt. "As soon as it was heard of, several of them appeared immediately, constructed in different manners of wood," he added.

Peale's iron draisine was one of the two "curious machines" that so fascinated the reporter that May night in Washington Square. And the riders were probably Peale's sons Rubens and Franklin, according to a letter Peale wrote a friend. The young men had likely liberated the iron draisine from its display after hours to show it off, along with a wooden one built by Franklin.

The draisine wasn't just a curiosity, though. It was a kind of jet pack in an immobile age. Even Peale's clunky metal specimen—which amounted to deadweight when pushed up a hill—flew downhill "like the very devil," as yet another son, Charles Linnaeus, put it to his baby brother Titian. (Among his other activities, Charles Willson Peale fathered seventeen children, naming most of the boys after artists.) Peale himself was too afraid of falling to coast down hills, but that summer he wrote of watching younger men on Franklin's wooden draisine tear down them "in a swiftness that dazzles the sight." The machines bumbled along fine on flat land, too, allowing riders to scoot and glide as fast as nine miles per hour, a horse's trot.

Only the well-to-do had the resources and leisure time to build or buy such machines, just as only the well-to-do could afford to keep horses. But the sight of draisine riders inspired predictions of a form of personal mobility that would be affordable to all. A newspaper reporter who had heard of a velocipede ride from Germantown—the site of Peale's estate, Belfield—to Philadelphia during the summer of 1819 wrote that "several grave and learned gentlemen" rode the eight miles "in as short a time as real horses could have done." That year saw a financial panic in the United States, and horse fodder was expensive, the reporter noted. "We should be happy to see these 'animals' introduced into this country. . . . Whilst oats are selling at sixty-two cents a bushel, it would be a serious saving to our Sunday equestrians."

During the rest of the year, a series of American cities picked up the velocipede fashion. Boston, New Haven, New York, Washington, DC, and Savannah saw the machines exhibited or rented by the day or month in public parks. Specimens were spotted as far west as Cincinnati, then a frontier boomtown. Newspapers were full of mentions. The sensation of balancing in a line by shifting body weight was new to most Americans—ice-skating being a seasonal pursuit for Northerners willing to risk breaking through the ice and drowning—and riding schools cropped up to serve the need. "A few lessons are sufficient to overcome the difficulties necessarily attendant on its novelty," wrote a New York newspaper contributor identified as Gymnasticus, "after which it is not only agreeable, but even fascinating."

But for all its fascination, the draisine died a quick death, both in the United States and in Europe. It is estimated that fewer than a thousand were ever made in this country, which had a population of more than nine million, and their use was restricted almost from the start after an outcry over collisions with pedestrians. In July 1819, for example, a New York man wrote to a newspaper about a four-year-old boy he had seen knocked down and injured by two fops riding velocipedes on the sidewalk. "Is it not enough to be annoyed by mud, dust, chimney sweeps, hogs, mad dogs, hot corn [that is, corn on the cob hawked by street urchins], and all the evils necessarily attendant on a great city like ours," he asked, "but that our peaceable citizens, our wives and our children, cannot enjoy a walk in the evening, without the danger of being run over by some of these new-created animals?" Within months, draisine riding was against the law on most American city sidewalks.

With sidewalks off-limits, you might think that riders would simply take to the roads, but in most places in America, that wasn't a realistic option. Most city streets weren't paved, and when they were, it was usually with cobblestones or bricks, which made for a bumpy ride. Not to mention the obstacle course created by horses and their droppings. Unpaved city streets were rutted and dusty in dry weather, gloppy after a rain.

In the countryside, it was even worse. More than 70 percent of the US population still lived on farms, and rural roads, where they existed, were notoriously bad, "hardly more than broad paths through the forest," according to a 1951 economic history. "In wet places, they presented a line of ruts with frequent mud holes, and, where dry, a powdered surface of deep dust." One early Ohio law decreed that stumps left in the road should be no more than one foot high. Coaches and wagons routinely got stuck in ditches and overturned or broke their axles, which made overland travel slow going; in 1813, a cargo wagon drawn by three horses was noted for taking only two weeks to make the trip from Boston to Philadelphia, "notwithstanding the wretched state of the roads," as a Baltimore business journal reported. Unless you had a hilly country estate to get around, as Peale did, you couldn't count on draisines for transportation. And if you had an estate, you also had horses to ride.

Then too, the heavy velocipede was a workout. The British cycle historian Cally Callomon has called it "the pogo stick of its day," more suited for recreation than transportation. As a horse substitute, therefore, it couldn't last. Within a year of its introduction in the United States, it had nearly disappeared, as it soon did in Britain. In May 1820, a wag rewrote Hamlet's soliloquy as

> To ride—or not to ride—that is the question—
> Whether 'tis nobler in the mind to flatter
> The whims and follies of outrageous fashion—
> Or to ride horseback, and not stride away
> On a Velocipede!

He published the poem in a Boston paper with the caveat that the velocipede was "not yet wholly obliterated from the minds of all," an admission that it had been forgotten by most. And even that poem, in the end, came down on the side of not riding the mechanical horse.

The word "velocipede" stayed in use during the following decades, referring to a series of three- or four-wheeled carriages that inventors fitted out with treadle or hand-lever drives, none particularly efficient. But the two-wheeled, human-powered vehicle was widely agreed to be a technological dead end.

Meanwhile, Americans continued to develop other ways of getting around. Some private highways were built starting in the 1790s; these were called "turnpikes" because of the pointed spikes that gatekeepers turned aside for travelers after their tolls were paid. And the federal government built a road from Maryland to Illinois to encourage westward development. But the quality of these roads varied. There was no such thing as asphalt pavement; some early turnpikes were built on solid stone, and others consisted of gravel or just dirt. In any event, turnpikes connected only certain cities. Elsewhere, rural roads tended to serve a few communities and then just stop, lending truth to what would later be a punch line: "You can't get there from here."

In America, the chief method of long-distance travel in the early nineteenth century was by water. Most trips between East Coast cities were from seaport to seaport, and in the continent's interior, rivers and lakes were the only paths to take; there were no connecting roads at all. (This is why Americans came to use the verb "to ship" for "to send a package.") Originally, traveling upstream meant rowing, sailing, or using poles as leverage against the river bottom, but steamboats—first invented in 1787—gained power and popularity early in the nineteenth century. By 1820, there were fifty steamboats operating on the Mississippi River, churning upstream at the unheard-of rate of ten miles an hour. That year, one small steamboat that began running regular trips on the Ohio River was named the *Velocipede*.

The river voyage from New Orleans to Cincinnati, which took ninety days before the use of steam power, "is now performed, with the greatest ease and safety, in eleven or twelve days," wrote one Englishman who made the trip in 1827. ("Safety" was a relative term: steamboat boilers routinely exploded, killing passengers and crew alike.) The speed of steamboat travel fit the restless American spirit, one French visitor wrote in 1835. The typical American "is devoured with a passion for locomotion, he cannot stay in one place," the visitor opined. "He is always disposed to emigrate, always ready to start in the first steamer that comes along."

Boats were getting faster, and water routes were multiplying. At around the same time as the draisine's brief appearance, America embarked on a frenzy of canal construction. Starting with the Erie Canal's groundbreaking in 1817, states and private investors began digging channels linking Atlantic Ocean tidewater areas to the Ohio and Mississippi Rivers and the Great Lakes. These new water avenues eased inland travel and vastly reduced the cost of bringing goods to market. Too narrow and shallow for early steamboats, canals were traversed by barges hitched to horses or mules that trudged along towpaths on the banks. In 1827, our English traveler continued from Cincinnati by stagecoach to Lake Erie, and from there by boat to New York City via the partially completed Erie Canal, which he described as "crowded with boats of considerable size, laden with the various produce of the western and northern states, and returning with numerous emigrants, moving westward with their families and effects." Starting with only about 100 miles of canals in 1816, the nation had developed more than 3,300 miles' worth by 1840.

And of course railroads entered the picture in 1830, when the Baltimore and Ohio opened its first thirteen miles of track. Built mainly by private investors, with liberal assistance from states, these transit lines developed in a scattering of short segments that, over time, began to connect and thereby threaten the primacy of water transit. Though rickety by modern standards, trains were often twice as fast as steamers, and they could operate year-round; boats were stymied by frozen winters in the North and parched summers in the West. By 1840, there were almost exactly as many miles of railroad track in the United States as there were of canals: more than 3,300. But while domestic canal construction never went much further—in part because most of the obvious connections between waterways had already been made—railroad builders kept laying track.

Even more than canals and steamboats, trains seemed to collapse the country's vast distances by shrinking the time it took to cross them. In 1859, a Boston writer predicted that the Adams Express Company would soon be able to send parcels from New Orleans to New York via rail in four days: "How much such extraordinary dispatch by the Adams Express will do to increase the trade and communication between the two great cities of the North and Southwest, it is impossible, of course, to estimate; but we look for wonders."

Just two years later, the Civil War severed trade and communication between North and South for four gruesome years and left many Southern cities and rail lines in ruins. But the perception that technology—including the telegraph, introduced in 1844—was shrinking distances and accelerating American life endured. People called the phenomenon "the annihilation of space and time."

In July 1865, a few months after the South surrendered at Appomattox, a French mechanic by the name of Pierre Lallement arrived in Brooklyn, bearing the parts of a machine that he had built in Paris. The seventy-pound device, which had wooden wheels and a wrought-iron spine, was very similar to an old-timey two-wheeled velocipede he had seen in France, but with one key addition: there were foot pedals attached to its front wheel. Lallement, a quiet, dark-haired, unibrowed young man, soon moved to Ansonia, Connecticut, for a factory job, and he continued tinkering with the device until it was ready for short rides to and from his workplace.

That fall, Lallement conducted a road test of about four and a half miles, pedaling the velocipede mostly uphill to the nearby village of Birmingham (now part of Derby) and then doubling back home to Ansonia. As he told a journalist twenty years later, his delight during one bumpy downhill stretch turned to panic when he realized that his brakeless vehicle was about to rear-end a horse-drawn wagon. He yelled a warning to the two men in the wagon, then veered and tumbled into a roadside culvert filled with water, cracking his head in the process. The terrified men, meanwhile, whipped their horses into a run and took off.

Lallement collected himself and rode to Ansonia's main street, where, drenched and bleeding, he stopped in a tavern. "There he found the two men," the journalist wrote, "relating between drinks how they had seen the dark Devil, with human head and body half like a snake, and half like a bird, just hovering above the ground which he seemed no way to touch, chase them down the hill." Lallement approached the men and, in his thick French accent, exclaimed, "I was the Devil!"

Lallement secured a US patent for the device in 1866, but wasn't able to attract a manufacturer, and he returned home to France in early 1868, leaving his velocipede behind. When he arrived in Paris, though, he discovered that others were making and selling a pedal-cranked velocipede very similar to the one he had left in the States. Worse yet, one of the manufacturers was claiming to have invented it. How this happened is still "murky," says David Herlihy, author of the indispensable 2004 book *Bicycle: The History*. Herlihy thinks it likely that one of the French maker's backers had seen Lallement riding his pedaled velocipede in Paris years before and decided to copy it.

Whatever happened, the French claimed ownership of the crank-propelled velocipede—by then also called a "bicycle," from the Latin word for "two" and the Greek word for "circle"—and a new craze erupted, both in Europe and in the United States. In the summer of 1868, the world-famous Hanlon Brothers acrobatic troupe included velocipede races in their act during a North American tour. Soon, American carriage makers, wheelwrights, and blacksmiths were producing them.

Americans greeted the pedal-cranked velocipede with the same shocked amazement as the two Connecticut men who had witnessed Lallement's diabolical downhill ride. Spectators filled Cincinnati's Pike's Music Hall for an exhibition race in January 1869, "all agog to fathom the mysteries of the wondrous bicycle," a local paper reported. Few people alive had seen the velocipede's predecessor of fifty years prior, the draisine, in action—and those who had seen it could understand how that old machine operated. This was different, though. A rider on a pedal-cranked velocipede could seemingly go for as long as he wanted without visible means of support. And going faster didn't make the machine wobblier, as one might expect; paradoxically, it made it steadier. As a reader wrote in a letter to *Scientific American* in 1868, "That a carriage or velocipede with but two wheels . . . should maintain an upright position is, to the superficial observer, one of the most surprising feats of practical mechanics."

Cycling rinks and academies cropped up across the country as the public clamored to learn how to ride. *Scientific American* diagnosed a "velocipede mania" and proclaimed that "walking is on its last legs." This, finally, was a machine for shrinking the city as earlier machines had shrunk the countryside.

"Space has been a sort of enemy to enterprise, and a great part of our energies has been devoted to what is called the annihilation of space," wrote the editors of a bicycle-industry magazine in early 1869. "To this end steamboats have been invented, railroads have been projected, which answer very well for the longer distances, where many miles have to be traversed, but for the shorter distances, up to the invention of the velocipede, we have had nothing adequate to our wants." Stagecoaches were crowded with germy strangers and didn't take you door-to-door, the editors added, and horses were expensive and couldn't be risked on slippery pavement. "The two-wheeled velocipede is the animal which is to supersede everything else."

Two

THE NEED FOR SPEED

At the same time that Americans felt the Earth shrinking, they saw their country expanding. Fifteen states joined the union between 1820 and 1870, including Texas and California. Also during that half century, a torrent of immigrants helped quadruple the country's population. And the development of railroads put huge swaths of the continent's interior within travelers' reach for the first time. Recalling a trip he took on America's first transcontinental rail line—which was completed in 1869—the novelist Robert Louis Stevenson described the vastness of the Nebraska plains. "The line of railway stretched from horizon to horizon, like a cue across a billiard-board; on either hand, the green plain ran till it touched the skirts of heaven," he wrote. "The train toiled over this infinity like a snail."

Americans' daily spheres were expanding, as well. Before 1820, people spent most of their time at home or near it—and most people's homes were working farms. Families made their own clothing, soap, candles, and other household necessities unless they could afford servants to do it for them. Craftsmen such as cobblers and blacksmiths made their wares in home workshops, and sawmills, flour mills, and other small industries pro-cessed raw materials for neighbors, sometimes using the labor of enslaved workers.

But this so-called household-handicraft-mill economy quickly began to fade in the 1820s as steamboats and trains made it possible for manufacturers to reach far-flung buyers. Craftsmen enlarged their shops to serve broader areas, and factories began producing cotton and woolen fabrics, carpets, paper, and other consumer goods. New labor-saving technologies such as power looms and sewing machines made factory workers more productive than traditional artisans, and work progressively left the home for the plant and the office. It was the birth of the wage earner as a social and political force. The end of slavery by 1865 added four million potential earners to the mix.

As the workplace became something Americans could leave at the end of the day, though, an unfamiliar problem arose: what should people do with the strange new commodity of leisure time? The hours in factories were often just as long as those on farms—or even longer—but the quality of free time was different. Workers who were clustered in towns and cities, miles or oceans away from family and familiar rural pastimes such as fishing, needed new forms of distraction. "The people must be amused," wrote one former New York mayor in his diary. "They must have some way of passing their evenings besides poking the fire and playing with the children."

Into this void rolled the pedal velocipede, appearing after croquet (1866) and before roller-skating (1870) in a series of breathless national obsessions. "Never before in the history of manufactures in this country has there arisen such a demand for an article as now exists in relation to velocipedes," reported the *New York Times* in early 1869. "No sooner does a man try a machine anywhere than out comes the exclamation of, 'I must get me one of these.'" Nationwide, carriage makers were churning out bicycles at a rate of a thousand a week, which reportedly

Balancing on a pedal velocipede required practice—and there were no training wheels to ease the way. This engraving of wobbly students in a New York velocipede-riding school appeared in *Harper's Weekly*, February 13, 1869.

filled only one-tenth of the orders being placed for them. Makers soon added refinements such as solid rubber tires to cushion the ride (somewhat), and hollow iron tubing in place of solid iron supports in order to reduce the vehicle's weight.

The pedal velocipede had appeared on the US market in the fall of 1868, and until the following spring, riding was mainly an indoor sport. Impresarios converted warehouses and ice-skating rinks into cycling schools and taught mastery of the "fiery steed" to an eager public. "The expert riders of Brooklyn are multiplying rapidly," the *New York Times* reported. "The funny side of the picture is also exhibited nightly in the form of the collisions, falls, narrow escapes and the wabbling movements of the tyros in the art." Schools expanded their space and their hours and still couldn't keep up with the demand from men and women, young and old.

Along with those who wanted to ride came others who just wanted to watch. Schools created galleries for spectators and hosted races in which competitors circled the wooden-floored parlors. In Nashua, New Hampshire, in February 1869, a former telegraph operator won a silver cup for riding the quickest half mile at his cycling school: sixteen laps in two minutes and fifty seconds, or about twelve miles an hour. That same month in Des Moines, Iowa, two velocipede riders braved near-zero temperatures to race back and forth along an unpaved four-and-a-half-block segment of Walnut Street. Three thousand to four thousand people turned out for the contest, which ended when the competitors crashed into each other head-on, the *Daily Iowa State Register* reported: "No bones or spokes were broken, and the riders came out of the wreck with smiling faces and amid thundering cheers from the crowd."

Watching races—and betting on them—was nothing new, of course. Horse racing in open fields or on "Race Streets" in urban areas was a time-honored pastime. Also popular were professional footraces. In 1850, a large crowd gathered at the parade ground in Savannah, Georgia, to see which of two men could more quickly collect 100 scattered potatoes and place them in a basket. The winner earned $100, about $3,030 in today's dollars.

As Americans in cities sought ways to spend their off hours, new mass spectacles developed. Investors built the first US racing tracks with grandstands, where both equine and human sprinting contests attracted thousands. And baseball, descended from earlier stick-and-ball games, gained standard rules during the Civil War as soldiers from different states played each other in camps. After the war, amateur baseball teams flourished, and the sport spread "like wildfire," as one magazine noted in

1868; it was first professionalized in 1869, when the Cincinnati Red Stockings hired players for a national tour. Cincinnati beat every ball club it played that summer, and in the following year, ten thousand spectators showed up in Brooklyn for a rematch between the Red Stockings and the hometown Atlantics. (Brooklyn won.)

Also drawing big crowds were long-distance walking exhibitions that lasted for days or even weeks. In 1867, a slight twenty-seven-year-old Yankee named Edward Payson Weston sparked interest in the sport, called "pedestrianism," by walking from Portland, Maine, to Chicago to win a $10,000 prize offered by a wealthy patron. Because professional pedestrians often walked themselves into staggering, bleeding heaps in order to win a purse, some people criticized Weston's trek as no better than bare-knuckle boxing—a brutal, illegal, and sometimes fatal underground spectacle in which two contestants vying for a money prize pummeled each other until one dropped. Weston indignantly rejected the comparison. "This is a slander on an honest man," he wrote. "I fail to see wherein I am doing wrong. If baseball playing or boat racing is a crime, then I am wrong; otherwise, I am right." Wearing a cropped jacket, tight black pants, and short boots with red tops, Weston covered the distance in twenty-six secular days—that is, thirty days minus Sundays—drawing clots of spectators in each town he reached. In Providence, Rhode Island, "the crowd was so great the police had to open a passage for him through the streets," *Harper's Weekly* reported. By 1869, walking 100 miles within twenty-four hours (or attempting to, at least) was a common pedestrian feat.

That year, bicycle racing seemed certain to become the next mass amusement. "When the bright pleasant weather of spring comes," predicted the *New York Times*, "the streets will doubtless be alive with velocipedes, while [Central] Park and all country roads will be converted into regular race courses."

The newspaper warned two well-known racehorse owners to "look to their laurels." Ball fields added wood-plank velocipede tracks to accommodate exhibitions of speed and skill. One such retrofitted park was dubbed an "amphicyclotheatron"; a similarly whomped-up cycling venue might be called a "gymnacyclidium," a "velocipedrome," or a "bicyclocurriculum."

But when the warm weather came, the new machines couldn't deliver the speed they seemed to promise. Although some cities had begun paving streets with wood blocks soaked in creosote, most American roads were still in woeful shape—"one unending mud-hole opening into another unending mud-hole," as an Iowa newspaper complained. On such surfaces, the bicycle's rigid construction and wooden wheels made for a bumpy and arduous ride. Machines that went "easily and fast" on wood floors "went very slow, and only by the most exhausting efforts of the rider" on the street, the *Baltimore Sun* reported. Outdoor velocipede races staged in the spring of 1869 were unexpectedly dull. One April event at a Long Island horse track forced riders to struggle over a thick bed of sandy dust. "This was the first series of [velocipede] races on a horseback course, and no doubt it will be the last," wrote a disappointed reporter. "Our roads are a disgrace to the nation, and our race-courses but little less."

The pedal velocipede didn't vanish from the United States entirely, as its 1819 predecessor had, but the machine's faddishness quickly fizzled. Velocipede schools closed, and manufacturers who had been frantic to keep up with orders just months earlier got stuck with stock they couldn't unload. Wags began referring to the machines as "boneshakers" in honor of their unforgiving ride. "The excitement which followed [the bicycle's] introduction here has almost completely subsided," the *New York Times* reported in July 1869. "The field is now open to the next 'rage.'"

Over the following few years, Americans raced velocipedes at track meets and county fairs, but usually as a curiosity, not a main event. Bans on sidewalk riding were revived, and any public enthusiasm for the velocipede was reported with an eye roll. The hard, clattering machines that had been expected to annihilate space within cities instead annihilated the patience of city dwellers. "The velocipede mania rages in South Norwalk, greatly to the disgust of the sedate citizens," a Connecticut newspaper noted in May 1873; in September of that year, a Washington, DC, paper scoffed, "The velocipede idiocy has again broken out." Renewed outbreaks were also noted in New Orleans; Jerseyville, Illinois; San Francisco; and Maine. Boneshaker technology couldn't deliver on the promise of fast, independent transportation, but hopeful Americans kept needing to discover this sad fact for themselves.

In Europe, by contrast, better roads made the new self-propelled machines somewhat more practical for outdoor use, and the lack of a European patent—or related royalty charges—made them more profitable to manufacture or refine. So bicycles there got faster. Makers knew that the larger the wheel, the farther a bike would go on each rotation of the pedals. But wood-spoked wheels couldn't be enlarged much: they would get too heavy to crank. Then in 1869, a German mechanic in Paris patented a wire-spoked wheel. This weight-saving innovation allowed wheel diameters to expand to their logical outer limit: sixty inches, double the length of a tall rider's legs. Buyers ordered bicycles by wheel size, the way men now buy pants by inseam length.

The start of the Franco-Prussian War in 1870 put a temporary halt to French bicycle production, but that year a British manufacturer refined the wire-spoked wheel and produced the first commercially successful high-wheel bicycle. The Starley

Bigger wheels meant faster bicycles, but those cycles were difficult for women in long skirts to ride. Makers used the towering wheels on one- and two-person tricycles to accommodate female riders. New York's Riverside Drive, depicted here, was a popular cycling route. This engraving, from a drawing by T. de Thulstrup, appeared in *Harper's Weekly*, July 17, 1886.

Ariel had a chest-high front driving wheel, a knee-high rear wheel (shrunken to reduce the bike's weight), and a mounting step to help the rider clamber up to the seat. "One of the more interesting awkwardnesses of the tall bicycle was the trouble of mounting," recalled one British early adopter in a memoir. "You had to get the procession moving first, then swarm up the backbone into the saddle and catch the pedals before the thing lost steerage-way." (As with modern children's tricycles and fixed-gear bikes, the pedals on these direct-drive machines turned along with the front wheel; there was no gliding.)

Riding speeds doubled. As one British bicycle maker wrote in late 1870, "The machine of the present day is a very different affair from the old clumsy articles with wood wheels which were in vogue two years ago. We thought we were doing well when we covered a mile in 7 minutes," about 8½ miles per hour. "Now the time for a mile run on a course is 3½ minutes," which works out to 17 miles per hour.

Big-wheel bikes began to win all the European races, and before long, French and English racers had all converted to the spindly new machines, as had other riders strong and brave enough to try to mount them. High-wheel bikes weren't only difficult to get on, though; they were difficult to *stay* on. The rider's center of gravity sat so far forward that any small obstacle or quick stop might send him—and it was almost always a him—flying headfirst over the handlebars in a spill called "taking a header." "You were perched, remember, on the exact top of a wheel about five feet high, with an inconsiderable little roller of a trailing wheel to weigh down behind," our early adopter explained. If a jolt to the front wheel upset this balance, "you were flung forward with your face to the ground, hammer-fashion, and a nice, straight iron handlebar close across your waist to imprison your legs and make quite certain that it should be your face, and no less tender spot, that first reached the surface of this unyielding planet."

A few high-wheelers made it across the Atlantic as part of traveling European acrobatic shows during the early 1870s, and a few Americans built the newfangled machines for themselves, but it wasn't until 1876 that the high-wheel bicycle started to gain traction in the United States. That year, a Baltimore importer showed a few British high-wheelers at the Centennial International Exhibition in Philadelphia, a sprawling world's fair that introduced visitors to Alexander Graham Bell's telephone,

Heinz ketchup, Hires root beer, and the torch-bearing right hand of the future Statue of Liberty.

Newspapers made little note of the bicycle exhibit, but one entrepreneur famously did. Albert A. Pope, a thirty-three-year-old manufacturer of air pistols, cigarette rollers, and other patented devices, visited the Philadelphia exhibition as a representative of the city of Newton, Massachusetts, where he served as an alderman. A portly young man with a luxuriant moustache and muttonchops, Pope strolled the fair's pavilions, surveying the latest technology from around the world. When he saw the display of English bicycles, Pope was hooked. "They attracted my attention to such an extent that I paid many visits to this exhibit," he later recalled, "wondering if any but trained gymnasts could master so strange and apparently unsteady a mount."

In 1877, Pope hosted an English houseguest who was in the bicycle business. The guest commissioned a local tradesman to build a high-wheeler; then he taught Pope how to ride it. The machine cost $313 to construct—about twice what a Newton street railway company paid to buy two new horses the same year. That fall, after Pope had mastered the device, he imported several high-wheelers from England to sell, and in 1878 he contracted with a Hartford, Connecticut, sewing machine factory to begin manufacturing them. Other American entrepreneurs were importing high-wheelers by then, but by getting a jump on production—and by scarfing up every bicycle-related patent he could find, including Lallement's—Pope and his Columbia Bicycle brand came to dominate a growing US market. In 1878, just 50 high-wheeled bicycles were produced in the United States; by 1888, the number had reached 16,750, of which Pope's firm built about 5,000.

As in Europe, these precarious machines were ridden almost exclusively by young, strong men. It is easy to view these Victorians tootling around on their high-wheeled contraptions as comically precious, but as the cycle-racing historian Andrew Ritchie argues, cycle riders then were about as precious as a Formula One driver is now. "Riding the high-wheel bicycle, far from being a quaint or romantic activity (as it is compulsively portrayed in retrospect), was for the riders of the 1880s an expression of modernity and mobility," he writes in his 2010 book *Quest for Speed*. "There was nothing 'primitive' about early bicycle technology, which advanced with intense technological logic and precision."

Technology of all sorts developed at a mind-blowing pace in those years. In the United States, along with the telephone, the 1870s saw the invention of the commercial typewriter (1873), the structural steel bridge (1874), the electric dental drill (1875), the mimeograph (1875), the phonograph (1877), and the incandescent light bulb (1879). Meanwhile, railroad and telegraph lines burgeoned in tandem—telegraph poles lined railroad rights-of-way—and delivered goods, people, and ideas to their destinations ever faster.

And as the world was speeding up, the concept of time was shifting. Traditionally, "noon" had always meant "when the sun reaches its highest point of the day." Naturally, this moment gets earlier the farther east one goes: about one minute earlier for every thirteen miles. Through the 1870s, every city set its local time by the sun, so when it was noon in Chicago, it was 12:17 in Toledo, 12:24 in Cleveland, and 12:31 in Pittsburgh. Wisconsin alone had thirty-eight local times. Such differences of minutes weren't a problem before the nineteenth century—in fact, before then, clocks didn't even have minute hands—but railroad schedules and factory hours required more precision. In the chaotic years just before 1883, when US railroads agreed to operate on four standard time zones, clocks in the main Pittsburgh train station displayed six different times in order to track the arrivals and departures of railroads using different cities' standards.

In a world where even the simple question "What time is it?" didn't have a simple answer, the pace of change could be dizzying. "Everyone is familiar with the warning that we are living too fast and must pay a serious penalty," wrote a South Dakota newspaper columnist in 1888. "The visiting foreigner continues to hold up his hands in amazement at the breathless rapidity of American life." Some people started to complain of a newly identified mental illness, neurasthenia, characterized by fatigue, anxiety, and depression. The disorder, also called "Americanitis," was thought to be caused by the stresses of modern life. As one San Francisco humor writer explained, "In this telegraphic, high-pressure age, there are a great many more things to occupy one's attention than there were twenty years ago, but the brains ain't any bigger now than they were then."

While some Americans felt overwhelmed by the changes, many others were exhilarated. "An honest investigation will convince even the most confirmed pessimist that our country is advancing in material progress, and also in the arts and sciences, as never before," wrote one Baltimore business journalist about the 1880s. "History affords nothing with which to compare our marvelous advancement." One overt celebration of this rapid technological progress was the sport of bicycle racing, which flowered in the 1880s and eventually produced some of the nation's first athletic superstars. Bicycle manufacturers on both sides of the Atlantic fought to make their machines the fastest, and they sponsored races and riders to showcase their innovations to an amusement-hungry public.

One early high-wheel contest took its format from the then-current pedestrian rage: the six-day race, a grueling 24/6 slog to see which contestant could walk the most laps around an indoor track without collapsing from exhaustion. (The reason for the six-day duration was that racing on Sundays was forbidden.) The first six-day bicycle race in the United States, billed as a contest for the "Bicycular Championship of the Universe," was scheduled for November 1879, under a tent in a vacant lot in Boston's Back Bay. Two visiting European racers, one British and one French, had challenged all American comers, and five signed on. Fierce winds and freezing temperatures forced organizers to shorten the race to four days, and the winner, a "plucky little Frenchman" named Charles Terront, won by riding 660 miles around a wooden track, according to a bicycling industry magazine. Second place went to the Brit, even though both he and the winner had spotted the American contestants ten miles for every hundred they rode. The Americans' riding improved during the week, but only two of them finished; three withdrew. "It is hoped that before long America will be able to name men of equal endurance and speed," the magazine stated.

US riders and technology soon caught up with the Europeans, and bicycle racing caught on. At the end of 1886, a Chicagoan named Albert Schock set a world record inside a huge Minneapolis exhibition hall, riding 1,405 miles in six days with only short breaks for sleep. During the race's first twenty-four hours, Schock lost three and a half pounds off his slender, five-foot-six-inch frame, despite eating constantly. He spent much of the race behind, but eventually edged out his two competitors after one suffered a violent vomiting attack due to exertion and the other fell asleep while riding and crashed into a railing. Schock credited his Victor bicycle with the win, calling it "a vast improvement on all other wheels ridden by me," but the manufacturers of the rival American Champion bicycle claimed that Schock had ridden two-thirds of the winning distance on their machine and had switched to the Victor only "on account of a pecuniary inducement." That is not hard to believe; competition among manufacturers was keen, as Ritchie says, and in a foretaste of what would become a "modern dynamic," "the question of who sponsored who was right in the front line of media interest."

While professionals raced high-wheelers at indoor events (where admission could be charged), hobbyists raced the machines outdoors. Starting with the Boston Bicycle Club in 1878, military-style men's groups began to form, organizing joint rides and rallies featuring half-mile, one-mile, and two-mile sprints. The bicycle—then also called a "wheel"—was still a luxury item: the first of Albert A. Pope's high-wheelers cost $90, and imported English bikes ran about $125, at a time when a laborer might earn $1.30 a day and a skilled carpenter $2.25. Not surprisingly, club members were an upscale bunch, as they happily pointed out. "The bicyclers of England and America are a superior class of men," wrote one Connecticut enthusiast in 1882. Except in rare instances, women and people of color were excluded from club membership. Each club adopted its own knicker-pantsed uniform and code of courtly behavior, which usually included the stipulation that members be "gentleman amateurs" who had never competed for money. This rule tended to filter out anyone who could use an extra buck.

People had to be well off to afford a high-wheeler, and riding one made them feel nobler still—sometimes obnoxiously so. Much like a gargantuan SUV, a bicycle was a lofty, pricey perch from which to look down on others. "From the saddle we perceive things which are hidden from them who only walk upon the earth. Our senses are more acute, the sunshine seems brighter to us, and nature is more lovely," our Connecticut enthusiast continued. "We dash across the plain with a wild sense of freedom and power which no one ever knows until he rides the magic steed."

That sense of freedom and power was real. But this magic steed was not the practical, affordable people's nag envisioned by riders of the draisine or the boneshaker. The acrobatic and exotic high-wheeler was a plaything—a sort of mechanical giraffe. More physically accessible, though also more expensive by half, was the tricycle, built to capture the female and older-male markets. These came in many configurations, but in most, the rider sat sandwiched between two large wheels, with a third, smaller wheel at the front or rear. These devices weren't crash-proof; in fact, their need for three relatively smooth tracks in the road, rather than just one, made them prone to tipping over. But tricycles were considered safer than high-wheeled bikes: unlike bikes, they stood up by themselves, were easy to mount, and could accommodate the heavy, floor-length skirts that all respectable women wore at the time.

The first spider-wheel tricycles were weighty and slow, but engineers kept improving them, even as the form of the high-wheel bicycle stabilized. (An English tricycle of 1878 was the first vehicle to successfully use the chain drive, a standard feature of modern bicycles.) In the early 1880s, tricycles began to overtake high-wheelers in popularity in England, where two hundred styles of tricycle were in production. Given the limitations and perils of high-wheelers, many predicted the same trend would occur in the United States. "Certainly no one at all familiar with the marvelous English record for the year can doubt that a wonderfully rapid introduction of the tricycle is commenced in America," wrote an observer in 1882. That spring, one lady tricyclist in a white straw hat drew a crowd of gawkers to the curbside in Washington, DC, but the vehicles were becoming so common in the city that riders were confident they would soon excite only "the same quiet interest that any other method of self-propulsion gets," reported a *Baltimore Sun* correspondent.

It seemed as if America were gearing up for a steampunk idyll, its citizens churning through the streets inside cubicle-sized tricycles on five-foot wheels. But that never happened.

And why not? In part, because of the sorry state of the country's roads, which weren't smooth enough to support a British-style tricycle boom. In larger part, though, tricycles failed in the United States because they pointed the way to something better. Women's growing interest in tricycling hinted at a massive potential market for a safe and affordable self-propelled vehicle. Within just a few years, cycle builders responded with technological advances that brought the bicycle back down to earth and transformed it from a toy for the rich into a catalyst for unimaginable social change.

Three

THE WHEEL, THE WOMAN, AND THE HUMAN BODY

Angeline Allen must have been pleased. On October 28, 1893, the twenty-something divorcée, an aspiring model, made the cover of the country's most popular men's magazine, a titillating journal of crime, sport, and cheesecake called the *National Police Gazette*. Granted, the reason wasn't Allen's "wealth of golden hair" or "strikingly pretty face," though the magazine mentioned both. Rather, the cover story was about Allen's attire during a recent bicycle ride near her Newark, New Jersey, home. The "eccentric" young woman had ridden through town in "a costume that caused hundreds to turn and gaze in astonishment," the *Gazette* reported.

The story's headline summed up the cause of the gaping: "She Wore Trousers"—dark blue corduroy bloomers, to be exact, snug around the calves and puffy above the knees. "She rode her wheel through the principal streets in a leisurely manner, and appeared to be utterly oblivious of the sensation she was causing," according to the reporter.

It is unlikely Allen was truly oblivious, having already shown an exhibitionistic streak over the summer when she appeared on an Asbury Park, New Jersey, beach in a bathing skirt

Women had to shorten or abandon their traditional long skirts if they wanted to ride a bicycle. A New Jersey divorcée named Angeline Allen drew hundreds of gawkers when she cycled in tight blue pants, according to the *National Police Gazette* (October 28, 1893). This engraving of Allen's provocative ride appeared on the magazine's cover. Courtesy of William A. Mays, *National Police Gazette*.

that "did not reach within many inches of her knees," according to a disapproving newspaper report. ("Her stockings or tights were of light blue silk," the report added.) Allen didn't mind people noticing her revealing outfits—"that's what I wear them for," she told one reporter—and she kept cycling around Newark in pants despite the journalistic scolding. As another paper reported that November, "The natives watch for her with bated breath, and her appearance is the signal for a rush to all the front windows along the street."

For a grown woman to reveal so much leg in public was a staggeringly brazen act. What was noticeably unnoteworthy by then was Allen's choice of vehicle. Ten years earlier, all bicycles had been high-wheelers, and riding one had been largely the province of daring, athletic men. The women who had attempted it were seen as acrobats, hussies, or freaks; one female performer who rode a high-wheeler in the early 1880s was perceived as "a sort of semi-monster," another woman reported. But by the early 1890s, the bike had undergone a transformation. Allen's machine—a so-called safety bicycle—had two thigh-high wheels; air-filled rubber tires; and rear-wheel drive, with a chain to transmit power from the pedals. In fact, it looked a lot like a twenty-first-century commuter bike, and it had become nearly as acceptable as one. Even the fashion police who scorned Allen's riding *outfit* didn't object to her riding.

What had happened to the bicycle in the interim? Market expansion. In the 1880s, when bicycle makers had begun to saturate the limited market for high-wheelers, they sought products to entice other would-be riders, particularly men who had aged out of the strenuous high-wheel lifestyle. In the United States, where bad roads made tricycle ridership impractical, the sales potential for an easy-to-ride bicycle looked stronger than in Europe. In response, manufacturers on both sides of the Atlantic created a profusion of high-tech two-wheelers, including models with foot levers instead of pedals; "geared up" bikes with chains and sprockets that spun the driving wheel more than once for each rotation of the cycle's cranks; and a supposedly header-proof version with the small wheel in the front and the big wheel in the rear. Riders and makers started calling the standard high-wheeler an "Ordinary" to distinguish it from experimental models.

Several of the new bikes used geared-up rear-wheel drive as a way to bring the rider closer to the ground. The most influential of these was the English Rover, with a rear driving wheel only thirty inches tall that had as much force as a fifty-inch Ordinary wheel. (Even today, American bicycle gears are measured in "gear inches," which indicate how tall an Ordinary wheel of equivalent force would be.) At thirty-six inches, the Rover's front wheel was slightly bigger than its rear one, but apart from that, the machine looked as streamlined as some models of fifty or a hundred years later.

Introduced in England in 1885, the Rover Safety Bicycle delivered the speed of an Ordinary, but with a greatly diminished risk of skull fracture from flying over the handlebars. The Rover's manufacturer made some quick refinements, and a model with same-sized wheels caught on in Britain and inspired a fleet of imitators: low-mount, rear-wheel-drive bikes also called "safeties."

The major US manufacturers weren't impressed by this new low profile, though; they dismissed the safety style as a mistake. In 1886, after a two-month tour of England's bicycle factories, the US industry titan Albert Pope expressed confidence in his high-wheeler: "I looked at nearly all the principal [English] makes and I could not find a point that was in any way an improvement over our own." Echoed his lieutenant, George H. Day, who also made the trip, "Every innovation is regarded as a trap."

But when imported safeties hit the US market in the spring of 1887, the machines found eager buyers; Pope and other American cycle makers scrambled to put out their own versions of the header-resistant devices. By November, the safety bicycle was established in the United States as the modern option for men, even though its low wheels evoked the laughably old-timey velocipede of twenty years prior, as one bard made clear in the accented voice of an immigrant child:

In days of old, full many a time
You've heard it told, in prose and rhyme,
How down the street a wheelman came,
And chanced to meet his beauteous flame
Just where a pup in ambush lay,
To tip him up upon the way,
And make him wish that he was dead,
While gyrating upon his head.
In days of old
You've heard it told.

But nowadays, it's otherwise.
The safety craze new joy supplies;
The boulders lose their terrors grim,
Stray cans and shoes are naught to him;
He laughs at rocks, he kicks the pup,
But, in the end, things even up;
For, as his maid he gayly greets,
Some unwashed urchin always bleats —
"Hi, look at der big man on der melosipetes!"

For a short time, Ordinaries and safeties coexisted like Neanderthals and *Homo sapiens*, with the bigger, older species continuing to inhabit its traditional niche while the smaller, nimbler creature carved out a new one. "I do not think that [the safety] will hurt the sale of the Ordinary bicycle," predicted one US industry watcher in late 1887. "It will open the pleasures of cycling to a great many who have been afraid to venture upon a high machine." The writer was thinking of physicians and other "professional men" for whom an Ordinary was too dangerous, but some enthusiasts suspected that the safety would also appeal to female riders. Offering women "a clumsy wheelbarrow of a tricycle" to ride while men zip around on slender bikes, wrote one sympathetic man, "is offering a woman a stone to eat while men have soft biscuit."

And the safety bicycle's low profile *did* intrigue many American women, especially after the spring of 1888, when makers offered a drop-frame version, in which the bike's top bar scooped downward to make room for a lady rider's long skirts. As one woman reported that year, "A sudden desire began to awake in the feminine mind to ascertain for itself by personal experience, what were those joys of the two-wheeler which they had so often heard boastfully vaunted as superior, a thousand times, to the more sober delights of the staid tricycle."

With the safety's smaller wheels, its ride was bumpier than the Ordinary's at first. But then came the pneumatic tire. Devised in Ireland in 1888 by a veterinarian named John Boyd Dunlop, who was seeking a faster ride for his son's trike, the air-filled rubber tube cushioned the road's ruts and bulges in a way that springs and other early shock-absorbing devices never could. This marvel arrived in the United States by 1890 and became standard equipment on American safeties within a few years. "It permitted travel on streets and roads previously thought unridable," recalled an American journalist of the time, "and added to cycling a degree of ease and comfort never dreamed of."

In the 1890s, bikes got lighter as well as more comfortable. The average weight of a bicycle dropped by more than half during the decade's first five years, falling from fifty pounds to twenty-three. And since new gearings were able to mimic wheels larger than those of the largest Ordinary, speed records fell too. In 1894, while riding a pneumatic-tired safety around a track in Buffalo, New York, the racer John S. Johnson went a mile in just over one minute and thirty-five seconds, a rate of nearly thirty-eight miles an hour. He beat the previous mile record for a safety by fourteen seconds and the record for an Ordinary by nearly a minute; more impressively, he beat the mile record for a running horse by one-tenth of a second.

The Ordinary—which had by then acquired the derisive nickname of "penny-farthing," after the old British penny and much smaller farthing (quarter-penny) coins—became obsolete. High-wheelers that had sold for $150 to $300 just a year or two earlier were going for as little as $10.

The first safeties, meanwhile, cost an average of $150 during a time when the average worker earned something like $12 a week. At such prices, the new bikes targeted the same upscale demographic as the tricycle. But a strong market for safeties among well-to-do women goosed production, and competition among manufacturers reduced prices, making the bikes affordable to more would-be riders—and further fueling demand. In 1895, America's three hundred bicycle companies produced 500,000 safeties at an average price of $75, according to one encyclopedia's yearbook. Even manufacturers were surprised at the demand among women, who thrilled to the new machine's exhilarating ride. As one female journalist wrote, "If a pitying Providence should suddenly fit light, strong wings to the back of a toiling tortoise, that patient cumberer of the ground could hardly feel a more astonishing sense of exhilaration than a woman experiences when first she becomes a mistress of her wheel."

It wasn't just that women enjoyed the physical sensation of riding—the rush of balancing and cruising. What made the bicycle truly liberating was its fundamental incompatibility with many of the limits placed on women. Take clothing, for example. Starting at puberty, women were expected to wear heavy floor-length skirts, rigid corsets, and tight, pointy-toed shoes. These garments made any sort of physical exertion difficult, as young girls sadly discovered. "I 'ran wild' until my sixteenth birthday, when the hampering long skirts were brought, with their accompanying corset and high heels," recalled the temperance activist Frances Willard in an 1895 memoir. "I remember writing in my journal, in the first heartbreak of a young human colt taken from its pleasant pasture, 'Altogether, I recognize that my occupation is gone.'" Reformers had been calling for more sensible clothing for women since the 1850s, when the newspaper editor Amelia Bloomer wore the baggy trousers that critics named after her, but rational arguments hadn't made much headway.

Where reason failed, though, recreation succeeded. The drop-frame safety did allow women to ride in dresses, but not in the swagged, voluminous frocks of the Victorian parlor. Female cyclists had to don simple, "short" (that is, ankle-length) skirts in order to avoid getting their feet caught in their hems as they pedaled. And to keep their skirts from flying up, some women had tailors put weights in their hems or line their skirt fronts with leather. Other women, like Angeline Allen, shucked their dresses altogether and wore bloomers. The display that reporters had deemed shocking in 1893 became commonplace just a few years later as more and more women started riding. "The eye of the spectator has long since become accustomed to costumes once conspicuous," wrote an American journalist in 1895. "Bloomer and tailor-made alike ride on unchallenged." (For her part, Allen may well have given up riding, but not scandal; she progressed to posing onstage in scanty attire for re-creations of famous paintings, a risqué popular amusement.)

Bicyclists' corsets changed too, though less publicly. The corset of the 1880s was an armpit-to-hip garment stiffened with whalebone stays, which helped the hips support heavy skirts that hung from the waist. But while corsets braced women's torsos, they also weakened their wearers, squeezing women's lungs and displacing other internal organs, making deep breaths impossible. Out of necessity, female cyclists looked for alternatives, and many chose another garment that had been advocated by dress reformers decades earlier: a sturdy, waist-length cotton camisole with shoulder straps. When introduced in the 1870s, this garment was called an "emancipation waist," and it featured a horizontal band of buttons at the hem, to which drawers or a skirt could be attached. Later versions were named "health waist" or, finally, "bicycle waist." One 1896 model included elastic insets; its maker promised the wearer "perfect comfort—a sound pair of lungs—a graceful figure and rosy cheeks." All for $1, postpaid.

If women's clothing constrained them, so did their role in society. More Americans than ever worked outside the home; by 1880, farmers made up a little less than half of the country's labor force. But even among the urban working class, married women typically stayed home during the day to cook, clean, tend to children, and often manufacture homemade goods for sale. Meanwhile, their husbands, sons, and unmarried daughters toiled in factories, shops, offices, and other people's houses. Many Americans came to believe that men and women naturally inhabited two separate spheres: men held sway in business, politics, and other public arenas, and women took charge of the home. For most middle-class women, respectability meant appearing in public only under certain circumstances—such as while shopping—and making as small an impression as possible. "A true lady walks the streets unostentatiously and with becoming reserve," instructed an 1889 etiquette manual. "She appears unconscious of all sights and sounds which a lady ought not to perceive."

In addition, an unmarried young woman didn't go out without a chaperone, usually an older female relative. Being seen on an unchaperoned date, even at a restaurant or other public place, could be cause for social ruin. An 1887 etiquette guide warned against sailing excursions, for example, lest the boat be becalmed overnight: "A single careless act of this sort may be remembered spitefully against a girl for many years."

The bicycle challenged all that. Wives who had stayed close to home—venturing out only on foot, by trolley, or, if wealthy, with a driver and horse-drawn carriage—were suddenly able to travel miles on their own. Being so mobile, and so visible, was a revelation to many. "The world is a new and another sphere under the bicyclist's observation," wrote one female journalist. "Here is a process of locomotion that is absolutely at her command." If a woman's sphere begins to feel too small, wrote another, "the sufferer can do no better than to flatten her sphere to a circle, mount it, and take to the road."

As for unmarried women, manners mavens urged them to cycle only with chaperones, but the rule didn't take. "New social laws have been enacted to meet the requirements of the new order," reported one newspaper editor in 1896. "Parents who will not allow their daughters to accompany young men to the theatre without chaperonage allow them to go bicycle-riding alone with young men. This is considered perfectly proper." According to the editor, the reason for this difference was the "good comradeship" of the bicycling set. Fellow enthusiasts looked out for one another on the road, he wrote—so in a way, every ride was supervised. The historian Ellen Gruber Garvey suggests a second possible reason: propriety already allowed unmarried women to ride horses unchaperoned. Bicycles, as a less costly equivalent, may simply have extended this freedom down the economic scale.

But the same things that made the bicycle liberating also made it threatening. Moralists warned that skimpy costumes and unsupervised travel would lead to wanton behavior. "Immodest bicycling by young women is to be deplored," declared Charlotte Smith, founder of the Women's Rescue League, a group that lobbied Congress on behalf of "fallen women." "Bicycling by young women has helped to swell the ranks of reckless girls, who finally drift into the standing army of outcast women." Smith reported that her tours of brothels and interviews with prostitutes confirmed this.

Physicians—who at the time shouldered responsibility for patients' moral as well as physical well-being—had their own concerns. One visited New York's Coney Island and saw a sixteen-year-old cyclist get drunk on wine provided by a beautiful but nefarious older woman. "She looked like an innocent child, but was away from home influence," the doctor reported. Many physicians fretted that pressure from the bicycle seat would teach girls how to masturbate, a practice thought to lead to spiritual and psychological decline. Climbing hills on a bike could excite "feelings hitherto unknown to, and unrealized by, the young girl," wrote one doctor in 1898. (Boys faced the same danger: pressure on the perineum would call their attention to the area, warned one doctor, "and so lead to a great increase in masturbation in the timid [and] to early sexual indulgence in the more venturous.")

The bicycle's peril was medical as well as moral. In the late nineteenth century, many saw physical energy as a finite resource that had to be carefully parceled out, not a power that could be renewed through exercise. The fashionable malaise of neurasthenia was only one of the disorders thought to be caused by a depletion of energies. Overexertion could also cause tuberculosis, scoliosis, hernias, heart disease, and other maladies, doctors believed. Safely sedentary middle-class women, who frequently suffered from varicose veins and other consequences of annual pregnancies, were prone to fatigue; one Boston writer called them "a sex which is born tired," adding that "society sometimes seems little better than a hospital for invalid women." Particularly for women in heavy dresses and constricting corsets, any activity that raised the heart rate could seem more likely to be the cause of fainting and listlessness than their remedy. Opponents of the bicycle latched onto this perception, arguing that riding would cost women more effort than they could afford. "The exertion necessary to riding with speed . . . is productive of an excitation of nervous and physical energy that is anything but beneficial," Charlotte Smith warned. "If a halt is not called soon, 75 per cent of the cyclists will be an army of invalids within the next ten years."

But even as Smith made her dire predictions, Americans' fear of cardiovascular exercise was beginning to lift. For decades, health reformers had trumpeted the benefits of fitness, and during the 1880s, the United States saw a spike in organized physical activity. Citizens of America's growing cities tried new sports such as baseball and football, and exercise advocates built the first public playgrounds and pushed for physical education for both boys and girls. Doctors continued to caution against overexertion, but they acknowledged that, in moderation, fresh air and exercise tended to improve patients' health. The high-wheel bicycle of the 1880s proved the benefits of regular exercise to those who could ride it; proponents made extravagant claims for the risky machine's ability to restore well-being. "For constipation, sleeplessness, dyspepsia, and many other ills which flesh is heir to, not to speak of melancholy,—all are curable, or certainly to be improved, by the new remedy, *'Bicycle,'*" wrote a Texas physician in 1883. "It is always an excellent prescription for the convalescents, and nearly always for chronic invalids."

Not everyone could take the prescription, though. High-wheeled cycling and rigorous team sports were acceptable only for young men. The new games deemed suitable for mixed company, such as lawn tennis and golf, were far less taxing—and therefore far less likely to lead to noticeable improvements in fitness. As for working out on your own, the recommended options were either too costly (horseback riding) or too boring (indoor calisthenics) to gain much popularity. As a result, many more Americans of the 1880s thought they *ought* to exercise than actually did it. So when the safety bicycle appeared at the end of the decade and Americans began riding in large numbers—an estimated two million by 1896, out of a population of about seventy million—few were certain how such vigorous physical activity would affect them.

Doctors were wary. Most US physicians believed that each patient's condition was based largely on his or her habits and experiences, the weather, and other environmental factors. Good health was a reflection of proper balance among bodily systems and energies. "A distracted mind could curdle the stomach, a dyspeptic stomach could agitate the mind," writes the medical historian Charles Rosenberg. It was a doctor's job to know each patient well enough to restore balance when something was out of whack, using laxatives, diuretics, and other purging drugs to reboot the system. Even contagious diseases could not be treated in a cookie-cutter fashion, argued an 1883 medical journal editorial: "No two instances of typhoid fever, or of any other disease, are precisely alike. . . . No 'rule of thumb,' no recourse to a formula-book, will avail for proper treatment even of the typical diseases." To many doctors, advocating a specific drug to cure a specific disease seemed the height of quackery.

And just as there were no one-size-fits-all medical treatments, many physicians believed there were no one-size-fits-all exercise routines. While cycling enthusiasts rhapsodized about the safety bicycle's benefits for riders of both sexes and all ages, doctors fretted that many of their patients would be harmed by the new machines. Even seeming success stories were suspect. In an 1895 paper on heart disease, one doctor reported that a patient who had panted for breath after climbing one flight of stairs was now able to cycle up hills with ease. "It would be wrong to conclude from this that cycling is not injurious," the doctor wrote: there hadn't yet been time to observe the bicycle's long-term effects. Moreover, as an unfamiliar activity, cycling tended to catch the blame for pretty much anything bad that happened to a new rider afterward, up to and including death.

Logically, acute injuries were a concern. Though the safety bicycle did greatly reduce the risk of head wounds, it didn't obliterate that risk, particularly among "scorchers"—thrill-seeking youngsters who hunched over their handlebars and pedaled as fast as they could. "It might seem almost impossible to fracture a skull thick enough to permit indulgence in such practices," reported the *Boston Medical and Surgical Journal*, "but the bicycle fool at full speed has been able to accomplish it." Medical journals also noted the danger of road rash and broken bones.

More insidious than crash injuries, though, were new chronic complaints attributed to cycling. The bent-over posture of the scorcher was thought to cause a permanent hunch called "kyphosis bicyclistarum," or, familiarly, "cyclist's stoop." Repeated stress to the cardiovascular system—that is, regular workouts—could lead to the irregular heartbeats and poor circulation of "bicycle heart." Gripping the handlebars too tightly might cause finger numbness, or "bicycle hand," and a dusty ride could trigger "cyclist's sore throat." Practically every body part seemed to have its own cycle-related malady; at least one New York doctor devoted his entire practice to treating such ailments.

Of all the physical woes attributed to the bike, the one that most strained credulity was the "bicycle face." Characterized by wide, wild eyes; a grim set to the mouth; and a migration of facial features toward the center, the disorder was said to result from the stress of incessant balancing. A German philosopher claimed that the condition drained "every vestige of intelligence" from the sufferer's appearance and rendered children unrecognizable to their own mothers. The bicycle face hung on, too, warned a journalist: "Once fixed upon the countenance, it can never be removed."

The doctors raising these alarms were careful to state that many of the new diseases affected only cyclists predisposed to them—which would explain why so few of their fellow physicians might have encountered the disorders. "Whilst thousands ride immune, a small percentage will suffer," wrote one doctor. Another, who blamed cases of appendicitis, inflammatory bowel disease, and the thyroid condition Graves' disease on excessive riding, said it didn't matter how many people believed that cycling had improved their health: "It would not affect my argument in the least if swarms of them had been rescued from the grave."

Nevertheless, the more Americans took to bicycling, the more tenuous these claims of danger came to seem. The machine made physical activity both practical and fun. "The bicycle is inducing multitudes of people to take regular exercise who have long been in need of such exercise, but who could never be induced to take it by any means hitherto devised," one doctor wrote in *Harper's Weekly* in 1896. And all that activity had an effect. Riders quickly noticed improved muscle tone, increased strength, better sleep, and brighter moods. Women, especially, transformed themselves, wrote the novelist Maurice Thompson in 1897: "We have already become accustomed to seeing sunbrowned faces, once sallow and languid, whisk past us at every turn of the street. The magnetism of vivid health has overcome conservative barriers that were impregnable to every other force."

The empirical evidence of cycling's health value began to overtake conservative doctors' concerns, as the rhetoric scholar

Sarah Overbaugh Hallenbeck argues. Though many physicians continued to raise objections to the sport, their voices were increasingly drowned out by those of more observant—and pragmatic—practitioners. "The bicycle face, elbow, back, shoulders, neck, eroticism," wrote one military doctor in 1896, "I pass as not worthy of serious consideration." Rather than discourage bicycle use, most physicians came to cautiously endorse it. "So long as the cyclist can breathe with the mouth shut," wrote one such doctor in 1895, "he is certainly perfectly safe." Some went further, citing evidence of the bike's benefits for heart patients, migraine sufferers, diabetics, and others with chronic conditions. In Chicago, the demand for injectable morphine dropped as patients with anxiety or insomnia "discovered that a long spin in the fresh air on a cycle induces sweet sleep better than their favorite drug," the *Bulletin of Pharmacy* reported.

This shift paralleled a transformation in medical thinking during the 1890s, when American physicians increasingly embraced the scientific method. Some clinics in Continental Europe had adopted this evidence-based approach early in the nineteenth century, using statistics to determine the efficacy of treatments and evaluating patients' conditions according to universal norms, rather than trying to divine what was normal for each individual patient. In the United States, however, doctors arguing for this approach were long in the minority. According to Rosenberg, the rift between medical traditionalists and empiricists "provided an emotional fault line which marked the profession throughout the last two-thirds of the century." Only at the very end of the nineteenth century did a research-based curriculum take hold at US medical schools.

It would be folly to suggest that the bicycle alone caused this transformation. Many other factors were at play, such as improved trans-Atlantic communication; an influx of European immigrants, including scientists; and a snowballing of evidence for new medical concepts such as the germ theory of disease. For centuries, Western healers had believed that contagion could erupt spontaneously, but between 1870 and 1900, researchers disproved this theory by isolating the microscopic causes of illnesses including typhoid, tuberculosis, cholera, diphtheria, meningococcal meningitis, plague, and malaria.

But even if the bike did not independently modernize American medicine, its unprecedented impact on fitness—and the clash this revealed between what doctors said and what experience showed—may well have accelerated the shift. Much as the bicycle triggered changes in women's dress that high-minded advocacy could not, it bolstered scientists' then-radical argument that what is good for one human body tends to be just as good for another.

To the bicycle faithful of the 1890s, this seemed to be just the beginning of the changes that the machine would bring about. The gulf between social classes would recede under the influence of this "great leveler," one enthusiast wrote in the *Century Magazine*: "It puts the poor man on a level with the rich, enabling him to 'sing the song of the open road' as freely as the millionaire, and to widen his knowledge by visiting the regions near to or far from his home, observing how other men live."

And while women may not yet have had full access to higher education—or even the right to vote—the unchaperoned, self-propelled bloomer girl seemed to be pedaling in that direction. "In possession of her bicycle, the daughter of the nineteenth century feels that the declaration of her independence has been proclaimed," wrote one female journalist, "and, in the fulness of time, all things will be added to complete her happiness and prosperity."

The first-wave feminist Susan B. Anthony was born in 1820, the year after Charles Willson Peale built his iron draisine. By the time of the safety bicycle boom of the 1890s, she was a snowy-haired eminence, too old to risk riding, but she had an opinion of the sport. "I'll tell you what I think of bicycling," she said in an 1896 newspaper interview as she leaned forward to lay a hand on the reporter's arm. "I think it has done more to emancipate woman than any one thing in the world."

Four

PAVING THE WAY FOR CARS

December 1891 was unseasonably warm in the Midwest, but the balmy weather trapped farmers at home just as effectively as any blizzard could have. Ordinarily, country roads—almost all made of dirt—would have been hardened by packed snow, but that month, rain dissolved rural routes into a squishy, muddy stew. Trying to get goods to market was useless: wagon wheels sank to their hubs. And so farmers in much of Iowa, Illinois, and Missouri stayed home with their produce while store shelves in towns sat bare. "The farming communities have been virtually padlocked on the farm," reported the *St. Louis Republic* that Christmas. "It is feared many failures among country merchants may result." By the time the so-called mud blockade ended in a cold snap on December 28, it had cost the Mississippi Valley region an estimated $1.5 million in lost business.

If the timing was unusual, though, the situation was not. Spring and fall rains routinely gunked up the roads and brought rural life to a standstill. "A million voters are disfranchised at every general election through bad roads," the *Clinton (NY) Courier* reported in 1892. Nearly one-third of the country's spending on public schools was being wasted, the writer added, since "30 per cent of the school children are kept at home by the mud." In fact, many roads in the United States at the end of the nineteenth century were even worse than they had been a hundred years earlier. Private turnpikes built in the early 1800s stood abandoned except for local traffic, having been superseded by railroads. Other country roads—when not sloshing with mud—bore deep sunbaked ruts in the summer and treacherous ice slicks in the winter. Vehicles often toppled over; in February 1885, one Minnesota newspaper noted that a particular farmer's horse-drawn sleigh-load of wheat had overturned seven times during a five-mile trek—"and he is a good teamster, too." Across the nation, roads were so unreliable for travelers that most state maps did not even show them.

Why did farmers put up with such dismal circumstances? For one thing, they saw no alternative. Road conditions seemed as uncontrollable as the weather. But another reason was that farmers had no one to blame but themselves. At the time, federal and state governments took no responsibility for road building. City halls levied taxes on abutting properties to pave city streets, but farmers themselves maintained country roads, usually working a day or two each year to pay local road taxes that were calculated in days of labor rather than dollars. Under the guidance of an elected but untrained supervisor called a "roadmaster," male citizens age sixteen to sixty would report for duty on an appointed day, usually with the enthusiasm of your average juror. "The farmers assemble and make a holiday affair of scraping a little dirt in the middle of the road, where it will do least good and most harm," wrote one critic of the system in 1882. "The roadmaster is elected for his popularity on account of his letting the farmers off easily." This compulsory roadwork was often so poorly done, wrote another critic in 1889, that "the experienced traveller who finds himself at the beginning of a newly mended road will betake himself to the nearest house" to ask about a detour and "escape the danger of the repairs."

When most roads were unpaved, a few days of heavy rain could halt all travel and commerce. This illustration from *American Highways* by N. S. Shaler (1896) depicts a scene just two miles outside the city limits of Cleveland, Ohio, along the main road to Warrensville Township, site of present-day Shaker Heights.

In Europe, water-shedding technological advances such as stone-foundation Telford pavement and convex, crushed-stone macadam (McAdam) pavement—each named for its Scottish inventor—made highways usable in any weather. But these developments hadn't reached rural roads in the United States, in part because no local road district could afford the equipment or the foreign expertise required. In America at the time, there were few formal training programs for civil engineers.

City streets hadn't improved much by the 1880s, either. As urban populations boomed, mayors rushed to slap down cobblestones or wood-block pavers. Smooth, flexible asphalt pavement—in which a semisolid form of petroleum was melted and mixed with pebbles—had been pioneered in the 1870s but was still a rarity. Meanwhile, horse-drawn streetcars (invented in the 1830s), steam-powered cable car systems (invented in the 1870s), and electric trolleys (invented in the 1880s) sliced up streets with their jutting metal tracks. In 1892, the novelist Rudyard Kipling savaged New York's streets in a travel essay, noting their "gullies, holes, ruts, cobblestones awry, [and] kerbstones rising from two to six inches above the level of the slatternly pavement." Raised tram tracks, discarded building materials, unregulated traffic, and "more mixed stinks than the winter wind can carry away," he added, made the city's streets "first cousins to a Zanzibar foreshore."

These execrable conditions might have persisted indefinitely. But just as bicyclists helped transform Americans' thinking about gender roles and fitness, their indignation over the state of the country's roadways altered how those roads were built and used. In the 1880s, the only self-propelled vehicles on any US roads were a few steam-powered buggies—and it would be decades before cars came into common use—but cyclists had already begun laying the groundwork for the interstate highway system. It was only one of several ways in which the bicycle would make American car culture possible.

High-wheel bicycles were the first bikes that could be ridden outdoors for any distance, and as soon as they appeared in the United States, cyclists began kvetching about the roads. "The majority [of Americans] do not know what a good road is," wrote one bicyclist in 1882, "and their horses—who do know and could explain the differences in roads—are debarred from speaking." The bike rider, on the other hand, was "the perfect road tester," the cyclist added. "From no other vehicle does a rider descend with so much suddenness and *aplomb*, and with such serious emotion, to investigate a defect in the surface of the highway."

And cyclists could not only speak: they could organize. The first bicycle clubs, which formed in the late 1870s, may have been upper-crusty fraternities for racing and socializing, but they quickly developed a political agenda. Cyclists had to fight for a place to ride. With the arrival of the Ordinary in 1878 had come renewed enforcement of old bans on velocipede riding. In Boston, police stopped cyclists and shooed them off the streets; riders in Hartford, New York, and other cities faced similar treatment. So cyclists banded together to press for access to public thoroughfares. A national organization founded in 1880, the League of American Wheelmen (LAW), sought to make the country safe for wheeling. Colonel Albert A. Pope, the Columbia Bicycle impresario who first popularized the high-wheeler, helped drive this civic effort, which dovetailed conveniently with his business interests.

Early court cases regarding road use went against bikers—in 1881, three cyclists who very publicly defied a ban on riding in New York's Central Park were briefly jailed, and their civil suit went nowhere, despite attorneys retained by Pope—but with continued pressure and mounting evidence that bikes were not uniquely dangerous, the cyclists eventually prevailed. In 1887, New York governor David B. Hill signed a controversial bill allowing cyclists access to all public thoroughfares in the state; in exchange, the LAW backed his (successful) reelection campaign. In 1890, the landmark Kansas case *Swift v. Topeka* established bicycles as vehicles with the same road rights as any other conveyance. "They are not an obstruction to, or an unreasonable use of the streets of a city," stated the Kansas Supreme Court in its ruling, "but rather a new and improved method of using the same."

But being allowed to use public roads and being able to use them were two different things. As one reporter noted of urban cyclists in 1896, "In Chicago they scurry over wooden blocks, and also perpetually dodge cable cars engineered by maniacs; in Cincinnati and Kansas City they pedal up altitudinous hills, over stony streets and muddy paths; in Boston and Philadelphia and San Francisco their spines are daily impaired by rattling over the deadly cobblestone."

Riders trying to escape the crowded city for the countryside faced other perils. Unmarked—because the farmers who maintained them already knew where they led—and uneven, rural roads stymied cyclists. In July 1896, one biker wrote the *L.A.W. Bulletin* to warn other wheelmen about conditions he found in the Shenandoah Valley in Virginia. "Smooth stretches of road, free from broken stone, were few and far between," he wrote. Encountering wet clay near Staunton, he added, "My companion and myself spent a whole afternoon in covering fourteen miles, and gave up in despair. It required a dismount every few minutes to dig the mud out of the front fork, so the wheel could revolve."

When they ventured out into the countryside on their pricey, futuristic vehicles and discovered the blighted state of the roads, many cyclists—who already regarded themselves as a superior breed—felt obliged to bring conditions up to their higher standards. It wasn't, cyclists insisted, that they selfishly wanted better places to joyride. It was that the progress of society required such places. As one advocate wrote during the high-wheel era, the reform of highway laws was inevitable, "for the bicycle is the vehicle of luxurious roads, and of the highest civilization." The 1887 advent of the low-profile safety bicycle in the United States swelled cyclists' ranks, and the demand for smoother pavements began to go mainstream.

Farmers weren't buying it, though. The dirt roads that had been good enough for the country's founders were good enough for them, many felt, especially if the alternative was swinging sledgehammers to break rocks for unfamiliar Euro-style pavements during planting season. As long as farmers could get a fair price for their crops, wrote one New York state farmer in early 1892, "they will manage to get to market without the aid of fancy roads." The friction between cyclists and farmers was illustrated by a gag in one Idaho newspaper that summer:

> Bicyclist (in disgust): Why do you have such abominable roads in this section?
>
> Farmer: Wall, you see, we're afraid if we made 'em any better, you bicycle fellers will be usin 'em.

Some city residents felt no differently. In New York's Lower East Side and Brooklyn, where children had the run of the streets, parents opposed asphalt pavements for fear of attracting dangerous scorchers.

By the mid-1890s, though, farmers had made common cause with cyclists to press for better roads. What had turned the tide? A full-bore PR campaign, one of the first of the modern era. Both in books such as *The Gospel of Good Roads: A Letter to the American Farmer* and in a new monthly magazine called *Good Roads*, the LAW made the case in pocketbook terms. Because pulling loads through muck or over ruts required extra horsepower, American farmers owned—and fed—at least two million more horses than they would need if the roads were smooth, Isaac B. Potter informed his rural reader in *Gospel*. "A bad road is really the most expensive thing in your agricultural outfit," he wrote. Photos of American horse carts abandoned in mire were published alongside images of horses pulling towering loads of hay over flat dry roads in France, where taxes on city dwellers helped pay for rural road construction. Potter argued that the people who depended on America's country roads deserved a cut of their urban countrymen's taxes too: "The farmer has the same right to demand a means for saving time, space, power, materials and expense as are accorded by the Government to other divisions of society." As a result of such advocacy, some state governments began funding rural road construction, and the federal government took its first tentative steps toward oversight of interstate highways.

While cyclists urged farmers to lobby for better roads, they also lobbied governments directly. LAW representatives monitored local and state government hearings and rallied grassroots support for reform, inspiring the first cash road taxes, which could be applied to highway construction. In mid-1892, Pope printed thousands of copies of a petition demanding that Congress create a federal department to promote "knowledge in the art of constructing and maintaining roads." He enlisted cyclists' help to collect signatures and return signed copies, which he had pasted into an enormous scroll. In 1893, Pope delivered this scroll to the US Capitol on a pair of hand-cranked oak spools that stood seven feet high. The so-called monster petition bore 150,000 signatures. That same year, Congress authorized the creation of the Office of Road Inquiry, a two-man fact-finding office that was a precursor of the Federal Highway Administration.

In 1896, the US Postal Service boosted rural support for good roads by launching the first rural free delivery routes, in response to lobbying by farmers' unions and the LAW. Rather than having to trek miles over iffy roads to the nearest post office just to check for mail, farmers could now receive the same daily drop-off service as city residents. The catch was that the postmaster would authorize home delivery only if the local roads were passable—a strong incentive for farmers to see that they were.

It had begun to seem that whatever bicyclists wanted, bicyclists got. When railroads in New York started charging extra to transport passengers' cycles, the bicycle lobby persuaded the state legislature to ban the practice. When pedestrian safety advocates sought to require that all bikes in New York City have brakes, the bicycle lobby shot the measure down as an unfair burden, since skillful riders could stop without brakes. In an unsigned 1896 editorial, *Harper's Weekly* noted cyclists' collective political power and implored them to use it gently: "Whatever you insist upon having you can apparently acquire. Do not insist upon having the earth, but be content with such right of way over its surface as may make its primitive uses still feasible, and life upon it still worth living even for folks who do not go on wheels."

But the sheer number of bicyclists—an estimated three million by the late 1890s—was altering life for everyone, on wheels or off. "All mankind is a-wheel apparently and a person on nothing but legs feels like a strange animal," wrote the poet Stephen Crane in 1896. On New York's Western Boulevard (now Broadway) above Columbus Circle, "the bicycle crowd has completely subjugated the street. The glittering wheels dominate it from end to end." Cafés were full of riders in cycling togs; billboards advertised bikes and accessories "with all the flaming vehemence of circus art," and repair shops lined the street, Crane noted. "Everything is bicycle."

At the time, the United States was enduring an economic depression triggered by the pop of a railroad-industry bubble in 1893. In the financial panic that ensued, banks and businesses failed, the price of farm goods plummeted, and the unemployment rate spiked, remaining above 10 percent for five years. Bicycle manufacturing seemed to be the only industry thriving, and other businesses blamed their sorrows upon it. "The watchmakers and jewelers say they are nearly ruined; that all pin money which the young people saved formerly with which to buy watches and jewelry now goes for bicycles," wrote one

Indiana newspaper in 1896. "The tailor, the hatter, the bookseller, the shoemaker, the horse dealer, and the riding master all tell similar tales of woe." Tobacconists, saloon keepers, and accordion salesmen complained they were losing their share of Americans' idle time and, hence, their spending money.

According to that same Indiana newspaper article, the only winners seemed to be innkeepers on the country's long-forgotten turnpikes, who "awakened from a sleep of half a century almost, to find prosperity once more rolling in at their doors." As roads slowly improved, bicycle tourists increasingly explored the fly-over country of their day: the terra incognita between railroad stations, "numberless nooks and corners of the civilized earth that the locomotive rushes by," as *Scribner's* magazine described it in 1894. Wayside inns that had averaged one guest a week for years were suddenly overrun with wheelmen, some of whom installed signposts and created road maps to help other cyclists find their way. And as the historian James Longhurst notes, turn-of-the-century cyclists also led a briefly successful "side-path movement," creating hundreds of miles of separate cinder- or gravel-covered bike paths in jurisdictions across the country. St. Paul, Minnesota, for example, had 115 miles of such paths in 1902, and Monroe County, New York, had 200 miles. (Most of these sidepaths were eventually paved over as roads widened.) When automobile tourists took to the roads in large numbers more than a decade later, they found the way marked, mapped, and paved by cyclists who had gone before.

Cars themselves were in some ways fathered by bicycles. True, inventors had been constructing ungainly steam-powered overland vehicles since the late eighteenth century. And scientists had started tinkering with small internal combustion engines fueled by gunpowder, coal dust, and other solid explosives nearly that early. In 1859, the birth of the US petroleum industry introduced a lightweight liquid fuel called gasoline, and around the same time, a French physicist invented the lead-acid battery—a rechargeable technology still used in cars today. So by the mid-1860s, both gasoline engines and lead-acid batteries showed the potential to power land vehicles. And as the historian Clay McShane argues, steam cars built in the 1870s had the potential to replace horse-drawn vehicles, but could not surmount public fears of coal-dust pollution and the prospect of boiler explosions.

Still, many of the mechanical devices needed for a practical horseless carriage had to wait for the bicycle. Pneumatic tires, differential gears that allowed two tires on the same axle to spin at different rates (as when making a turn without tipping over), ball bearings that reduced friction and wear on the axles, and other technological improvements to land navigation had been developed for bicycles and tricycles starting in 1869; these advances formed the basis of early automobile chassis. The brothers Charles and J. Frank Duryea, who built America's first working gasoline-powered car in Springfield, Massachusetts, in 1893, were bicycle mechanics. In fact, most early car builders, including Henry Ford, had worked on bicycles first.

Even many of the mass-production methods associated with the early automobile industry had been employed by bike makers, as the historian David Hounshell described in his influential 1984 book, *From the American System to Mass Production*. When Pope started manufacturing high-wheelers in the late 1870s, he adapted a process known to Europeans as the "American system of manufacture": instead of one artisan making each unit from scratch, piece by piece, Pope's factory workers used machine tools to crank out uniform parts that other workers then assembled into chains, frames, wheels, and completed bicycles. This time-saving division of labor originated with New England rifle makers in the 1820s and had spread to the makers of sewing machines, clocks, and other small devices by the 1860s. As Hounshell showed, Pope and other bicycle manufacturers refined and expanded the system, especially after demand for the safety bicycle exploded into an unprecedented sales opportunity. By 1897, US makers were producing more than a million bicycles a year, using innovations that included electric resistance welding (a way to fuse two metal pieces that required less skill than arc welding); sheet metal stamping (a practice adapted from plow-making in which bike parts were cut from rolls of steel rather than individually forged); and "scientific testing" (an attempt to identify design flaws by stressing products until they failed). The geographer Glen Norcliffe has noted that Pope's vast Hartford factory complex, which housed every stage of bicycle production and included a corporate headquarters as well, "served as a prototype for a Fordist plant." Not every automotive innovation came from the cycle industry, of course: Henry Ford claimed to have based his groundbreaking 1913 moving assembly line on the grisly "disassembly line" conveyors at Chicago meatpacking plants. But much of what early automakers knew about building cars, they learned by building bicycles. (Pope himself started producing electric cars in 1897.)

Bicycles made cars feasible. They also made cars *necessary*. Their popularity helped spark a collective leap of imagination, showing Americans the promise of self-powered travel and forging a crucial link between horse-drawn carriages and automobiles. Inventors in Europe, where intercity distances were shorter and roads smoother, took the lead in early automotive development; the first gasoline-powered vehicle—a tricycle—was patented in Germany by Karl Benz in 1886. In 1891 and 1892, though, dozens of Americans began trying to invent their own cars. Why did so many Americans suddenly want to build cars then, when the gasoline engine had been around for decades and the rudimentary car itself for five years? Surely, news of advances by Benz and other European motorcar tinkerers had something to do with it. In addition, electric trolleys had accustomed city dwellers to the idea of faster street traffic, and the spread of smooth asphalt pavements in cities seemed to invite it. But crucially, American inventors were inspired by the bike's new example of everyday automobility. Before 1890, "the bicycle had not yet come in numbers and had not directed men's minds to the possibilities of independent, long-distance travel over the ordinary highway," recalled the automotive pioneer Hiram Percy Maxim, who began work on his own gasoline-powered tricycle in 1892. "We thought the railroad was good enough." And before the bicycle, it was. A writer for the *New York Times* recalled in 1925 what the arrival of the bike meant: "All the little human entities which had followed steel tracks in streets and roads suddenly found themselves released. They tasted the power of locomotion in their own right. After that, how could they be content with timetables?"

But soon, just like the boneshaker mania of 1869, the safety bicycle boom of the 1890s collapsed without warning. By 1898, the glittering hordes that had clotted Broadway just two years before were vanishing. Prices for the machines plunged from over $100 to less than $20 as manufacturers rushed to dump their inventory and get out of the market. Between 1899 and 1902, US bicycle sales plummeted by 80 percent. From its peak of more than 102,600 members in 1898, the LAW shrank to 77,000 members in 1900 and fewer than 8,700 by 1902.

It is commonly assumed that cars caused this bust, muscling cycles off the streets. But in reality, cars remained a rare luxury long after bicycles had lost their allure. Wrote the *Washington Post* in 1906, "Not more than one-hundredth of the people who formerly rode wheels can now afford automobiles." In 1908, a Model T Ford cost $800; you could have bought fifty bicycles for that. And in 1910 there were still nearly two hundred Americans for every motor vehicle in use.

Nevertheless, by 1900 the bicycle craze had given way to other manias, including euchre and Ping-Pong (which came complete with dire warnings of "the weird and woe-begone ping-pong face"). Even the most fervent society cyclists couldn't explain why they had quit riding. "I have tried to discover just why we put our wheels away," William H. Arthur, a former president of the Illinois Cycling Club, told a reporter in 1902. "No one can give any good, logical reason." Arthur did admit that uncultured "rowdies" had given the sport a bad name—at country inns, these clods insisted on "eating in their sweaters" rather than changing into dining attire—but added that their behavior was "not enough so to actually kill bicycling."

And indeed, bicycling had not been killed at all. Hundreds of thousands of urban workers continued to use bicycles for transportation. But the wheel had been demoted: it wasn't classy anymore. As one observer noted in 1901, "Fashionable society, in one of its whims, takes up this or that novelty and makes it the fad because it is comparatively scarce. The rage stimulates production until the thing sought becomes so common that everybody can enjoy it, which in turn kills the fad." In the process, the writer added, investment and competition lead to technological advances that remain after the fever has broken: "The bicycle fad disappeared, but it left behind it a perfect machine of great practical utility and within the reach of even a poor man's purse."

But the bicycle boom's legacy went beyond that. While it flourished in the 1890s, the bicycle helped midwife a major transformation in American society, one that is still felt today. From its beginnings as a turbocharged rich boy's toy to its downgraded status as a throwaway steed of the masses, the bicycle ushered in the beginnings of consumer culture as we know it.

Five

FROM PRODUCERS TO CONSUMERS

Historians of technology have a rule called the "principle of symmetry." Basically, it says that if you're going to blame external factors for a machine's failure—as you might pin the boneshaker's demise on America's horrible roads—then you have to give external factors credit when a machine succeeds. In other words, a new technology doesn't catch on by being intrinsically superior to its predecessor; it catches on because the world is ready for it. The air-filled tire, for example, was first patented by the Scottish engineer Robert William Thomson in 1845, more than forty years before his countryman John Boyd Dunlop came up with the same idea for his son's tricycle. But despite successful public demonstrations on horse-drawn carriages, Thomson's inflatable "aerial wheel" was just a curiosity. In 1854, the bicycle hadn't yet brought a large group of people into close communion with joint-jangling cobblestone roads, so most people saw no need for an air-filled tire. By the time the cycles of the 1880s inspired Dunlop to seek a cushier ride, Thomson's invention had been forgotten.

As discussed in the last chapter, Dunlop's reinvention of the pneumatic tire completed the bicycle's transformation into a machine for all ages and both sexes. It offered a faster, smoother, safer ride than the Ordinary. Still, the ensuing decade-long bike boom that followed was hardly inevitable. In a different context, the safety bicycle might well have been a one-summer fad in the United States, just as its low-rise predecessors, the draisine of 1819 and the boneshaker of 1869, had been. Here is what gave the latest bike staying power: cities bursting with new citizens eager for amusement; middle-class housewives itching for autonomy; doctors endorsing exercise. And crucially, the birth of America's first mass medium—national general-interest magazines—in the early 1890s. These publications became powerful persuaders that both fed off and nourished the new bicycle industry. Together, they helped give rise to a faith in the ability to buy happiness that remains ingrained in American culture.

The country did have a few national publications before the 1890s, but they appealed to limited audiences. Lofty journals of politics and literature such as *Harper's* and the *Atlantic*, both launched in the 1850s, spoke to an educated elite. Priced as high as thirty-five cents an issue (equal to about $9.50 today), they were "leisurely in habit, literary in tone, retrospective rather than timely, and friendly to the interests of the upper classes," according to *A History of American Magazines*, Frank Luther Mott's magisterial 1957 chronicle of the industry. Meanwhile, starting in the late 1860s, so-called mail-order magazines such as the *People's Literary Companion* and women's magazines, including the *Ladies' Home Journal*, wedged a bit of homey advice for farmwives among copious ads for soap powder, patent medicines, and other household products to be sent away for. These circulars, which cost only five or ten cents each, reached hundreds of thousands of subscribers. Their publishers benefited from a confluence of propitious developments: an 1879 drop in postage rates; the invention of new printing technology such as halftone photoengraving for illustrations (which cost one-tenth as much as wood engraving); and the engineering of industrial-scale processes for turning wood pulp into paper, much cheaper than traditional paper made of fibers from old rags. But there was no national newspaper, and between the high- and the low-brow, no national magazine unified the reading public.

This changed in 1893, when Samuel S. McClure—a thirty-something striver whose first job had been as a window washer at a bicycle rink owned by Albert A. Pope, and who had worked his way up to editing two of Pope's cycling magazines—launched *McClure's* magazine at fifteen cents an issue. With his new venture, McClure sought to compete with the high-minded *Century* magazine. In response, *Cosmopolitan*, a seven-year-old family magazine, soon dropped its price from twenty-five cents to twelve and a half cents, and four-year-old *Munsey's*, a "light, bright, timely" (according to its publisher, Frank A. Munsey) general-interest magazine, cut its price from a quarter down to a dime. *McClure's* and *Cosmopolitan* quickly matched *Munsey's* lower rate, and circulation for all three magazines leapt, as did advertising revenue, more than making up the losses in subscription income. What these publishers realized was that the big money wasn't in selling magazines to readers; it was in selling readers to advertisers. Some American corporations were growing into national entities that thrived on brand recognition, and national magazines could provide that. Within a few years, publishers launched scores of ten-cent magazines, characterized by lavish illustrations, lively writing, varied subject matter, and a fascination with newness and progress that suited the tastes of advertisers flogging merchandise. Between 1890 and 1905, the circulation of monthly periodicals in the United States spiked from 18 million to 64 million in what was called a "magazine revolution." (Local newspaper circulations also rose, thanks to the same technological advances.)

And who were the advertisers that bankrolled this revolution? The manufacturers of patent medicines, cleaning products, foods (including Quaker Oats and Nabisco), and clothing were well represented. But right behind them were bicycle makers, who sought to lure readers to their dealers' local showrooms. The March 1896 issue of *Cosmopolitan*, for example, contained ads from thirty-eight bike companies. In 1898, bike ads constituted 10 percent of all national advertising. During the economic downturn of the 1890s, the flourishing cycle industry's support was key to the survival of general-interest magazines—and of the splashier, more image-driven ad formats the new printing technologies made possible. "To the bicycle manufacturers of the 1880s and '90s advertising owes that which all owe a trail-blazing pioneer," wrote Frank Presbrey, a historian of the advertising industry, in 1929. "The bicycle gave the magazine a measure of recognition as a medium."

Naturally, bicycle makers also benefited from their ads, which stoked the country's sudden and ravenous hunger for their products. In cartoony illustrations and dreamy art nouveau tableaux, these ads portrayed the bicycle as a portal to a world of adventure and freedom. "I never enjoyed summer more," exults one lady rider in an 1892 Columbia ad as she waves to two neighbors on a porch. "I'm simply happy." Some bicycle ads didn't depict their products at all, choosing instead to create an elegant mood. One 1894 ad for Chicago's Crescent Bicycles features a serene maiden in Grecian garb perched on a crescent moon, peering down at a presumably Crescent-filled world. If you buy a Crescent, the ad implies, her grace can be yours.

The articles in these magazines were predominantly bike friendly, too, as publishers whipped up editorial content to entice their best advertisers. In one overheated 1896 short story, a would-be burglar redeems himself with a harrowing nighttime bicycle ride to warn an oncoming train of a washed-out bridge; in another, a young girl defies her overbearing father by hopping a bike to her own elopement. Nonfiction articles lauded cycling's health and social benefits, abandoning the debate over

The bicycle industry pioneered the use of image advertising, which focused less on a product's actual characteristics than on how ownership would make the consumer feel. This ethereal Grecian maiden appeared widely in advertisements for Crescent Bicycles in the spring of 1894, including in the *Youth's Companion* (March 22, 1894).

whether women should ride in favor of tips on what to wear while awheel. Readers couldn't avoid the suggestion that buying a bicycle would significantly improve their lives. As Albert A. Pope later recalled to a journalist for *Profitable Advertising* magazine, "We created the demand for bicycles with one hand, and the supply with the other."

The message that buying a particular product will make you happier or cooler or more loveable is still so entrenched in American society that it is hard to imagine an America without it. But as the Columbia University historian William R. Leach argues in his influential 1993 book *Land of Desire: Merchants, Power, and the Rise of a New American Culture*, that message was brand-new in the 1890s—and it was a conscious creation of the era's industrialists and marketers. Before then, ads typically announced the availability and price of a product, or at most touted its merits compared to its competition's. Ads didn't play on readers' self-images to create demand where there was none.

What allowed the change, Leach writes, was a shift in how Americans made their living. For much of the nineteenth century, wealth meant owning land that could produce food and raw materials such as tobacco and cotton. But as the country's economy became more industrial and more urban, wealth came to depend less on what you could make than on what you could buy. The rich were those with money to build factories and pay wages. And members of the middle class, increasingly, were clerks and managers in someone else's corporation, dependent upon capitalists for their living. Lower-income workers lost autonomy too, writes the scholar Richard Ohmann: "Clock in, clock out, follow the pace of the machine, give over to your boss the tasks of conceiving and planning."

With all these new wage earners, the cash in circulation in the United States shot up: total personal income, adjusted for inflation, nearly doubled between 1880 and 1900. Capitalists craved this money to fuel factories, and workers needed it to buy products they no longer had time to make at home. Advertising connected the two groups, urgently instructing readers in the most modern ways to spend. For example, instead of cooking up all-purpose soap using animal fat and wood ash, as their grandmothers had done, or buying chunks of generic soap cut from blocks at the grocer's, as their mothers had, women now learned from ads that they ought to shell out for multiple cleansers: packaged Pears' or Ivory brand soap for their faces; Sapolio or Soapine for scouring; Pearline or Wool Soap for laundry. "Some soaps are quick and sharp; too sharp, they bite; the skin becomes rough and tender," read an 1891 ad for Pears' that instructed readers on the new categories. "Washerwomen suffer severely from soaps no worse than such; indeed the soaps are the same." For a gleaming complexion, though, "Pears' is perfect."

Industry didn't just offer replacements for homemade products. It devised tantalizing new must-have objects, with the safety bicycle topping the list. "Are you satisfied to move along as your grandfathers did before you: patient and plodding, so long as you get there some time," asked one 1892 ad for the Victor brand, "or would you rather keep pace with the world as it rolls on?" An 1895 ad for the Stearns brand assured readers that they deserved splendor: "The best bicycle is none too good for you." Bicycle advertisers were the first to successfully market a costly luxury to the masses, inspiring unprecedented levels of getting and spending, and turning youngsters into eager earners. The lust for money to buy a bicycle, wrote Presbrey, "made many a boy useful to others and himself who might have been a failure" otherwise.

Fresh frills for middle-class households included parlor organs, gramophones, cameras, laundry wringers, carpet sweepers, and indoor plumbing fixtures. "If your new house has no bath room, don't let that annoy you," counseled one 1894 ad in the *Ladies' Home Journal*. "Buy a Mosely Folding Bath Tub"—a Murphy bed–like appliance that hid a water heater and a fold-down tub within a mirrored wooden cabinet. Ads on the same page flogged a gas-powered iron; an Oriental floor cushion ("No well appointed home is complete without one"); and Cottolene shortening, an "entirely new food product" made of suet and cottonseed oil. The issue also contained thirteen ads for cycles, including one that promised to attract "wheeling companionship," that is, suitors.

As households increased their spending power, manufacturers' offerings grew more and more extravagant. One 1897 issue of *Munsey's* noted the advent of diamond bracelets for dogs. "Every day brings some novelty, tending to put into ever more grotesque array the 'refinements' of luxury," wrote one fed-up commentator. "There is no end to the restless seeking after new excesses, new frivolities, and new follies." Fashionable cyclists obsessively traded in year-old bicycles for the latest models. Some even stopped riding till they could afford to upgrade. Being seen on an outdated bike might raise eyebrows. "Is it true that Bigley has met with business reverses?" asks one character in an 1898 newspaper gag. "Couldn't say," comes the reply, "but his wife is riding a last year's wheel."

It is easy to see why capitalists wanted the American public to buy, buy, buy—and equally easy, from a twenty-first-century vantage point, to see the value in telephones, running water, and other luxuries that soon became necessities. But dog bracelets? A new bike every year? What was driving the public to consume beyond its needs? To be sure, humanity had indulged in plenty of greed and ostentation in the past, but this widespread acquisitiveness seemed novel. In 1899, the economist Thorstein Veblen labeled it "conspicuous consumption." In peaceful societies, he wrote, the rich had traditionally distinguished themselves through idleness and self-indulgence. But among the wage-earning bourgeois of the 1890s—whose breadwinners couldn't slack off without sacrificing their status—the way to lay claim to a higher social standing was to accumulate and display unnecessary possessions. The proper middle-class home became encrusted with superfluous objects: doilies, tapestries, curios, ashtrays, tea services, multiple sets of china. (Because bicycles were a current fad, many decorative items featured their image, as did unrelated consumer products such as Bicycle playing cards.)

The way people acquired things had changed, too. Since the Civil War, a few dry-goods stores—including Bloomingdale's, Lord & Taylor, and Macy's—had burgeoned into multicategory downtown "department" stores, and shopping was transformed from a neighborhood chore into a destination pastime for middle-class housewives. For the first time, people shopped for the sake of shopping. They even shopped in order to go shopping. As one woman confided to another in an 1898 conversation overheard by a *New York Times* reporter, diamond solitaire earrings were too flashy for a refined woman to wear to parties or to church, but they were "invaluable for making an impression upon the clerks."

Spurred in part by the bicycle industry, Americans had begun to see themselves as consumers rather than as producers. No longer in control of their workdays, the middle-class reveled in what they *could* control: their cash. The eventual result, Leach writes, was "a society preoccupied with consumption, with comfort and bodily well-being, with luxury, spending, and acquisition, with more goods this year than last, more next year than this." It is a value system familiar to anyone who has ever swapped a working smartphone for one that works a smidge better—or has endured teasing for clinging to a familiar old cell, the modern equivalent of "last year's wheel."

At the same time that bicycle advertising stoked Americans' passion for new household belongings, bikes and better roads were helping create a whole new housing pattern on the outskirts of cities. The first commuter suburbs had emerged early in the nineteenth century, organized near ferry lines like the one that linked Brooklyn's Fulton Street to Manhattan's, or along locomotive tracks like Philadelphia's Main Line. (Originally, "commuters" were passengers who commuted—that is, reduced—their fares by buying monthly or quarterly passes.) But most of these early suburbs were leafy retreats for the well-to-do: an escape from the noise, smell, and sheer humanity of urban areas. Some city dwellers did shuttle to work via horse-drawn streetcar or, after 1873, steam-powered cable car, but many workers couldn't afford the daily fares, and on jammed city streets, those vehicles often moved no faster than pedestrians anyway. Most people still needed to live within an hour's walk of work. But then two swifter alternatives arrived—the safety bicycle in 1887 and the electric streetcar the following year—and the space and quiet of suburbia became a middle-class option.

It is well known that electric trolleys triggered the growth of American suburbs during the 1890s, when metropolises splayed out like starfish along the new transit lines, reaching nearby towns such as Evanston, Illinois (Chicago), and Santa Monica, California (Los Angeles), with their arms. Increasingly, ordinary Americans could live on placid tree-lined streets and work at jobs downtown. What is less well known is that the bicycle preceded—and then competed with—trolleys as a way to pursue the picket-fence life. In 1892, while the first streetcar companies hustled to secure rights-of-way and install their tracks, the bicycle was already being hailed by one booster as "a leading factor in the building up of attractive suburbs." The writer singled out New Jersey, an early builder of state-funded asphalt pavement, as a place where good roads encouraged cyclists to settle and commute from: "This consideration has been largely effective in giving to the Oranges a goodly proportion of their population." (Angeline Allen, the Newark rider who so notoriously wore trousers in 1893, lived in nearby East Orange until her divorce.) Suburban land values rose, and advocates gave the bicycle credit. "Man's legs have been lengthened and his speed increased by the introduction of the bicycle," read a report in the *L.A.W. Bulletin and Good Roads.* "Property that was once denominated as 'outside' [the metropolis] may now be termed 'inside.'"

The bike and the streetcar blossomed in tandem, and for much of the 1890s, it wasn't clear which would become the dominant mode of urban transport. All that was clear was that horse-drawn travel was on its way out. The price of horses dropped, and an 1898 report by the State of Pennsylvania's secretary of internal affairs blamed "the very extensive introduction of electricity and the bicycle for the purposes for which animal power has always been used." At that point, between the trolley and the two-wheeler, the latter seemed to be winning: streetcar fare receipts in the state had fallen in 1897, whereas bike use rose. "Many more persons travel the streets on bicycles than patronize the [street]cars," the Pennsylvania report states, adding that the bicycle "has become a most formidable competitor of the street railway companies." It was like that all over. In Springfield, Massachusetts, bike commuters thronged downtown streets every workday evening. "In the few minutes which succeed the happy hour of 6 there is a rushing tumult there which it is hazardous for the pedestrian to breast," the local newspaper reported. "The two streams of bicyclists pass each other with bewildering rapidity." Horse-drawn trucks and carriages mingled with the bikes and trolleys, though automobiles were still rare, hinky, and way too expensive for daily commuting. In 1899, one science writer allowed that the stratospheric cost of the auto would probably drop eventually, but added that the vehicle "will never, of course, come into as common use as the bicycle." Another writer predicted that "some other invention" would one day take the bike's place, but "as yet the 'some other invention' has not made itself known."

Streetcars soon won out over bikes as the latter's fashionability faded away. In 1901, the *L.A.W. Magazine* suggested that cyclists had switched to streetcars because they had gotten lazy, but the historian Paul Rubenson raises another possibility: that American manufacturers' preference for fussy, high-maintenance single-tube racing tires made their bikes much less dependable for commuting than the heavier but more practical tires used overseas. Cars and buses would later supplant streetcars, extending the suburbs' tentacles far into the countryside. But it was the bicycle that first promised American office workers a daily retreat from urban grit—and a house and yard in which to display their burgeoning collections of machine-made stuff. The safety bicycle may have caught on because Americans were ready for it, but the bike, in turn, helped ready America for the next technological leap.

Six

THE INFINITE HIGHWAY OF THE AIR

The bachelor brothers who owned Wright Cycle Company in Dayton, Ohio, were known for their eccentricities. Both of them lanky and reserved, one of them rumpled and the other fastidious, they lived with their father—a bishop in the Church of the United Brethren in Christ—and their unmarried sister in a white clapboard house a couple of blocks from their shop. When not building or repairing safety bicycles, the thirty-something brothers tinkered obsessively, devising a calculator, an improved typewriter, and other mechanical oddities. Once, when stuck with two old high-wheelers they had accepted as trade-ins, the brothers welded the monsters into a tandem and rode it around their neighborhood. Others who tried to ride the treacherous machine were quickly and amusingly ejected by its tricky steering system.

So when Orville and Wilbur Wright emerged from their brick storefront shop one calm fall day in 1901 with another funny-looking bike, the neighboring shopkeepers probably weren't surprised. This bicycle had started out as a regular safety, but the brothers had taken a third wheel, laid it on its side like a pizza, and mounted it that way above the front wheel.

This third wheel had two pieces of sheet metal sticking up from its rim. One, a curved piece about the size of a legal pad, was positioned at about twelve o'clock; the other, a flat piece about the size of a business letter, was at nine o'clock.

As one of the brothers pedaled the bike fiercely up the red-brick pavement of busy West Third Street or down one of the unpaved residential streets nearby, the bike's third wheel spun in the breeze. And this revealed a big problem: once the cycle got up to speed, the wheel wasn't supposed to turn at all. According to the most advanced science of the day, the curved sheet at the bike's front should have caught just enough air to counterbalance the flat one, and the wheel should have stopped spinning. With their peculiar contraption, the Wrights had just confirmed that the most advanced science of the day was wrong.

There was no such thing as an airplane yet, but many people—including the Wright brothers—were trying to invent one. Indulging their natural curiosity, the Wrights had already spent two summers in the remote fishing village of Kitty Hawk, North Carolina, where rolling sand dunes and breezy weather made it possible to test gliders. That fall, they had returned home dejected, unable to understand why their latest model behaved erratically, sometimes bucking its pilot into the sand. "When we left Kitty Hawk, we doubted that we would ever resume our flying experiments," Wilbur, the rumpled brother, later recalled. Although their glider had coasted as far as 389 feet—farther than any other they knew of—he considered their overall efforts a flop. The two-day trip home by sailboat, steamer, and train was glum, as Wilbur noted: "At this time I made the prediction that men would sometime fly, but that it would not be within our lifetime."

But there was something about the *way* their glider failed that irked Wilbur. The wind required to keep the apparatus aloft turned out to be much stronger than Wilbur's calcula-

In 1901, the Wright brothers used one of their St. Clair brand bicycles to fashion a device for testing the effect of air pressure on flat objects. When the cycle was ridden, the two metal airfoils caught the wind and caused the horizontal wheel to spin. This image is from the collections of the Henry Ford (37.724.1/THF17497).

tions had predicted it would be. Either his calculations regarding lift—the force that holds a moving object in the air—were off, or the principles they were based on were wrong. Growing suspicious of a traditional coefficient related to air pressure, the Wrights built their three-wheel test bicycle and disproved the coefficient, which had been in use by scientists for 150 years. With that, their passion for aeronautics returned, and they built a wind tunnel on the second floor of their bike shop to test the lift of various wing shapes, assembling their own charts of coefficients. The six-foot-long wooden tunnel featured a fan powered by a gas engine; the shop had no electricity.

The following summer, the Wrights returned to Kitty Hawk to test a new glider that proved to be more predictable and twice as efficient as the previous year's model. In 1903—convinced that they had discovered how to keep a flying machine in the air—the brothers built a double-decker airplane with a twelve-horsepower engine, linking the motor to the plane's two propellers with a bicycle-style chain-and-sprocket transmission. The wings were braced with bicycle-spoke wires. Orville was particularly proud of the plane's propeller design, which the brothers had devised based on their own data. As he wrote in a letter to a fellow would-be aviator, "Isn't it astonishing that all these secrets have been preserved for so many years just so that we could discover them!!"

In Kitty Hawk on December 17 of that year, this *Wright Flyer* rattled down a sixty-foot wooden track on three bicycle-wheel hubs and lifted off, with Orville on his belly at the helm, to make the first powered, controlled, heavier-than-air flight in history. "I don't think I ever saw a prettier sight in my life," recalled one of five locals who had turned up to watch. "The sun was shining bright that morning, and the wires just blazed in the sunlight like gold. The machine looked like some big, graceful golden bird sailing off into the wind."

It might seem strange now that the millennia-old problem of how to fly was solved by two bicycle mechanics, but at the time it made sense. Cycling was already seen as the closest man might ever get to speeding through the air. The first passenger hot-air balloon had flown in 1783, and the first fully controllable airship—a hydrogen-filled blimp called *La France*—in 1884, but these ponderous floating cushions couldn't replicate the soaring and darting of birds the way cycling seemed to. Wilbur Wright later said that he thought the human yearning for avian flight was as old as humankind. Our prehistoric ancestors, he said, "looked enviously on the birds soaring freely through

The Wright brothers used tools and materials from their Dayton, Ohio, bicycle shop to build their experimental aircraft. This photo shows Wilbur Wright at work in the shop in 1897. From the Library of Congress Prints and Photographs Division, Washington, DC.

space, at full speed, above all obstacles, on the infinite highway of the air."

Many in the scientific establishment insisted that a true flying machine was physically impossible. Nothing big enough to carry a person could ever be strong enough to withstand the resistance of the air, wrote the prominent astronomer Simon Newcomb in October 1903—just two months before the Wrights' first flight. "And, granting complete success, imagine the proud possessor of the aeroplane darting through the air at a speed of several hundred feet per second!" Newcomb added. "It is the speed alone that sustains him. How is he ever going to stop?"

Nevertheless, cyclists could already "fly" at an altitude of five feet or so. The owners of mechanical horses had no need of flying machines, wrote one magazine editor in 1894. "There be steeds that neither eat nor drink, yet Bucephalus in all his glory could not go as fast or as far as they," he opined. "Shall we presently fly? Why fly? Surely we are going fast enough now." Many bikes even had the word "flyer" in their names: White Flyer, Belleville Flyer, Flying Yankee. Bicycle advertisements featured riders coasting merrily through the air, and one ad showed a nonrider plummeting. This ad depicted Darius Green, a popular children's book character known for building his own Icarus-style flying machine—with Icarus-style results. "Darius Green would never have sighed for a flying-machine if he had seen a '95 Victor bicycle," the ad copy noted snidely. Ministers even likened cycling to heavenly flight. "We are riding upon the wind," preached one Brooklyn pastor in May 1895. "What Job did in his figurative escape from trouble, riding on the air, the weary and confined toiler at the desk and counter performs when he shuts the door behind him, comes forth into God's pure air, and mounts his scientific angel."

So whereas many respectable scientists saw heavier-than-air flight as a fantasy, some cyclists felt it was the natural next step. Just as the bicycle had created a demand for powered land transportation, it created a thirst for powered flight. "The bicycle no longer satisfies the longing of mankind toward a freer movement over the face of land and water," reported a writer for the *New York Times* in 1893. "Who is the man to lift us finally clear of the earth?" Some went so far as to say that powered flight would eventually make the bicycle obsolete. As the *Minneapolis Jour-*

nal asked in 1895, "Who will stay on the ground bicycling when it is possible to maintain a flight mid-air?"

And who would create these revolutionary new vehicles? The same people who created the last ones, many thought. "The flying machine problem is liable to be solved by bicycle inventors," wrote a Binghamton newspaper editor in 1896. "The flying machine will not be in the same shape, or at all in the style of the numerous kinds of cycles, but the study to produce a light, swift machine is likely to lead to an evolution in which wings will play a conspicuous part." The bicycle maker Charles Duryea designed a pedal-powered helicopter, though he probably never built it. Said Duryea of the 200-pound machine he imagined: "It is right in our line; is in fact really a development of the bicycle."

There was logic to the editor's prediction that bicycle mechanics would solve the mystery of flight. The bicycle introduced humans to the sensation of flying; its technological development created a precedent for the process of inventing the airplane. Rather than tinker in isolation and emerge with complete, radically new devices to test—as some visionary or crackpot aeronautical inventors had been doing—bicycle manufacturers competed, collaborated, copied each other, and moved together inchwise toward a consensus on how to build the lightest, fastest, and safest vehicles. In other words, the bicycle evolved. The German gliding pioneer Otto Lilienthal, whom Wilbur considered "without question the greatest of [our] precursors," argued in 1896 that the development of flying machines should follow the same pattern. Through methodical experimentation, Lilienthal had developed the first controllable hang glider and could travel more than eight hundred feet through the air. He urged other would-be aviators to try to best him. "The greater the number is of such persons who have the furthering of flying and the perfecting of the flying apparatus at heart the quicker we shall succeed in reaching a perfect flight," he wrote in an (awkwardly translated) article in the *Aeronautical Annual*, a Boston journal for would-be aviators. "The rivalry in these exercises cannot but lead to a constant perfecting of the apparatus, the same as, for instance, is the case with bicycles."

The journal's editor, James Means, made an even stronger link between the two technologies. "The admirable wheel of today is the product of more than eighty years of careful thought and experiment," he wrote. "If the world is to make rapid progress in manflight it must have a much greater confidence in the value and importance of the Lilienthal soarer than it had in the wonderful balancing wheel of 1816." Sadly, Lilienthal died in a gliding accident in August 1896. It was news of his death that reignited the Wrights' childhood interest in aviation. After reading all the aeronautical literature he could get his hands on, Wilbur wrote to the Smithsonian Institution, requesting more material. "I believe that simple flight at least is possible to man," the letter read, "and that the experiments and investigations of a large number of independent workers will result in the accumulation of information and knowledge and skill which will finally lead to accomplished flight."

At the time, most aeronautical experimenters—including Samuel P. Langley, then secretary of the Smithsonian—sought to build airplanes that would automatically balance themselves in buffeting winds. Though scientists had long believed that air moved pretty much like water, with uniform waves and currents, Langley had revealed in 1893 that the atmosphere is much more chaotic than the ocean. Within each puff of wind are eddies, hollows, shears, and other unpredictable movements that can quickly flip or stall a floating object. "Whirlwinds go corkscrewing up and down and to and fro, spinning like tops, or rolling like barrels or scaling at every angle like a boomerang," explained one reporter in 1909. "The air never sticks to one given line or plane of direction." For Langley and like-minded researchers, the answer was to design a flying machine that could right itself like a punching clown. No human pilot could be expected to compensate for wind gusts the way birds do, they believed. As Joseph Le Conte, the president of the American Association for the Advancement of Science and an aviation skeptic, wrote in 1894, "In the bird we have the last perfection of skill acquired by constant practice and inherited through successive generations. Even if the science of aviation were perfect, the exquisite art necessary to manage such a machine seems almost hopelessly unattainable." It seemed Le Conte was right. The self-balancing airplane proved elusive, and its pursuit led to some spectacular crashes, including the catapulting of Langley's four-winged, 750-pound "Aerodrome" straight into the Potomac River on December 8, 1903, nine days before the Wrights first flew.

The Wrights, by contrast, had an insight that came straight from cycling. They understood that a plane didn't need to be stable. Like a bicycle, it could be inherently unstable and could be flown in the same way a bicycle is "flown": by a rider making constant, tiny, unconscious adjustments. "It has been a common aim of experimenters with the aëroplane to solve the problem of equilibrium by some automatic system of balancing," stated the brothers in a 1908 "as told to" story in *McClure's*. "Our idea was to secure a machine which, with a little practice, could be balanced and steered semi-automatically, by reflex action, just as a bicycle is." The Wrights studied the movements of soaring birds and designed a steering system that copied the way birds torque the tips of their wings when they turn. In the *Wright Flyer*, the pilot steered by pushing on levers that warped the plane's wings. (Wilbur first got the idea for the wing-warping system while idly twisting an empty inner-tube box.)

And like a cyclist, a pilot would need practice, the Wrights realized. "If you are looking for perfect safety, you will do well to sit on a fence and watch the birds," Wilbur said in 1901, "but if you really wish to learn [to fly], you must mount a machine and become acquainted with its tricks by actual trial." This is why the brothers built a working glider before they even tried to add an engine: they wanted to learn how to fly. In 1909, after the Wrights had publicized their invention and other aviators had built working planes of their own, one journalist compared the airplane pilot to "the bicycle-rider on a slack wire, armed with a parasol"; like the cyclist, "he must exercise incessant vigilance lest he lose his balance." But the Wrights had developed such skill, another journalist wrote, that they "are often able to remove their hands from the levers, and glide along like the bicyclist who leans back and lets go of the handle bars."

The Wright brothers were not the only wheelmen to succeed in aviation. Lilienthal was an enthusiastic cyclist who once built a high-wheel tricycle rickshaw with his brother. Glenn H. Curtiss, an early Wright competitor who pioneered the use of seaplanes, had been a bike shop owner and bicycle racer. Many early barnstormers were cycle racers first. According to Tom D. Crouch, the author of *The Bishop's Boys: A Life of Wilbur and Orville Wright* and several other books on early flight, the bicycle prepared these aviators both practically and psychologically. Along with introducing people to the sensation of swift flight and proving that any ordinary person could develop balancing skills, the bicycle afforded an unprecedented sense of independence and control that translated into the confidence to fly, Crouch says. Of course, not every cyclist had the vision or drive to accomplish what the Wrights did. "They were engineers of genius who happened to be bicycle makers," Crouch writes. "They demonstrated the insight, perseverance, skill, and courage required to move from a basic conception to the development of a practical, working airplane."

People would no doubt have figured out how to fly eventually even without the bicycle, but it was the bike that made it happen when it did and made America the birthplace of aviation.

Just two years after the Wrights' first flight was Albert Einstein's "miracle year" of 1905, during which he published four papers that shattered previous thinking about space, time, mass, and energy. One of those papers laid out Einstein's special theory of relativity, which gave rise to the famous equation $E = mc^2$. There is no direct connection between the Wrights' work and Einstein's, other than that both took place during an unprecedented flowering of science and technology in which the bicycle had played an instigating part. In fact, Einstein's ideas on the relative nature of time are rumored to have been inspired by the bicycle. In one very widely reported—but apparently apocryphal—quotation, Einstein claimed that he "thought of [relativity] while riding my bicycle." According to the legend, Einstein cooked up his idea while contemplating the speed of the beam from his headlight. Einstein's biographers have found no basis for this appealing myth, but it is true that Einstein rode a bicycle in his youth, like most of his peers—he turned twenty in 1899. And since his experiments were "thought experiments" in which he imagined the behavior of physical bodies and forms, it is likely that the experience of moving and balancing on a bike informed his thinking. In any event, the bicycle clearly had an influence on how he saw the world. As he once wrote in a letter to his son, "Life is like riding a bicycle. To keep your balance, you must keep moving."

The 25th Infantry Bicycle Corps was stationed at Ft. Missoula, Montana. In August 1896, it rode to Yellowstone National Park to demonstrate the bicycle's value in military troop movements. This photograph, of the corps at Minerva Terrace, is from the Haynes Foundation Collection of the Montana Historical Society Research Center Photograph Archives.

Seven

THE CYCLES OF WAR

Their shirts were blue gingham and their canvas knickers a pale, dead-grass green—or at least they had been once. By the time the nineteen soldiers rolled into St. Louis, Missouri, on July 24, 1897, weeks of sun, grit, toil, and sweat had faded their US Army uniforms to a dull, tattered gray. "Their natty blue coats couldn't be sold for dust rags in a second-hand clothing store," one journalist reported. "[The men] are actually a lot of weather-beaten scarecrows." The troops of the 25th Infantry Bicycle Corps, who had just ridden 1,900 miles, wore their rifles slung over their shoulders. As they glided in four-man platoons up one last hill to their final destination—a restaurant in the city's central Forest Park—their steel bayonet scabbards clanked against the muddy frames of their bikes.

These African American enlisted men belonged to the segregated 25th Regiment. Six weeks earlier, they had left their fort in Missoula, Montana, along with two white officers, on a road trip meant to demonstrate the military value of the bicycle. Each soldier toted about forty pounds of camping and combat gear strapped to his bike, which weighed more than thirty pounds on its own. During their rolling march, the men had surmounted the Continental Divide; sloshed through ankle-deep slush; blistered their soles in broiling desert sands; forded chest-high rivers with their bikes on their shoulders; and trudged through a sticky black clay mud known as "gumbo" that they had to slice from their gunked-up spokes every few feet. In Wyoming, they encountered hailstone drifts eight feet high; in Nebraska, vast, parched expanses where any trickles of water were poisoned by mineral salts. Over one rough patch between resupply points, the going was so slow that the troops staggered on for forty-five hours without sleep, some hallucinating as they went.

"We have endured every hardship except being shot at," said James A. Moss, the twenty-five-year-old lieutenant who led the expedition. The thin, wiry young officer had aggressively lobbied army brass for permission to make this trial run, but not out of any love of cycling. "The truth is, I find no pleasure in riding," he told a reporter along the way. "I take up my wheel as I would the handle of a plow. My only interest in it is its use in military science."

And where military science was concerned, the US Army was lagging behind. The service's standard-issue firearm had only recently changed from a single-shot rifle designed in 1873 to a newer repeating rifle that could fire five shots between reloads. (European soldiers had been issued repeating rifles since the 1880s.) Even when American arms manufacturers invented deadlier weapons, such as the rapid-fire Gatling gun, they sold most of their inventory to European countries. Those Old World powers had tetchy neighbors to intimidate and colonial rebellions to quell; the United States, for the moment, had no such problems. By 1890, America's western frontier was closed, and the wars between settlers and native peoples had largely ended. Neither Canada nor Mexico threatened to invade over land, and the country's sea borders were defended by the navy, not the army. Some lawmakers didn't even see the point of having a standing army, and the army's slim budget and outdated technology reflected this. "While being the most progressive nation on earth in matters civil, we are among the most conservative in affairs military," complained Lieutenant Henry Whitney, a future brigadier general, in 1895. "Old ideas are regarded almost as a fetish; we shrink from making new experiments."

So it was with bicycles. European powers had begun using the machines in military exercises as early as 1875, when Italian commanders dispatched cyclists as messengers during field maneuvers. Quieter, cheaper, and faster than horses (at least on paved roads), and raising no telltale cloud of dust, bicycles proved useful for stealth missions. An English colonel first employed bike scouts in 1885; within a few years, as many as 5,100 cyclists were attached to British volunteer regiments. By the mid-1890s, the armies of France, Germany, Switzerland, Belgium, Austria, Spain, the Netherlands, and Russia all included cycling soldiers, who acted as couriers, scouts, gofers, and spies. Motorized trucks and tanks were still more than a decade away, so most military equipment moved by horsepower, but some European soldiers pedaled artillery guns into position on four-wheeled bike-based carriages or transported injured comrades on stretchers slung between two safeties.

The US Army and some state militias, meanwhile, had only begun to test bicycles, with stunts like an 1891 Connecticut race that pitted a bike messenger against traditional flag signalers. (The wheelman got his message through in ten minutes, compared to forty minutes for the flag signal service.) Still, civilians took notice. "That the bicycle possesses advantages for military use cannot be denied," stated a newspaper in Toledo, Ohio, in 1893. "It may come to pass that the bicycle will totally supersede the horse in time of war." While most observers weren't quite that bullish, many lauded the cycle's potential as a tool of warfare. "[The bicycle] will before long be a military accessory," predicted one Massachusetts pastor during an 1895 sermon. "This imponderable antelope will dash from point to point conveying the soldier and his valuable message like an armored knight of old." A few forward-thinking army officers, including the 25th Infantry's young Lieutenant Moss, urged their superiors to adopt the machines. While the bicycle would never do away with the cavalry completely, Moss wrote in a June 1897 opinion piece, it could perform better than a horse in some situations. "Should not a modern, up-to-date army have both?" he asked.

The following month, when Moss's team of exhausted Buffalo Soldiers rode into St. Louis, it seemed that the answer was yes. The group had averaged fifty miles of travel a day, far faster than the ten daily miles that infantry troops could march over long distances; faster, even, than the thirty daily miles that mounted cavalry could ride, since horses needed frequent rest. It was, in the words of the *St. Louis Star*, "the most rapid military march on record." Moss himself called it "the greatest march known of in military history."

At the top of that final St. Louis hill, Moss called, "Halt!" and the soldiers broke into broad grins and dismounted. After standing for inspection, the relieved and proud—and buff—troops piled their bikes against trees and marched to a restaurant annex for a meal of steak and tomatoes. Then they pitched their dingy tents on a hill near the restaurant to await orders on where to ride next. The following day, thousands of St. Louis cyclists descended on the park to congratulate the men and question them about their odyssey. "Now we're happy," one soldier identified only as "Black Jack" told a reporter. "We get three square meals a day."

Lieutenant Moss wrote to Washington, requesting orders for the troops to ride 500 miles north to St. Paul, Minnesota, but the general who had OK'd the St. Louis trip was out of town, and his subordinate denied Moss's request to extend the journey. Instead, the group was ordered to return to Fort Missoula by train. Six months later, Moss again wrote to Washington, asking whether his men could ride 1,200 miles from Missoula to San Francisco on another test, but the War Department said no to that too. Military leaders were gearing up for war with Spain over control of Cuba, and they didn't have the patience or manpower for bicycle experiments. "The Acting Secretary of War regrets his inability at this time to approve your request," the adjutant general wrote to Moss, "as in his opinion sufficient experiments to meet all knowledge of its merits have been made with the bicycle at present."

The Spanish-American War broke out in April 1898. Moss was transferred to a new infantry battalion and sent to fight in Cuba, where he earned a silver star for gallantry in action and then developed a debilitating case of malaria. By mid-August, the United States had won the war, gaining control of Cuba as well as Puerto Rico, Guam, and the Philippines, which had all been Spanish territories. That October, while still recuperating from malarial fever, Moss wrote to his superiors to propose a 100-soldier bicycle company to keep order in US-occupied Havana. Such a force, he wrote, "could be moved to the seat of a disturbance with inconceivable rapidity." Once again, though, his proposal was rejected, and Moss, who spent the rest of 1898 on sick leave, was in no condition to press the case.

Other military bike advocates in the United States were no more persuasive. Howard Giddings, a major in the Connecticut National Guard, whose cycle messenger had so trounced a signal-flag team back in 1891, lost traction with his troops. As the bicycle boom waned nationwide and the machine's charm dwindled, Giddings gave in to his cyclists' demands that they be allowed to switch back to horses. "It is an open question which mount is most desirable," Giddings wrote defensively in his 1901 annual report. "I have seen both used; both in peace and war, and each has its advantages." Still, he added, "there is a strong and unanimous desire on the part of the members of this Corps to be mounted on horses instead of bicycles." And so they were. The US military establishment didn't see a tactical role for the bicycle in the twentieth-century army and decided to sideline it. That decision would haunt the country many decades later and half a world away.

European armies, on the other hand, continued to develop the bicycle as a tool of war. Both the French and the Russians built folding bikes that soldiers could strap to their backs when crossing rough terrain—or could lay down as leg-breaking obstacles in the path of enemy horses. Though few Europeans seriously imagined cyclists charging into battle like horsemen, many touted the bike's use for rapid, unobtrusive troop movements. In 1896, the French magazine *L'illustration* predicted that the country's cycling soldiers would become like the gnat that drives the lion crazy with bites in an ancient fable: "The lion will be the enemy, disdainful at first, but soon put upon the defensive, and finally conquered by the sorry insect that has tormented it without truce or mercy."

In the bike's first true wartime test, both sides cast themselves as the gnats. During the Second Boer War of 1899–1902 in what is now South Africa, British imperial forces fought to annex two independent republics inhabited by Afrikaans-speaking Boers, the descendants of Dutch settlers. Along with more conventional cavalry, the Brits used cyclists to lay temporary telegraph lines, patrol the railways, and scour the open grassland ahead of columns of soldiers on horseback. Messengers hid rolled-up communiqués inside the seat tubes of their bicycles. The Boers, vastly outnumbered, waged a furious guerrilla war against the British, who horse-proofed the countryside with crisscrossing barbed-wire blockades. The Boers' bikes could go where horses could not, and Boer fighters kept the resistance going for two gruesome years, despite the British tactic of torching their farms and imprisoning their families in brutal concentration camps. When the British finally prevailed and declared martial law, they seized all the bicycles in some Boer strongholds and banned citizens in other towns from riding after dark. To European minds, at least, the bike had enough military value to merit banning.

Early in the twentieth century, the bicycle's motorized descendants began to emerge, and by the start of World War I in August 1914, fighters could theoretically travel by motorcycle, truck, and airplane, though these internal combustion options were still rare, costly, and fragile. Horses—the traditional engines of warfare—still had their uses, and bicycles, too, played a role. When Imperial German Army troops marched through Brussels on the way to attack France in August 1914, the three-day, round-the-clock procession of cavalry, infantry, and artillery soldiers in gray-green uniforms were preceded by a tiny advance team: a captain and two privates on bikes.

In one August 25, 1914, battle in northern France, a platoon of French cyclists made a suicidal attempt to hold a muddy beet field against a much larger force of advancing Germans. The cyclists, with their folded bicycles strapped to their backs, rushed into German rifle fire fifty yards at a time, "though at every rush cyclists fell moaning or motionless," according to one magazine account. When French cannons finally arrived to take up the fight, the few surviving cyclists were ordered to retreat. One French soldier trying to unfurl his bike found it jammed closed. A passing comrade helped free the cycle, and the relieved young man rode away from a battlefield still zinging with bullets. "Close behind sounded the fierce hurrah of the Germans," the magazine story stated, "but infantry at the double are no match for a pair of wheels."

German cycle troops sometimes fared better. On September 3, 1914, as their army marched farther south into France, an advance guard of German bicycle soldiers stole twenty-two miles ahead of their battalion, planning to cross the Marne River near the medieval village of Mont-Saint-Père, about seventy miles east of Paris. French soldiers guarding the Marne River bridge had wired it with explosives in case they needed to flee to the south and destroy the bridge behind them. But the French weren't expecting to see any enemy soldiers just yet. So when the German cyclists appeared and opened fire on the French encampment, they created "a terrible panic," according to one account of the skirmish. Though they greatly outnumbered the German cycle troops, French foot soldiers and horsemen jammed onto the bridge, which blew up before they could get across, sending men and horses to their doom in the river below. The invading cyclists proceeded across the river at the next town over, but they didn't get much farther. French and British troops soon stopped the German advance, and when Allied forces chased the Germans back north across the Marne a week later, it was the cyclists of the French 10th Cavalry Division who crossed the river first.

Before long, both sides had dug the first trenches on what became the western front, a broad, muddy gash of zigzagging ditches and coiled concertina wire. Day after day, soldiers took shelter in these trenches and then stormed out of them into enemy gunfire, sometimes gaining only yards of territory if they gained any at all. The front line moved no more than ten miles in either direction for three years.

In these mucky, savage daytime firefights, bicycles were of little help. But by night, cycles had their uses on the battlefield. One group of New Zealanders, who had come to fight as part of the British Empire, specialized in creeping through the dark to dig ditches and bury communication cables between the Allied forces' trenches. Cycles also continued to move soldiers and messengers behind the lines on both sides. "Horses are slow and quickly become frightened and exhausted," wrote an American reporter in 1915. "It is a common sight to see a patrol pedaling along on low gear on a heavy, muddy road, making good time in comparison to what a horse could do." Unmentioned was the fact that unlike bicycles, horses died in war. And also unlike bicycles, living creatures are not quickly manufactured.

As the war—and technology—progressed, trucks and airplanes increasingly supplanted draft animals and dirigibles. By 1916, British and French engineers had developed the first working armored tanks, which could trundle over the trenches in the scarred no-man's-land. When America joined the fight in 1917, its expeditionary forces brought 29,000 bicycles along, but their users were messengers and supply clerks, not combat troops. By then, it was clear that internal combustion could unleash far greater destruction than pedal power. The arrival of US reinforcements decided the war in the Allies' favor. Backed up to its own borders and blockaded at its ports, Germany agreed to an armistice in November 1918.

According to Jim Fitzpatrick, the author of *The Bicycle in Wartime: An Illustrated History*, the bike performed solidly in World War I, its first large-scale military challenge, but it offered too few surprises to be seen as a success, even by the victors. The cycle "proved to be a valuable tool," Fitzpatrick writes, but "in the final analysis it was totally overshadowed by the astonishing rate of adoption of the wide variety of mechanized transport."

For the Allies, the days of organized military bicycle units were over. Even some of the most storied units of the war, including the New Zealand cable-burying battalions, were disbanded after the armistice. The British army had dissolved all its cycle units by 1922. A history of the London Cyclist Battalion, which had been demobilized shortly after the war, called that force "an interesting military experiment, conceived, developed, and abandoned well within the span of a normal adult lifetime." The swift, silent bike wasn't completely banished from military service in these countries, but its uses were humbler. No one bragged any longer that the bike would supplant the horse, let alone the motorized truck. In the US Army in 1925, only 190 cyclists were assigned to each infantry division of about 20,000 soldiers. Each cavalry division merited one lone cyclist: a medical corpsman.

For the defeated Central Powers—Germany, Austria-Hungary, the Ottoman Empire, and Bulgaria—dismantling military units, including cycle units, was compulsory. The terms of the Versailles peace treaty required Germany to permanently limit the size of its army. But the impoverished and devastated Germans resented this "dictated peace," which many saw as a humiliation. Germany secretly began rebuilding its military almost as soon as the war was over, and its officers studied the war's lessons and errors, including the use of bicycle troops by both sides. In the early 1930s, in the midst of a worldwide depression, the Nazi party rose to power by promising to restore Germany's strength and dignity—and that meant rearming openly, in defiance of the Versailles treaty.

By 1936, Hitler was ready to reoccupy the demilitarized Rhineland region of western Germany. On the morning of March 7 of that year, the mayor of the Rhineland city of Cologne donned a Nazi storm trooper's uniform and proceeded to the town's Dome Square, where he was joined by a lieutenant general from a nearby province. Police cordoned off streets, and a curious crowd gathered. Around noon, three uniformed cyclists in steel helmets rode into the square as the crowd cheered. Behind the riders marched more than 1,500 German soldiers.

When Germany invaded Poland on September 1, 1939, the German army consisted of 100 infantry divisions, with a bicycle reconnaissance company attached to each. And though known for a rapid, mechanized strategy called "blitzkrieg" that shocked neighboring armies with tanks and airpower, Hitler's army relied heavily on horses, trains, and bicycles to transport troops and consolidate its gains after each assault.

France and Britain, which scrambled to catch up with German military production, deployed bicycle troops in World War II as well. One British commando wryly recalled staggering out of his landing craft on the beach at Normandy in 1944, overladen with a tommy gun, ammunition, grenades, clothes, a blanket, coiled rope, a spade, and rations. "With one hand I carried my gun, finger on the trigger; with the other I held onto the rope rail down the ramp," he told an interviewer. "And with the third hand I carried my bicycle."

As in World War I, bicycles proved useful to uniformed troops on both sides for gasoline- and forage-free transport. But in the European theater, it was civilians who used bikes to most memorable effect. The 400,000 Jews confined to the Warsaw Ghetto were banned from most streetcars—and from most of their old jobs—so in early 1940, people began building bicycle rickshaws to provide transport and earn a living. "In the beginning a few of them appeared and caused a sensation," wrote one resident of that doomed sector in his journal. "No one is any longer surprised by such manifestations of the primitivization of life." These hundreds of bike-based taxis offered more than rough transit, though: some were built with a deep under-seat compartment for smuggling as much as forty pounds of meat or butter to famished ghetto residents.

Throughout occupied Europe, bicycles became tools of the resistance, since cars and gasoline were nearly impossible to get. A young teenager in northern France, Eugenie Ceklarz, smuggled notes between coal-train saboteurs in the handlebars of her bicycle. In fascist Italy, the Tour de France winner Gino Bartali rode 110 miles from Florence to Assisi with materials for making counterfeit identification papers for Jews stashed in his seatpost. Even the French underground's Morse code radios were sometimes powered by bicycles rigged up to generators.

In much of occupied France, the Nazis forbade cycling after dark, in order to thwart surprise attacks on their soldiers. They made an exception to the rule, though, for twenty-nine-year-old Guillaume Mercader, a bike shop owner in Bayeaux who had been a professional racer before the war. The slim, taciturn merchant, who wore his dark hair parted down the center and slicked with grease, renewed his racing license so that he could ride the coastal road under the pretext of training. As a leader of the Resistance, Mercader used these "training" rides to gather intelligence about German fortifications and troop movements, which he drew on secret maps he would stash in his bicycle's handlebars and deliver to his undercover contact.

On June 5, 1944, the BBC's French-language service broadcast encoded messages to inform the Resistance that the D-Day invasion would start the following day. When Mercader heard his confirmation message—"The dice are thrown"—he grabbed his bike and rushed off "to alert my key people to an imminent landing," he later recalled. "The night was going to be long." As Mercader spread the word, one team after another took action. The saboteurs, many also on bikes, disabled locomotives at the rail yard, cut telephone lines, blew up train tracks, and otherwise made it as difficult as possible for German forces to communicate. In the largest seaborne invasion the world has ever seen, the bicycle played a crucial supporting role.

The folding bicycles that came ashore with Allied troops—and that wafted down while strapped to the backs of Allied paratroopers—often weren't much use off-road among Normandy's shrubbery-fence hedgerows. And riding on the road was too dangerous: it made troops visible to enemy gunners. The Germans, however, had no choice but to use their bikes.

With the train lines blown and no way to refuel their trucks and tanks, many companies retreated over the roadways by cycle, often with fatal results. Wrote a *New York Times* correspondent: "Daily we see the highways from which fighting has been heard dotted with dead Germans lying near their bicycles."

In the Pacific, by contrast, an Axis power rode the bicycle to (temporary) victory. Japanese cycling soldiers pulled off the biggest military upset of the war, and possibly of all time.

Bicycles had arrived in the Far East in the 1870s, brought by Western expatriates to trading ports such as Shanghai and Yokohama. Japanese craftsmen soon began manufacturing European-style bikes, and by the 1920s the country was exporting them. Ravenous for natural resources and arable land for its booming population, the Japanese Empire seized Korea and parts of China in the early decades of the twentieth century and then cast its eye on the western Pacific and Southeast Asia. In the years before World War II, Japan's military success owed much to its investment in massive battleships, submarines, and advanced aircraft, but its ground troops, often fighting with last-generation equipment, used trucks, horses, and bikes to secure the gains made possible by high-tech weaponry.

In early December 1941—Pearl Harbor Day, to be exact—Japanese landed at the northwest tip of the British territory of Malaya (now Malaysia). Their goal: to travel six hundred miles south and conquer the fortified island city of Singapore at the end of the Malay Peninsula. British leaders thought the feat impossible: protected by battlements and the mighty Royal Navy, Singapore was seen as impregnable. As the editor of the *London Sunday Observer* wrote just weeks before the Japanese landed, "No more formidable stronghold has been known than Singapore today. Malaya, as she is now fortified and manned, is a bristling and terrible obstacle."

And had the Japanese attacked the British on their own terms—by sea or over motor-vehicle roads—that might have been true. Instead, 6,000 soldiers in the Japanese force of 35,000 moved by bicycle over narrow paths through rubber plantations, outflanking the British imperial troops. Riding in groups of sixty or seventy, the Japanese soldiers talked or laughed with one another or sang quietly to themselves. Although the cyclists seemed lighthearted, they "had a resolute expression that reminded one of a touring club out for an arduous competition tour," a US Army intelligence bulletin noted.

When they encountered the mainly Indian or Australian troops who were defending this British imperial territory, the Japanese cyclists often attacked by subterfuge. More than once, Japanese troops dressed as Malay natives and watched an Indian regiment march by, then pulled out their guns and shot their enemies in the back. Meanwhile, Japan's tanks drove south over areas that the cycle troops had spearheaded, and its superior air force dominated the peninsula from above, especially after the Brits made the tactical error of failing to destroy their airfields in retreat.

The Japanese cycle troops' uncanny speed evoked dread. One Australian reporter described the fearsome soldiers as "often six-footers," though in reality their average height was only five foot three. When their blown bike tires couldn't be replaced, the Japanese soldiers would ride on the metal wheel rims. At night, a company of such tire-less bikes created a creaking, rumbling racket that sent British imperial troops scattering and yelling, "Here come the tanks!" Newspapers suggested that the Japanese had learned their shock-attack strategy from their Nazi allies; the commander of Australian forces in Malaya later called the Japanese campaign there "a blitzkrieg on bicycles."

In just ten weeks, British forces retreated all the way to Singapore. According to legend, the island's fortifications weren't designed for attack over the narrow channel that separated it from the mainland: all of Singapore's guns supposedly pointed out to sea to defend against naval attacks. That legend is false, but the true story is hardly more flattering to the British. They had guns pointing at the Japanese invaders, all right, but due to a supply error, they didn't have the proper ammunition. On February 15, 1942, the British surrendered the fort, and Japan took more than 130,000 soldiers prisoner. As Winston Churchill wrote after the war, it was "the worst disaster and largest capitulation in British history."

While the Malay campaign pitted empire (Japanese) against empire (British), it also hinted at the bicycle's advantages in a colonial struggle for independence to come. On bikes, the outmanned Japanese soldiers were nimbler than their adversaries, able to fade in and out of the tropical landscape and the local population. Although the Japanese bicyclists had the support of tanks and bombers, their six-hundred-mile rolling campaign was a prototype of asymmetric warfare.

Japanese troops occupied British Malaya for the duration of the war, just as they did the nearby French imperial territory of Indochina—now Vietnam, Cambodia, and Laos. After the United States dropped atomic bombs on the Japanese cities of Hiroshima and Nagasaki in August 1945, Japan surrendered, and the war was over. France got Indochina back, even as national independence movements agitated for change. Within a few years, Laos and Cambodia gained independence from France, but in their neighbor Vietnam—a country about the size of California with a long, curling coast on the South China Sea—the French hung on, fighting the communist Vietminh for control. The United States, fearing the spread of communism, began sending military aid to the French in 1950. And so it was that the two countries that had claimed credit for the pedal velocipede in 1865—France and the United States—each wound up opposing a bicycle-dependent uprising in Vietnam.

From 1950 to 1953, the United States joined other UN forces on the Korean Peninsula, battling the communist North Korean and Chinese armies to a stalemate that persists today. Both sides in the conflict used bikes—in fact, the Chinese brought in most of their supplies on foot, by pack animal, or by bicycle—but the war's deciding technology was the bomber, which used incendiary napalm bombs to blast the invading northern armies back to the thirty-eighth parallel, incinerating both landscape and civilians along the way.

As warring countries improved their ability to rain down devastation, it began to seem as if future military victories would belong to whoever controlled the air. So in 1953, when the French commander in Vietnam decided to lure his enemies, the Vietminh, into a decisive confrontation, he chose a remote valley in the mountains of northwestern Vietnam where he could build a base around an old colonial airstrip. In the bowl-like valley of Dien Bien Phu, General Henri Navarre reasoned, he could fly in supplies and bomb enemy soldiers on the ground. Navarre, an agile, silver-haired career army officer, felt certain the Vietminh would attack his new base, and certain he would defeat them there.

The Vietminh had a major logistical disadvantage beyond their lack of an air force: although China provided some heavy artillery, and the Soviet Union some trucks, they had few roads. In the steep jungle terrain, they had to move artillery with manpower alone; each piece required dozens of men to move and service it. It was perilous work: at least one man died by throwing himself under the wheel of an artillery piece to keep it from falling into a ravine. And feeding Vietminh fighters required a whole separate army of porters—peasant men and women who trailed the troops on foot. Since those porters also had to eat, on long marches it could take several people to carry enough extra rice for just one soldier.

The French had no such limitations. Their supplies were delivered by air. To feed the troops stationed in Dien Bien Phu, military planes flew in at least thirty tons of food a day, and the base's storerooms contained forty-nine thousand bottles of wine.

But Navarre didn't plan for his enemy's ingenuity. The military commander of the Vietminh, General Vo Nguyen Giap, was a small man with a gigantic forehead and a lively, intense intelligence. He had built his army slowly through scattered guerrilla actions against the French, accumulating new fighters after every successful attack. "We chose the positions where the enemy were relatively weak," Giap later wrote. "The more we fought, the stronger we became." By late 1953, the Vietminh had a force of fifty-five thousand soldiers to mass at Dien Bien Phu, where French troops numbered only fifteen thousand. Giap's plan was to surround the French encampment and systematically strangle it—a classic siege. And to do this, he relied on the bicycle, a common transportation mode for Vietnamese workers since the first safeties were imported from France decades before.

In December 1953, Giap called for a peasant force of twenty thousand to cut new pathways through the jungle for his troops to march along. He ordered communist party officials throughout the northern countryside to muster "brigades of iron horses"—that is, of bicycles—to bring in rice for the soldiers. The bikes were not to be ridden; they were to be laden with bulging canvas sacks holding as much as 440 pounds of food or ammunition, ten times as much as a person could carry. The bikes were then rolled, pushed, or shoved along the narrow mountain paths. "We had one day to make preparations," one village's brigade leader recalled. "We had to fix two hard bamboo sticks—one to form a long handlebar for easier steering, the other to extend the seat [post]" to act as a handle. Camouflaged from French bombers by dense foliage, tens of thousands of these cargo bikes, along with pack ponies and porters on foot, inched through the jungle to the rim of the French-held valley. After fifteen days, one Vietminh army officer recalled, "the colossal human serpent lay coiled up around Dien Bien Phu and awaited an order to tighten its grip." Under French fire and under cover of night, Giap's troops then spent three months digging trenches into the hillside above the encampment and positioning big guns for battle.

And when the Vietminh finally attacked, in March 1954, the French were stunned. They hadn't expected the communists to bring in long-range artillery, let alone burrow it into the slopes leading down to the fort. Moreover, the French hadn't known their enemy could feed an army so large. In the gory series of battles that followed, the Vietminh took heavy losses but still managed to rout division after division and close the main French airstrip, ending resupply flights and medical evacuations. Though French and American planes still dropped in supplies by parachute, much of that material fell into enemy hands. By May 7, the French were starving and broken. They had lost three thousand men, while the Vietminh lost eight thousand, but it was the French who were forced to surrender both the fort and the country.

At a peace conference held in Geneva that summer, the French, the Vietminh, and world powers including the UK and China established a border between North Vietnam and South Vietnam that was supposed to be temporary: a cease-fire line to cool tensions until a planned election could unify the newly independent country. But neither the United States nor anticommunist leaders in the South signed on. Soon, a new conflict sim-

The North Vietnamese Army used bicycles as mechanical pack animals to transport supplies to Vietcong fighters in South Vietnam over the Ho Chi Minh Trail. This photo, shot in North Vietnam in 1969 by Marc Riboud, appears courtesy of Magnum Photos.

mered as American and South Vietnamese Army troops fought communist guerrillas—the Vietcong—in the south. In early 1959, the North Vietnamese Army formally joined the fight; said the communist premier, Pham Van Dong, "We will drive the Americans into the sea." In May of that year, North Vietnam's Central Military Commission ordered the creation of a secret route south along which the country could supply the Vietcong with weapons and fighters. This pathway through the borderlands of Laos and Cambodia became the spine of the communist guerrillas' struggle in Vietnam. The trail was nicknamed the Ho Chi Minh Trail, after North Vietnam's charismatic, scraggly goateed president. As the conflict escalated in the following years, US forces assailed North Vietnam, Laos, and Cambodia with incendiary napalm and the defoliant Agent Orange; self-scattering cluster bombs and forest-flattening "daisy cutters"; armored attack helicopters and supersonic jet fighters: the most sophisticated nonnuclear military technology of the day. But like the French, the Americans were eventually bested by peasants on bikes.

"The bicycle convoys of Dien Bien Phu days are on the roads again, but in far greater quantities and carrying much heavier loads," wrote the Australian journalist Wilfred Burchett in 1966. When he rode the Ho Chi Minh Trail himself with one such convoy, Burchett found the path "never more than three or four yards straight, with roots and snags everywhere; tiny stumps where the undergrowth had been slashed close to—but not level with—the earth, jabbing at your pedals and ankles; overhead creepers waiting to strangle you while you are looking down to avoid a stump; trellises of bamboo banging at your head no matter how low you bent over the handlebars." But bikes were preferable to jeeps, he added, because bikes were silent. Cyclists could hear planes coming in time to scramble into the undergrowth to hide.

As the war bore on, communist forces developed the Ho Chi Minh Trail into a system of busy arteries, some of them multi-lane blacktops, where camouflaged trucks conveyed tons of donated Soviet and Chinese weapons and food south to the Vietcong. But at the end of the line, the trail still fractured into a maze of bicycle trails and footpaths. An insistent barrage of US bombs never neutralized the trail, because when the roads were bombed out or gasoline was scarce, bicycles still got through. Every year during the summer monsoon season, low-lying stretches of roadway lay swamped under standing water that halted all truck traffic, but bicycles rolled on.

In North Vietnam, where US bombers targeted roads, railway lines, and fuel stores, the bicycle was indispensable for everyday transportation and business. Without it, the country couldn't function, wrote Harrison Salisbury for the *New York Times* in 1967: "If by some magic weapon all the bikes in North Vietnam could be immobilized, the war would be over in a twinkling." When a bomb knocked out a railway line, a brigade of bikes would ferry each train's freight to a waiting train on the other side of the blast, he wrote.

The ubiquitous bicycle was also used as a weapon of terror. In the southern capital of Saigon (now Ho Chi Minh City), Vietcong agents would pack plastic explosives into a bicycle's hollow tubes and leave the cycle on a crowded street to detonate. One 1963 bicycle bombing rocked an Americans-only theater during a screening of Walt Disney's *Lady and the Tramp*. (Communists were not the only ones to use this tactic. In 1952, a nationalist warlord carried out a series of bicycle bombings in Saigon, events later fictionalized by Graham Greene in his novel *The Quiet American*.) And this tactic has endured: booby-trapped bikes still kill and maim in war and terror zones around the world.

In the late 1960s and early 1970s, the US public grew increasingly opposed to the long and seemingly unwinnable war in Vietnam. In 1973, the United States withdrew its troops, though North and South Vietnam fought on. In the following year, the actress Jane Fonda—whose earlier, sympathetic visit to the North Vietnamese capital had earned her the derisive nickname "Hanoi Jane"—returned to the communist country. While most of the bikes used there during the war had been imported from China, some were made by local workers. In Thanh Hoa City near the country's coastline, Fonda visited a factory where two hundred employees built four hundred bike frames a month, "mostly from scrap metal of downed US aircraft and bomb casings," as she reported in *Rolling Stone*. "The debris is melted down and hammered into spokes and frames. The factory director proudly showed us his own bike, part of which was made from the debris of the [Lyndon] Johnson bombing and part from [Richard] Nixon's bombing." The bicycle had become not only a tool of resistance to superior military power, but also a symbol of victory over it.

The gnat had conquered the lion. And the lion never forgot it. America's loss in Vietnam redefined its role in the world and cooled its military hubris. For decades afterward, before each US military action—or the threat of one—opponents would try to sway opinion against the action by predicting "another Vietnam."

In 1975, the North Vietnamese captured Saigon and united the country under communist rule. Today, portions of the Ho Chi Minh trail have returned to jungle. Other parts remain narrow, vine-choked mountain paths, while many broader, paved segments see regular visits from Western tourists on bikes. Giggling schoolchildren often rush to the road to shout "hello" and high-five the cyclists as they pass. In 2015, one American bicycle racer planned to ride the full eight-hundred-mile length of the trail to commune with the father she never met, a US Air Force pilot shot down during the Vietnam War.

Eight

THE KING OF THE NEIGHBORHOOD

On March 26, 1883, the showman P. T. Barnum opened his circus's season in the original Madison Square Garden, a brick arena that he had built from the shell of a decommissioned railroad depot. "The Garden was packed from the rings to the roof," the *New-York Tribune* reported of the 8,500-seat venue. "There was a wonderful array of elephants, giraffes and zebras, sacred cattle and some profane cattle. . . . Small children on bicycles performed marvelous antics on those peculiar machines."

The small children in question were the Elliotts: five English siblings and their cousin, ages five to sixteen. Dressed in tights and spangled costumes, the children astounded the crowd by circling the central stage on the high-tech, high-wheeled bikes of the day—scaled, of course, to their little legs. On these Ordinaries, they rode on a raised platform, traced figure eights with their wheels, and brandished parasols and whips.

In the audience that afternoon was E. Fellowes Jenkins, the chief administrator of the nine-year-old New York Society for the Prevention of Cruelty to Children. During the Progressive Era, which was then just beginning, this private agency defined and fought against child abuse and neglect. It agitated for the

Catherine ("Kate"), Thomas, James, and Mary Rand ("Polly") Elliott, circa 1884, wearing "unicycle skates" patented by their father. This cabinet card, by the New York photographer J. Wood, was provided by the Picture History photo service.

first laws limiting children's work hours (to sixty hours a week) and requiring guardians to feed, clothe, and supervise the children in their care.

As he watched the Elliotts perform, Jenkins felt troubled. What he saw struck him as dangerous and exploitative. Kindergarteners teetering on big wire-spoked wheels for onlookers' amusement? It was inhumane, Jenkins believed. A tumble from a cycle could result in a compound fracture or a hernia, and in any event, the strain of the act was too much for the children's small limbs, he thought.

The SPCC demanded that Barnum stop the Elliotts from performing again, but—after consulting his attorneys—the showman defiantly repeated the act. "A society claiming to prevent cruelty to children threatens cruelly to rob these children of their well-earned money and turn them into the streets to beg," he pronounced before the Elliotts' next performance. An agent for the SPCC then went to court and swore out a warrant against Barnum, and the showman was arrested, along with his two circus managers and the father of the five siblings, James Elliott. All four men were charged with violating section 292 of the New York State Penal Code by allowing the Elliott children to perform feats "that are calculated to injure them," according to news reports.

At the men's trial on April 4, 1883, Jenkins testified that he had seen ten-year-old Polly Elliott slip during her act, and that the other children had seemed out of breath. Clearly, he argued, the bicycle was no machine for a child.

Barnum, in his own defense, presented a series of physicians who endorsed the children's act. One of them, Dr. Louis A. Sayre, testified, "If all children took similar exercise, it would be better than doctors or drugs." The three-judge panel must have agreed, because the four defendants were acquitted. When Barnum heard the judges' ruling, he approached his accuser, Jenkins. "I'll give you $200 per week," Barnum offered, "if you'll let me exhibit you about the country as the man who would prevent children from earning their livelihood." ("Go about your business!" Jenkins angrily replied.)

It seems crazy now to think that someone could be arrested for letting a kid ride a bicycle. In the United States for much of the twentieth century, children were practically the only people who did ride them. But as Robert Turpin convincingly argues in his 2013 dissertation, "'Our Best Bet Is the Boy,'" the identification of cycling with childhood in the United States—and only in the United States—was in large part the result of a conscious and concerted effort by the bicycle industry to market to children.

This effort, which started in the early twentieth century, helped determine who bought bikes and also how the machines were perceived. As children moved from the periphery to the center of the middle-class American family, a process largely complete by the 1950s, the bicycle became an indispensable accessory for them, an emblem of parental love.

When Barnum was arrested in 1883, the bicycle was still a towering, costly machine, and cycling was "essentially a selfish sport for men," as one business reporter described it. Women and teenage boys were largely excluded from organized cycling; leaders of elite clubs deemed both groups unsuited to membership. One exception was a club in Burlington, Vermont, whose organizers welcomed teenage boys (though not women). In an 1884 letter to *Outing* magazine, an older member offered a feisty defense of his club's unusual age policy. "We do not think here that [teenage boys] take anything away from the good standing of our club," he wrote. "We are not ashamed of our boys." The prevailing snobbism of cycling started to erode in 1887 when the English-style safety bicycle swept the American market and brought the bike back down to earth. Suddenly women, older men, and children who *weren't* professional acrobats could ride bicycles. The adoption of the pneumatic tire in the early 1890s made the riding even easier.

But during the international cycling boom that followed, most bicycles were still built for adults. The cycle had been transformed from a luxury good into a vehicle of liberation; it was not a child's toy. While some manufacturers marketed junior-size safeties, they represented a small portion of the American bicycle market.

Childhood during this period was diverse, and its definition was rapidly changing. According to Steven Mintz, author of *Huck's Raft: A History of American Childhood*, "at no time in American history was children's play experience more varied along lines of class, gender, and region" than during the nineteenth century. Some children toiled in the factories of the industrial revolution and had little time for play; others helped with farm work and then romped freely in the rural countryside; still others attended school with peers in the country's first grade-segregated classrooms. In congested cities, reformers created playgrounds and organized the first youth sports leagues. "These sports were seen as a way to cultivate virtues important to a modern society—such as teamwork—and to foster and channel competitiveness and aggressiveness," Mintz told the *American Journal of Play* in 2010.

By the early decades of the twentieth century, crusading groups such as the SPCC had largely succeeded in shifting childhood from a time of labor to a time of education. Simultaneously, public health and safety efforts had reduced the infant mortality rate—which in turn inspired many parents to limit their childbearing. With fewer children born and a greater expectation that each child would survive to adulthood, American parents began, paradoxically, to see their kids as more precious and more fragile than earlier generations had, as the social historian Peter Stearns has argued. Rather than economic assets that would generate revenue for the household, kids had become a treasured cost center. In middle-class families, children were consumers, not producers, and the more valuable they came to seem to their parents, the more stuff they seemed to need.

Meanwhile, the great 1890s bicycle boom ended, and in the United States, many adults came to see cycling as embarrassingly downscale. In 1899, as the market for new bicycles collapsed, forty-five cycle manufacturers and parts makers—including Pope's company—joined forces in an ill-conceived conglomerate called the American Bicycle Trust, which failed within three years, leaving a fragmented and fractious industry in its wake. The League of American Wheelmen staggered on, but its monthly journal began to fill with the obituaries of its aged members. "Our two oldest veterans have left us," reads one plangent notice in the June 1917 issue of the *Official Bulletin and Scrap Book of the League of American Wheelmen*. "Who stands next in line?" (In August of that year, the *Bulletin* reported that the league's new senior member was Jarvis C. Howard of New Rochelle, then seventy-seven years and five months old.)

Bikes hadn't vanished from adult life completely, though. Six-day bicycle races continued to draw crowds of ten thousand or more to velodromes around the country, and racing stars such as the sprinter Frank L. Kramer earned more than baseball greats like Ty Cobb. But for most American adults, biking for pleasure was off the agenda. And the bike's practicality for city commuting waned, too, as automobiles became more plentiful in the 1910s. People may have preferred the swifter and more modern motorized carriages to bicycles, but they also feared riding in traffic. Fatal crashes became shockingly common as cars took over the roadways, and most of the casualties were pedestrians. If you persisted in cycling on streets clogged with cars and newbie drivers, you were taking your life in your hands. And the United States embraced automobiles like no other country. In 1933, there were seventeen cars for every bike in the United States, while in Europe there were seven bikes for every car.

US bicycle and parts manufacturers needed a new customer, and they found him in the schoolyard. Industry trade groups urged bike merchants to target suburban children, who couldn't drive cars but might well love a toy that they could ride on the sidewalk or in quiet cul-de-sacs. "Play to the kid all the time," wrote W. P. Farrell of the J. W. Grady bicycle company in 1917. "If you don't, you lose your best bet. . . . The bicycle is as much the expectation of every boy as an automobile is the expectation of every business man." As Robert Turpin argues, though, this strategy was a sort of time bomb. By painting bicycle ownership as a youthful expectation, merchants reinforced the perception that grown-ups didn't ride. As one 1926 Iver Johnson bicycle ad in the *Youth's Companion* told readers, "The selection of a bicycle is as important to you as the selection of an automobile is to your father." That a father might select a bike for himself was out of the question.

Ads touting car-like bicycle components such as the "New Multiple Disk Clutch New Departure Brake" prepared kids for the day when they could cast aside their ersatz cars and get real ones. "Dad discovers the reason you've set your heart on a bicycle," reads one 1927 New Departure advertisement. "He knows what this kind of a clutch means to the automobile." As part of a broader cultural shift, kids were being groomed as good consumers: they were learning to trade up.

By then, a bicycle wasn't anyone's idea of trading up. Small-town commuters and city delivery boys still routinely used bikes to get around, but for white-collar workers they had become ridiculous. In 1928, a *New York Times* reporter interviewed several businessmen riding stationary bicycles at gyms. "They tell me that they would like to go bicycling," he wrote, "but they imagine that they would be unpleasantly conspicuous." Girls tended to abandon riding as soon as they graduated from elementary school, the reporter added, and the typical teenage girl regarded the bike as "considerably beneath her dignity," an attitude with potentially devastating effects for would-be suitors: "If a youth would invite her to ride a tandem with him, he would probably destroy the friendship then and there." Grown women almost never cycled, though one 1925 writer thought it a shame, considering what the bicycle had done for their mothers thirty years earlier. "How they did blossom out on it!" he wrote. "How cleverly they did pedal out of that place of theirs so long said to be in the home!"

For children, though, biking became more than acceptable; it became desirable. Marketers encouraged parents to see the machine as a way to develop their children's bodies and also their charisma. "Give him a bicycle that he will be proud of," counsels one 1916 ad from *McClure's* magazine. "If he has one of these bicycles, he will be the king of the neighborhood." By publicizing the message that "boyhood without a bicycle is like a summer without flowers," to quote a 1922 ad in *Boys' Life* magazine, the bicycle industry helped make their product an essential aspect of childhood. Earning the money for a bicycle was a way to build character, as one financial journalist noted. "What normal boy wouldn't gladly work three hours a day—before and after school—to own a bicycle?" he asked. Any parent, he added, should be able to "look beyond the bicycle and behold what the boy gained in grit, persistence, self-confidence, and strength of character by his long-continued effort."

Unexpectedly, the Depression saw a resurgence in adult cycling. "Here comes back, freewheeling, the deposed, nigh-despised, almost forgotten bicycle," announced the *Wall Street Journal* in 1933. Bikes were cheaper to buy and operate than cars, and that fact sparked sales in the otherwise listless economy. Another attraction of cycling, one industry leader told *Fortune* that year, was "the urge of a weary people to return to the vanished past." And then there was stardust. Hans Ohrt, a Los Angeles bicycle merchant to Hollywood luminaries, dated the renewed interest in adult cycling to the 1932 Olympics, when some celebrities first glimpsed road racing—and weren't put off by the US team's medal-free performance in that competition. Big names like Joan Crawford and Douglas Fairbanks Jr. started cycling for exercise, and the fashion spread eastward. Bicycle rental spots cropped up across the country, and railroads began offering "cycle train" day trips that would ferry urbanites into the countryside for bike rides.

Bicycle production rose from 249,500 in 1932 to 1,250,000 in 1937, and by 1938, there were more than 6 million cycles on the streets, "far more than existed in the Gay Nineties," according to the *New York Times*. (Like other professional sports, bicycle racing lost much of its ticket-buying audience during the 1930s, though unlike ball sports such as baseball, basketball, and football, it never recovered from the loss.)

Despite the new interest in adult cycling, though, child cyclists outnumbered adult riders in the United States, and both kids' and adults' bikes grew ever more enticingly car-like. Makers adopted bulbous frames and fat low-pressure "balloon" tires copied from cars. (They also featured coaster brakes, which the rider could engage by pedaling backward, an especially useful technology for children, whose hands aren't strong enough to make hand brakes practical.) A 1936 ad for a Monark Silver King bike boasted of an "electric blast horn hidden in headlight" and an "automobile-type theft-proof wheel lock." The 1941 Columbia catalogue touted the company's new model

F9T, built with an "exclusive instrument panel" for its odometer, speedometer, and dashboard clock; an integrated luggage rack; and a "snug-fitting" faux gas tank. The bikes' ample tires and feature-laden frames made for a strenuous ride, but since the bikes were intended for neighborhood play rather than commuting, it didn't much matter how fast they could go.

By late 1941, when the United States entered World War II, 85 percent of the bicycles sold in the country were kids' bikes. That changed abruptly in March 1942 when the federal War Production Board prohibited the manufacture of all children's bikes and directed bicycle companies to ramp up production of drab, stripped-down adult machines instead. These so-called Victory bicycles were needed to help workers commute under the wartime rationing of gas, tires, and cars. In mid-August of that year, though, with thousands of new adult bikes in circulation, the federal government ended most bicycle manufacturing for the duration of the war and directed bike factories to make machine-gun tripods, searchlights, and other war materiel instead. War workers dutifully (or necessarily) commuted by bicycle, but throughout the war the idea of the bike as a childhood must-have endured.

In September 1945, one month after Japan's surrender, the *Wall Street Journal* reported that 97 percent of American children told pollsters they wanted their own bicycles. The postwar bike industry ramped up as quickly as possible to meet the demand for children's bikes, soon adding kiddie styles such as Monark's 1950 Gene Autry model, which came with a metal cap pistol and leather holster attached. American adults, on the other hand, aspired to own cars; they quickly returned to their pre-Depression disdain for two-wheeled transport.

Of course, as an object, the bike offered children the same sort of liberation it had offered adults in the days before automobiles. Not dependent upon grown-ups for transportation in the ever-expanding postwar suburbs, a kid with a bike in the 1950s and 1960s could range around his or her neighborhood looking for adventure. Encouraging this exploration was a new philosophy of child rearing, espoused by experts such as Benjamin Spock, that instructed parents to allow children to take risks, lest they develop neuroses arising from overprotective parenting. Counseled one University of Tennessee child development professor in 1954, it was "much better that [children] suffer for a month the inconveniences of a broken limb than that they suffer for life from undeveloped physical powers and immature personalities." Then, too, the large number of mothers who stayed home all day in the postwar years—in the interregnum between wartime production and women's lib—afforded a kind of collective supervision of suburban sidewalks and streets.

But just as a child could use a bike to gain independence, he or she could also use it to go looking for trouble. The 1950s saw a juvenile delinquency panic that offered bicycles both as a possible trigger for mischief (since bike theft fueled by envy was a standard starter crime) and as a potential deterrent to it. Along with scout troops and other organized activities, concerned adults formed bicycle touring clubs to occupy kids and render them too tired to transgress. "Keep a healthy boy busy and happy, and he stays out of trouble," said Wayman LaRue, the founder of Philadelphia's Safety Riders bicycle club, in 1959. The retired police officer had formed the fifteen-member group three years earlier as a means of "doing something about delinquency," he told the *Philadelphia Tribune*.

By the 1960s, the specter of the slick-haired, leather-jacketed juvenile delinquent had been replaced by a fearsome new teenage minority: the hippie, whose hallucinogens, campus activism, psychedelic music, and improvisational hygiene threatened to destroy the social order. Critics blamed the generation's wildness on parental overindulgence—such as handing out bikes to children without requiring work in exchange. "We have given our children a free ride since the day they were born, and now we can't understand why they demand so much," opined the California philanthropist Mrs. George Buccola in 1967. "We gave them that bicycle." Parents' desire to protect and develop their offspring, in other words, seemed to have gone a step too far.

Kids' cycles at the time underwent a drastic change in form. In the early 1960s, youngsters in California began customizing their bikes with high-rise handlebars that created a two- or even three-foot chrome U shape at the front of the cycle. This modification originally allowed newspaper delivery boys to sling bags of papers between the bars, where they would be within easy reach. With the addition of long "banana" seats borrowed from European bicycle polo, the reconfigured bikes caught on as a youthful imitation of chopper-style motorcycles. Manufacturers soon copied the trend, releasing the Huffy Dragster and the Schwinn Sting-Ray in 1963. The style, called a "wheelie" bike because of its facility for rear-wheel riding, overtook the market within a few years. Wrote one befuddled visitor to a New England bike shop in 1965, the looming handlebars "rose up so fantastically tall they suggested the antennas of giant Martian insects."

In 1969, 85 percent of US bicycle riders were sixteen or younger, and by 1970 almost three-quarters of the bikes sold in the country were children's high-risers, even though the awkward form raised safety questions because of its tendency to buck up and its unforgiving protuberances. "Anywhere you go, you can see the children struggling to keep from being garroted on the high-rise handlebars (known as monkey bars) or squirming on the thin, precarious seats," wrote a *Washington Post* reporter in 1971. These "monstrosities," she added, made children feel that the bicycle was "about to pierce them with its grasping iron limbs."

Phil Leon captured this image of a New Orleans or Texas neighbor performing a wheelie sometime in the 1970s. The photo was provided by Kumar McMillan under a Creative Commons Attribution-ShareAlike 2.0 Generic License.

In the rest of the world, the bike still looked very similar to the pneumatic safety of the 1890s, though with the addition of shiftable gears to ease uphill riding. Eighty years after its heyday, the machine was still a "vital mode of transportation" for adults outside the United States, as the *Chicago Tribune* reported with fascination. "People would starve, commerce would suffer, and populations would be virtually immobilized" in Africa without bicycles, and in Britain, "a lot of country mail (and some babies) would be delivered late," the paper stated. In England, France, Germany, Italy, Belgium, and Denmark, bikes outnumbered all other forms of transportation "by a sizeable margin" in 1971, according to the *Washington Post*. In Southeast Asia, as we have seen, bicycles had become trusty beasts of burden for US enemies.

Yet over the same eighty-year time frame, the American-made bicycle had morphed from a fashionably grown-up conveyance into something so spectacularly juvenile and impractical that no self-respecting adult would ride one. "What are we to make of these bikes, these flamboyant, ill-proportioned grotesques?" asked the journalist Arthur Asa Berger in 1972. "The development of the Sting-Ray and its brethren only carries to a somewhat mad conclusion what was evident in the old balloon tire bike." For Berger, the absurd showiness and inefficiency of high-rise bikes—and of balloon-tired bikes before them—reflected a "perversion of values, a somewhat monstrous application of merchandising and salesmanship." By turning into toys, American-made bikes had come to represent a "chrome-plated, plastic-coated" society that preferred mindless consumption to authentic experience, he wrote.

But if high-rise bikes took style to dangerously outlandish extremes, change was afoot—"some kind of a counter-revolution," Berger called it. In the mid-1960s, American adults had begun buying imported bikes: thin-wheeled multigeared roadsters. Within a few years—quite to the astonishment of the US bicycle industry—America was in the midst of a bike frenzy to rival that of the 1890s.

Nine

THE GREAT AMERICAN BICYCLE BOOM

"My husband, my girls, and even some of the neighbors, I guess, think I'm some kind of kook," confessed a thirty-two-year-old housewife in 1966. Her quirk? Riding a bicycle for exercise. "You should hear the catcalls and hoots I get," she wrote to the advice columnist Molly Mayfield. "My husband is disgusted." The housewife begged Mayfield for a reality check: "If you tell me I'm a crazy nut, I'll stay off that bike."

Three months earlier, Mayfield had fielded a similar question from the peanut gallery: a horrified fifteen-year-old girl had discovered her father on his back in the living room, churning his legs in the air as if riding a bicycle upside down. "Imagine an old man of 42 doing gym exercises like a teen-ager," she wrote. "If one of my girlfriends saw him like that, I'd be laughed out of the school."

Mayfield tartly stuck up for both exercisers, but their weirdness was real. The 1890s bicycle craze had proved that physical activity led to better health, but that lesson had been largely forgotten by the 1950s. Postwar prosperity and an increasingly car-centric lifestyle had made for a population that was plumper and more sedentary than their grandparents.

There were some outliers, of course. Fitness evangelists like the TV bodybuilder Jack LaLanne found a following—his show premiered in 1953 and ran for decades—but the conventional wisdom held that vigorous exercise was bad for adults. Just like Victorian housewives hyperventilating in their tight corsets and heavy frocks, many middle-aged desk workers of the mid-twentieth century avoided any activity that might make them pant or sweat. And while most doctors recognized the value of sports for children's developing bodies, a great many warned that adults who tried the same exploits would wear their hearts out prematurely. "After [age] 25 or 30, competitive exertion is superfluous—and hurtful," wrote the internist and author Peter J. Steincrohn. A middle-aged fat man who works out at a gym is "a victim of slow suicide," he cautioned. "Exercise is a joke."

Ridiculous as cycling seemed for many adults in the mid-1960s, it seemed even more ridiculous for teenagers. "In high school, it just wasn't done," recalled one young man a few years later. "We wouldn't be caught dead riding a bike in those days." "I walked two miles each way to high school to avoid the embarrassment of being seen on a bike," recalled another man of his midsixties adolescence. "We had bike racks at school without a single bike parked on them." These were teens who had cycled as children; in fact, their childhoods coincided with a national surge in bicycle sales. But at around age twelve or thirteen—years before they were eligible to drive—they had put their bikes away. Cycling was considered kid stuff, even if the standard adult bike was a beast no child could lift: the full-size 1959 Schwinn Phantom "deluxe spring fork balloon model," for example, had a shipping weight of more than sixty-two pounds.

Still, bit by bit, an army of bike nerds was mustering, spurred by economics, technology, medical science, and ecology. By 1972, that army would conquer the country and, for a few brief years, make the bicycle as cool as that sophisticated new sensation, the video game.

The trend started with postwar economics. In 1948, to help boost a British economy still struggling after World War II, the United States slashed the tariff on British lightweight bicycles from 30 percent to 15 percent or lower. The following year, to lower the price of its exports relative to those of other countries, Great Britain devalued the pound, which dropped the average wholesale price of an imported British bike in the United States from $45 to less than $37, a considerable drop in those years. The Brits also ramped up their production of bicycles for export. The result was a steady supply of affordable multigeared imports in American shops. Many of these cycles placed riders in the bent-over "down" posture of the racer, rather than the prim, upright posture Americans had by then become accustomed to. The imports were also among the first on the US market to feature derailleur gears, which allowed the rider to shift the chain between sprockets of different sizes in order to make riding faster (on flats and downhills) or easier (on uphills). Derailleurs had been in wide use in Europe since the 1930s, but in the United States they had been considered too complicated for children's use and not smooth enough for track racers, who preferred single-speed bikes.

Adult-size bikes still made up just a sliver of the US market, but increasingly, the ones that were selling were imported. As these high-tech lightweights found buyers, including military veterans who had ridden similar cycles in England during the war, American makers responded by developing midweight (fifty-pound), three-speed models—not as sprightly as the imports, but not as expensive either. By 1960, US companies were producing their own European-style eight- and ten-speed bikes, notably the Schwinn Varsity, which at forty pounds was "lightweight" compared to balloon-tired American monsters, even if not to Raleighs and other ten-speed imports, which weighed as little as twenty-two pounds.

If your only frame of reference was a one-speed balloon-tired bike, or even a midweight three-speed, then riding a ten-speed could be a revelation. First-time users reported that "the bike had a light, springy, alive feeling, not an inert heaviness," according to *Sunset*. As one rider told the magazine in 1965, "It's like a constant tail wind. Once you get that feeling, you never want to change." According to the *Los Angeles Times*, the difference between a three-speed and a ten-speed was "the difference between driving a tank and a sports car." The new technology began to make adult biking seem more worth the effort. As one 1964 ad for a Huffy brand ten-speed argued, "This Huffy is one reason you see more adults on bicycles today. . . . Your [old balloon-tire] bike was hard to pedal; this one skims over the ground."

That kind of lightness echoed the descriptions of pneumatic safety bicycles when they were first introduced. And, like an old safety, the new ten-speeds gave riders a refreshing sense of freedom. "So many of us have a Kafkaesque feeling that we have no power over anything in modern society," said the Chicago public relations man Eugene A. Sloane in 1970. "Bicycling offers a new feeling of independence." (Sloane was the author of *The Complete Book of Bicycling*, published that year.) Comparisons of cycling to flying also began to reappear. In 1974, an ad for the ten-speed AMF Roadmaster depicted the bike ascending a tightrope carried aloft by a gigantic blue butterfly. The ad's headline read, "Flying Machine."

In summery locales like Florida and Southern California, grown-ups began taking ten-speeds on day trips and multiday touring vacations. Unlike the "dead weight" of a balloon-tired bike, these new models "put joy in an adult journey," *Life* magazine explained. One young Southern California couple who typified the trend shipped their bikes five hundred miles north to San Francisco, flew up to meet them, and spent two weeks pedaling home along Highway 1. The pace gave them a new perspective on travel, they told a reporter. While a high-wheel cyclist of the 1880s might have exulted in the unprecedented speed of the overland jaunt, his 1960s counterparts exulted in the trip's leisurely pace. "You get a chance to notice little things—flowers, birds, trees," said the wife, identified as Mrs. William Rogan. "We talked to beatniks in Big Sur, to truck drivers in restaurants. It's a different world." In 1960, the *New York Times* noted the unexpected upswing in pedal-powered touring: "In this age of jet planes and tail fins, the bicycle would seem to stand about as much chance of survival as the sedan chair or the one-horse shay, but, strangely enough, the evidence is mounting that bike-riding is a growing outdoor sport." And bicycle ads started to target this full-grown, outdoorsy demographic. "Discover the call of far away places . . . romantic settings . . . and the total relaxation of the open road," urged a 1968 Schwinn ad (ellipses and all). "It's been there all along . . . just a short ride away on a new Schwinn bike!"

Plentiful imports and better gearing didn't fully explain the burgeoning bike revival, though. A changing attitude toward adult exercise also played a part. Prominent physicians—including, notably, the Harvard cardiologist Paul Dudley White—had been studying the effects of exercise on heart health. Their findings suggested that fitness buffs like LaLanne might have had the right idea. More doctors started encouraging older adults to stay active. "I'd like to put everybody on bicycles," White frequently proclaimed. "That's a good way of preventing heart disease."

White's pro-exercise position—and the bicycle itself—got a PR boost in 1955, when then-president Dwight D. Eisenhower had a serious heart attack. White flew to the president's bedside as a consultant and became the spokesman for his medical care team. Rather than the traditional postcoronary treatment of prolonged bed rest, White recommended exercise such as cycling, which he himself had done regularly since he was a Harvard freshman in 1904. "Some believe that vigorous exercise not only helps the general health but also helps a healthy person to delay the onset of serious coronary atherosclerosis," White wrote shortly after Eisenhower's heart attack. "We have inadequate information about this, altho[ugh] many of us, including President Eisenhower, have found that exercise makes them feel better." A few American adults took the hint and started cycling for heart health, though drivers didn't always appreciate the new obstacles in their midst. In Baltimore in 1956, catcalls from drivers to health-minded adult cyclists included, "What's the matter? Too cheap to buy a car?" and "Now ain't you ashamed—at your age."

The medical case for exercise gained even more credibility in the 1960s after a University of Oregon track coach introduced a new practice called "jogging" and advocated it for "anyone—six to 106—male or female." As the historian Alan Latham has ably documented, Coach Bill Bowerman largely created the phenomenon of nonathletes trotting around for fitness in the United States. Bowerman had been converted to the health benefits of noncompetitive running during a 1962 trip to New Zealand, and he wanted to spread the word. He and several medical researchers launched a series of studies, and they found that sedentary men over thirty who took up jogging could lower their blood pressure and lose weight without dieting. The group published their findings in 1967 in the *Journal of the American Medical Association* as well as in a guidebook that sold more than one million copies. By the following year, tens of thousands of formerly inactive adults had taken up the habit. Given the potential gains and low cost of the new regimen, the *Chicago Tribune* noted that year, "probably the only disadvantage to jogging is the feeling of looking ridiculous." (The wisdom of exercise for adults was still being debated, though. Speaking at a Washington, DC, Medical Society seminar on the topic in 1969, a skeptical Peter Steincrohn opined that "pushing 40 or 50 is exercise enough.")

As the sight of adults exercising outdoors became more common, both jogging and cycling began to lose their stigma. Eventually, many Americans who had started out as joggers switched to cycling out of boredom or discomfort. "Jogging might be good for you, but you feel like you're going to drop dead any minute," an IRS auditor named Henry Bernard told the *Washington Post* in 1970. "So one day I took my son's bike to work . . . I went through the park and I could smell the trees. . . . I'd been cooped up in the car for so long I forgot there was such a thing as honeysuckle."

And besides being easier than jogging and more fun than driving—at least in fair weather, for short distances, and without heavy cargo—biking in traffic-congested cities was often significantly faster than taking a car or a bus. "It's the swiftest way to get uptown," the Broadway producer Morton Gottlieb told the *New York Times* in 1970. Gottlieb, then forty-nine, enjoyed racing the No. 5 bus up the Avenue of the Americas. "I haven't lost yet," he said with a grin. For a Washington, DC, bike commuter named "Lucky" Wentworth, cycling was the only private conveyance that made sense. "I think most people are starting to realize that cars in the city are, well, insane," he told the *Washington Post* in 1971. Although bikers were still a tiny minority of commuters—no doubt less than 1 percent—they had become a noticeable presence on urban streets for the first time since munitions-factory workers rode their drab Victory bicycles in the 1940s.

After decades stuck in the schoolyard, the bicycle was reasserting its old usefulness for adults. As in the 1890s, grown-ups recognized that cycling was a fun way to get around and stay fit. And in the 1960s, a new crisis gave the bicycle an additional role to play: as a symbolic would-be savior of the planet.

Since the 1950s, Americans had grown increasingly troubled by pollution of the nation's air and waterways. Books like Rachel Carson's 1962 antipesticide opus *Silent Spring* and events like a disastrous 1969 oil spill off the coast of Santa Barbara drew attention to the toxic potential of poorly regulated industries. There were no federal emission standards before 1965, so cars spewed smoke. This mixed with fog to create a thick smog that killed hundreds of asthma patients and elderly people in repeated "smog episodes" across the country. At a building dedication in Cincinnati in the mid-1960s, the US surgeon general, Luther L. Terry, summed up the situation. "There is now nearly six times as much pollution in our rivers, streams, and lakes as 60 years ago, and the amount is still increasing," he said. "We are in danger . . . of creating an incredible disharmony in nature which will ultimately degrade and enslave us." The warnings were dire, some histrionically so. One 1968 best-seller, *The Population Bomb*, warned of overpopulation that would lead to environmental devastation and global starvation within ten years.

Among a public already mobilized to demonstrate for—or against—civil rights, women's rights, and an end to the Vietnam War, cleaning up the environment became just one more cause to pursue. Activists pushed for legislation to curb pollution, organizing demonstrations that included the first Earth Day, on April 22, 1970. During that event, some twenty million Americans gathered at sites around the country to demand action, helping bring about federal environmental protection laws such as the Clean Air Act (1970), the Clean Water Act (1972), and the Endangered Species Act (1973).

Nancy Pearlman (wearing a gas mask to protest smog), Janice Jones, Debbie Melville, and Kathy Briggs were captured in 1971 by *Los Angeles Times* photographer Don Cormier. This image was provided by the UCLA Library under a Creative Commons Attribution 4.0 International License.

As a nonpolluting vehicle, the newly un-ridiculous bike fit right in. For many, cycling became a political statement. "The alternative to sitting around and complaining about smog is biking when you can," Mrs. James Mahan, a mother of three, told the *Los Angeles Times* in 1971. By cycling, "we've done something, however small, to communicate that we believe in what we feel." Some political statements were small scale, such as the decision of twenty-something Nancy Pearlman to wear a gas mask during a 1971 bicycle ride in Los Angeles. Others were grander, such as a 1,500-person "Pollution Solution" ride that year, organized by the same Nancy Pearlman, founder of Concerned Bicycle Riders for the Environment. Activists like these saw the bike as more than a form of zero-emission transportation. They saw it as a chariot to enlightenment. In its 1971 manifesto, the Santa Barbara group Friends for Bikecology urged readers to take responsibility for the state of the planet by cycling rather than driving: "If we desire to change the world we live in, let's find the magnet which draws man to the land, in contact with its forces—the bicycle."

So in the same ten-year span, ten-speed bikes became more widely available, exercise for adults became more acceptable, and environmentalism entered the mainstream. What all this meant for the bicycle was a boom that started in the early 1960s and just kept building. Between 1960 and 1970, the number of bikes in use in the United States doubled, as did per capita ridership. Then in 1971, bike sales exploded, shocking retailers and manufacturers alike. At the sixty-four J. C. Penney stores in Southern California, bicycle shipments increased fivefold between July 1970 and July 1971. "No one could have predicted it," said the president of the Murray Ohio Manufacturing Company, which built store-brand bicycles for J. C. Penney and Sears. "We're not clairvoyant."

Producers couldn't keep up with orders. In 1971, Schwinn sold out its entire annual production run of 1,225,000 bikes by the third week of May. "If we could have increased our production by 50 percent or even 100 percent, we couldn't have met the demand," a Schwinn marketing executive said that summer. European and Japanese importers tried to fill the gap, but it was too vast. American bike stores became mob scenes, and by that fall ten-speeds were nowhere to be bought. A *Washington Post* reporter named B. D. Colen hunted for weeks before locating a shop owner who was expecting a shipment. Colen offered to pay for a bike in advance, sight unseen, but the merchant said no. "I've had 600 to 800 people calling asking for 10-speeds. I've had them offer me $25 to $30 over retail just to hold one. We just can't take any orders." The reporter eventually found a shop that would take an order for a French Gitane cycle to be delivered five weeks later—"and if you think I'll tell you where," he wrote in the paper, "think again."

By 1972, there were eighty-five million cyclists in the country: one out of every two people between the ages of seven and sixty-nine, according to a federal report. (In 1896, the year that "everything was bicycle," the US population was two-thirds smaller than it would be in 1970, but the number of cyclists was more than *forty times* smaller.) Bicycles outsold cars in the United States in 1972, and the year after that, and the year after that. And for the first time since the days of the Victory bike, most cycles sold in the United States were full-size. In 1971, 86 percent of Schwinn's bike sales were to adults, a complete reversal from just four years earlier. One New York City bicycle dealer jokingly estimated that if his customer ratio in 1970 was three children for every three adults, in 1971 it was "four-and-a-half kids to 300 adults." The bicycle had become more than acceptable for adults to ride. Unthinkably, it had become cool. In September 1971, the *New Yorker* writer Calvin Trillin took part in a 200-person ride down Manhattan's Fifth Avenue to demand bike lanes on city streets. "Most people who looked up at us smiled," he noted. "At 23rd Street, a young man walked over to me while we were stopped at a red light and, looking very somber about it all, informed me that bicycling was groovy." (Manhattan didn't get its first on-street bicycle lanes until 1978.)

In October 1973, Arab oil-producing countries gave Americans yet another reason to cycle: they cut off petroleum exports to the United States. This embargo, which lasted six months, was intended to penalize America for its support of Israel in that year's Arab-Israeli war, and the result was a punishing energy crisis. American drivers waited hours in line at gas stations, only to find that the pumps had run dry. Gas prices quadrupled. The pedal-powered bike looked more practical than ever, as marketers were quick to note. "The USA energy shortage?" asked a 1974 bike ad. "Think of how much gas you'd save" using "good ol' American leg power. . . . The Vista 10-speed Esquire . . . it's a gas!"

Cycling was especially appealing for college students. On campuses, the mix of strong young bodies, short commutes, and light vehicle traffic yielded thick swarms of bikes. At Cal State Fullerton in 1971, 10 percent of students arrived by bicycle. Although the school bought five new racks that fall, bicycle parking was hard to come by. "Students chain their bikes to any tree or pole or railing they can find," the *Los Angeles Times* reported. "Each lamp post on campus always has at least two bikes chained to it." At the University of Illinois in Urbana-Champaign in 1973, cycle paths coursed with endless streams of traffic; pedestrians complained of waits as long as fifteen minutes to cross. By 1975, it seemed that every scholar had a bike. "Take a look at the average college campus," wrote an essayist in the *Christian Science Monitor* that year. "Students cry poverty, but if any student is not able to satisfy his yearning for a 10-speed, it's not noticeable."

As it happened, though, that year marked the end of the 1970s bicycle fad. Sales fell 50 percent between 1974 and 1975, and by 1976, US manufacturers were starting to go bankrupt. "The 'boom' has turned into a 'bust,'" the president of the Huffman Manufacturing Company sadly testified before the Senate Finance Committee. Part of what popped the bike bubble may have been the poor quality of many of the machines people were riding. Due to the frantic demand, many ten-speeds sold during the 1970s were cheaply made and frustratingly prone to breakdown, as the cycle historian Frank Berto argues. "Anything with a derailleur could be sold," he writes in the book *The Dancing Chain*. "Some of these were truly horrid." Many once-coveted ten-speeds ended up in a corner of the garage—or at the dump.

Then, too, the high demand had created an easy secondary market for stolen bicycles. By 1971, bike thievery had become "a thriving business" nationally, as the *Los Angeles Times* reported; in 1975, *Time* magazine called it "America's fastest-growing crime." Many adults no doubt stopped riding their ten-speeds because they got tired of replacing stolen bikes—or just got tired of worrying that they would be stranded if a thief made off with their wheels.

And this points up a bigger change that seems to have contributed to the passing of the second great bike boom: the rising reality of urban crime. Because cities are densely built, they ought to be especially well-suited to the utility cyclist. Work, school, and shops tend to be located close enough to home to ride to; streets are paved; traffic is calmed by frequent stop signs and signals. But after the race riots of the 1960s—which began with protests against police brutality in Harlem and Philadelphia in 1964 and continued through the angry nationwide response to the assassination of Martin Luther King Jr., in 1968—the American middle class increasingly abandoned the urban core. The 1973–1974 energy crisis had helped trigger an economic downturn that knocked municipal governments on their heels; in 1975, New York City turned to the federal government for a bailout to avoid defaulting on its municipal bonds. (The feds obliged, but only after President Gerald Ford demanded that city leaders raise revenues and cut spending, a stance immortalized in the *New York Daily News* headline "Ford to City: Drop Dead.") The US crime rate doubled in the 1960s, and then nearly doubled again in the 1970s. Theft and assault became a fact of urban life.

Compared to cars, bicycles left riders more vulnerable to attack. On Easter 1974, for example, two young women were jumped by a gang of teenage boys with rubber tubes and clubs on a bike path in Washington, DC's Rock Creek Park. When one of the women went to the emergency room, an attendant there told her that they had been treating one injured cyclist a week due to assaults in the park. And during a 1980 transit strike in New York, office workers started commuting by bike across the Brooklyn Bridge—and criminals started lying in wait for them there. One night that July, four muggers attacked and robbed a cyclist and held him captive for two hours, during which time he watched them rob and beat another cyclist as well. "The situation there borders on barbarism," the president of the Federation of New York Bicycle Clubs said.

On-street cycling was already dangerous in the United States because roads had been built or rebuilt with cars in mind. Side paths had vanished; bike lanes were few. And the ubiquitous curb cuts that ease sidewalk riding today were nowhere in sight back then: most of them were installed after the passage of the Americans with Disabilities Act of 1990. So cyclists already had to be wary of drivers. With crime on the increase, some bikers must have felt they ought to begin fearing pedestrians as well.

And the baby boom generation that had fueled the ten-speed fad was starting to settle down. Some who had gotten caught up in the exhilaration of the ten-speed craze as childless young adults had become the parents of young children, for whom the risk-reward calculus was often different. Increasingly, it seemed that the risk of cycling wasn't worth the reward. Americans didn't completely stop riding bikes after 1975, of course. But given the frightening trajectory of the American city—the bicycle's natural habitat—maybe it was inevitable that the early-'70s mania wouldn't last.

Still, by the end of the boom, the bike had decisively shed its just-for-kids image. And some of the Americans who kept riding after 1975 ended up changing its identity further. Soon, a machine that had gone from trendy to dorky and back again would become the ultimate expression of gonzo individualism.

Ten

BIKE MESSENGERS, TOURISTS, AND MOUNTAIN BIKERS

The headquarters of Can Carriers Messenger Service was a dilapidated fourth-floor walk-up over a gypsy fortune-teller's shop in a sketchy area near Grand Central Station. "You don't find many landlords anxious to rent space to an outfit that's dragging bicycles up and down stairs all day long," said the owner, George E. Cooper, to explain the gritty digs. His company—one of New York's first bicycle courier services of the modern era—had opened in 1970. By 1976, when the *New York Times* ran a column on the still-unusual enterprise, the image of the bicycle messenger as a distinct urban species was already taking shape.

"Unlike most of the thousands of messengers who crisscross the city on foot or by public transportation—feeble retired people, former mental patients who tend to talk to themselves in elevators, or disgruntled beginners goofing off between errands—Can Carriers' bicyclists are blithe spirits," the *Times* reported. Young and artsy, wearing shaggy hair and cutoff jeans, these fifty couriers were individualists, "part Horatio Alger and part hippie," Cooper told the paper. As independent contractors, they set their own hours and earned half of the agency's fee for each package they delivered, whether it was a can of movie film, a set of advertising proofs, or a clutch of gems from the city's diamond district. Riding furiously on downtown streets that had been engineered for cars, the messengers constantly skirted danger or collided with it head-on. "Cabs are our natural enemies," one of the couriers told the reporter. "And Cadillacs. People who have Caddies think they own the world."

As both cycling and city life had begun to feel too perilous for many Americans, this new category of riders attracted people—mostly men—who embraced danger or even sought it out. The *New Yorker* called them "Evel Knievels" in 1975 and reported that while none of them had yet been killed on the job, close calls were "beyond counting." In the mid-1970s, similar services opened in other US cities, notably San Francisco.

By 1981 there were six hundred bicycle messengers in Manhattan, including at least one anthropologist doing fieldwork: Jack M. Kugelmass, who sought to understand why riders wanted such a tough, risky job. Most couriers were desperate people who signed up as a last resort and quit as soon as they had another option, Kugelmass discovered. But the few who chose to stick with it long-term were a special breed, he believed: "Like heroes of the West, they are mavericks, resentful of conformity and rebelling against it. They are romantic adventurers who prefer the exhilaration of danger to civilization's deadening routine."

While most messengers rode ten-speeds, the scholar counted dozens who rode what he called "track bikes" and what we would now call "fixies": single-speed, fixed-gear cycles originally designed for indoor racing. Like boneshakers and Ordinaries, fixies can't coast: the pedals turn along with the chain that turns the rear wheel. Since the most hard-core fixie riders don't use brakes, stopping such a bike can be tricky—the rider has to lock his or her legs to arrest the spinning pedals, without any assis-

In 1978, the *Village Voice* reported on the conflict between bikes and cars on newly striped Manhattan bike lanes. This rider, photographed by Harvey Wang for the story, wears typical messenger gear: a cross-body bag for cargo and a whistle at the ready to warn encroaching cars.

tance from a coaster brake that would use friction to stop the hub from spinning. Choosing to ride a fixed-gear bike in stop-and-go traffic might seem an odd choice, but couriers told Kugelmass they preferred the challenge. "It's hard. It makes your life harrowing every day. It's part of Zen," a messenger named Ahdullah said. After weaving through traffic on a fixie, "you're a bit keener and a bit swifter and a bit more relaxed about what just might come at you in life."

The unusual bike choice was just part of a developing subculture with its own distinct style. Unfettered by the expectations of a nine-to-five office job, messengers dressed for both function and effect. Practical measures such as rolling up one pant leg—to keep the fabric from getting caught in the bicycle chain—became flourishes worn socially and copied by nonmessengers. As punk rock emerged in the mid-1970s, rockers with piercings, purple hair, and other body modifications gravitated to courier work, which "allowed people with mohawks to earn a living," as a San Francisco messengers' association brochure later stated. Messengers developed what the anthropologist Jeffrey L. Kidder called a "bricolage" of attire that both reflected and influenced punk, skateboard rat, and hip-hop style.

Some office workers envied the messengers' fortitude. In 1982, the *Washington Post*'s Henry Allen called them "phantoms who materialize smug and dripping to remind us that it is sleeting outside our offices—offices that make cowards of us all." The 1984 Olympics helped burnish the bikers' heroic image. At those games, held in Los Angeles, America won its first Olympic cycling medals since 1912: four gold medals, two bronze, and three silver, including one for Nelson Vails, a bike messenger from Harlem. (It helped that a Soviet-led boycott of the LA games took many eastern bloc countries out of contention.) Hollywood films like Kevin Bacon's 1986 *Quicksilver*, in which a cocky young futures trader goes bust and finds redemption as a bicycle courier, reflected a benign view of the profession. Spike Lee's first film, the indie *She's Gotta Have It*, was released the same year; in it, Lee plays Mars Blackmon, a comically importunate cyclist in a messenger cap vying for the attentions of the titular "she." If not quite heroic with his tagline of "Please baby, please baby, please baby, baby baby please," Mars was at least unthreatening. And when Lee revived the character in a popular series of Nike ads featuring the NBA superstar Michael Jordan a couple of years later, Mars Blackmon became a b-boy cultural icon.

As bike messengers became more plentiful in American cities, though, their daring exploits quickly became less heroic to the drivers and pedestrians who had to dodge them. And although the annual number of bicycle-pedestrian collisions was never more than a tiny fraction of the car-pedestrian collisions, the sight of ever more messengers blasting through red lights or salmoning the wrong way up one-way streets could be unnerving. "There is a form of terrorism on the streets of Washington," stated a 1987 letter to the *Washington Post*. "This is the terrorism of the delivery or messenger bicyclists, the undisciplined intimidators who are subjugating our downtown streets." In New York in 1986, there were more than four thousand commercial bikers, and their presence made pedestrians feel unsafe. "The problem is not that their actual accident rate is so very high," one opponent admitted. "The problem is that this kind of riding causes so much stress to those sharing the streets with them."

Like citizens decrying scorchers ninety years earlier, politicians and activists agitated for laws limiting when and where messengers could work. In July 1987, New York mayor Ed Koch announced a midday ban on cycling on three major avenues in midtown Manhattan. The measure, scheduled to take effect that fall, was designed to constrain bicycle messengers without harming recreational riders on Central Park's bike paths or office workers commuting by bike in the morning and evening. "What [bike messengers] are doing is scaring the public to death," police commissioner Benjamin Ward said at the time, "and we've got to do something about it."

What Koch and Ward discovered, though, was that bikers stuck together. Throughout that summer, hundreds of cyclists would gather in the evenings to parade three miles up Sixth Avenue in an orderly but imposing mass. "Our stately pace, perhaps five mph, was slow enough that passersby could look past our bikes and see our bodies and faces," recalled the environmental activist Charles Komanoff in a recent memoir. "Cries of 'What do we want? Our streets back!' reverberated through the glass canyons, alternating with 'Join us!'" In the end, the ban's passage was delayed by a legal technicality, and Koch abandoned the idea of pushing it through. Bicycle messengers didn't completely shed their urban-warrior image after the protests—nor did many of them want to—but with collective action they quelled their most vocal opponents. Even during the relative bicycle bust of the 1980s, cyclists joined forces to wield the political clout that is part of the bicycle's legacy.

The arrival of the office fax in the late 1980s and of e-mail attachments in the mid-1990s thinned the messenger herd significantly, though their mystique lingered, and still does. The 2012 film *Premium Rush*, for example, starred Joseph Gordon-Levitt as a disaffected Columbia Law grad who delivers packages on a brakeless fixie and naturally encounters Hollywood-style intrigue along the way. "The pedals never stop turning," his character says as the film opens. "Can't stop. Don't want to either."

There were urban bicycle messengers before the 1970s, of course. In fact, UPS began as a foot-and-cycle messenger business in Seattle in 1907. And Western Union employed biking messenger boys (and some girls) from the 1890s until they mostly were replaced by fax-like technology during the 1960s. (A 1973 *Wall Street Journal* review of the corporation's "jazzy" new centralized telegraph office begins, "Without a bicycle in sight.") Traditionally, though, cycling couriers had the reputation of being poky and undependable, whether because they were paid by the hour or because they were too young to take the job seriously. That stereotype was reflected in news coverage from the beginning. For a story about an upcoming bicycle messenger race in 1896, for example, the *Buffalo Evening News* crafted the tongue-in-cheek headline, "For the First Time in History Messenger Boys May Be Seen Going Fast."

The bike messengers who began working city streets during the 1970s bike boom were different. As other Americans turned away from daily bike riding because they saw it as dangerous, some in this group turned toward the bicycle for the same reason. And they ended up forging an enduring outlaw mystique out of all proportion to their numbers.

The summer of 1976, when George Cooper was showing off his courier headquarters to the *New York Times*, was the nation's bicentennial summer. It was a time for celebration, but many Americans weren't feeling very celebratory. Crime and civic unrest were ongoing concerns. Then there was the economy. After World War II, the United States grew accustomed to its dominance as a manufacturing and political power. But its postwar aid programs gradually revived the Japanese and German economies, and by the early 1970s, US companies were facing formidable competition from their country's former foes. At the same time, steady wage gains for unionized American labor meant rising production costs for US manufacturers. So did new regulations intended to address the demands of environmentalists, consumer protection advocates, and civil rights and women's rights activists. These higher wages and added regulatory costs cut into corporate profits and, hence, hiring. By the bicentennial year, it all added up to an unusual and painful economic condition called "stagflation": high unemployment plus high inflation. Americans were hurting.

The country's military pride was hurting, too. US forces—stymied, in part, by the North Vietnamese Army's stealthy use of the bicycle—had withdrawn from Vietnam in 1973. When the South Vietnamese capital, Saigon, fell two years later, more than 1,300 Americans and 5,600 allies frantically evacuated the city via a chaotic scramble of ships and Huey helicopters. Distressingly, many South Vietnamese allies of the United States were left behind to face the fate of the vanquished. Even Americans who had opposed the war couldn't celebrate this outcome. Meanwhile, the unfolding of the Watergate scandal, leading up to Richard Nixon's resignation in August 1974, had rattled

Americans' faith in governmental authority. "We have been shaken by a tragic war abroad and by scandals and broken promises at home," announced future president Jimmy Carter when he accepted the Democratic nomination in July 1976. "There is a fear that our best years are behind us."

Into that dreary picture rolled—what else?—the bicycle. Because 1976 wasn't only the bicentennial. It was the Bikecentennial: the year 2,000 riders took up a challenge to cross the nation by bike, and another 2,100 rode part of the way. Following a meandering, 4,250-mile backroads route stretching from Astoria, Oregon, to Yorktown, Virginia (or vice versa), riders pedaled all day, then camped or slept in "bike inns" set up in church basements, school gyms, and college dorms. Cyclists could make their own way across or pay to join a group. Signing up solo cost $75; the deluxe "Odyssey Across America" option cost $965 for a guided eighty-two-day trip with lodging and meals included.

Small towns embraced the scruffy bands of middle-class adventurers who rolled through day by day. In Prairie City, Oregon, the sheriff tracked down a male rider who had been looking to buy a copy of the state seal and handed the tourist his seal-emblazoned badge. In Liebenthal, Kansas, a group of young women donned thrift-shop frocks to ride in a parade to mark the tiny town's centennial. "Not only are the cyclists enjoying America, but America is enjoying the cyclists," *Time* magazine noted. For some riders, Bikecentennial was a way to ignore the country's issues, or transcend them. One guide recalled picking up a new group of cyclists in Radford, Virginia, in August, just before the contested Republican presidential nomination had been decided in President Gerald Ford's favor. "The Republican National Convention was voting that night," he wrote. "But none of us seemed to care. We had a group that clicked, and we were headed to the Blue Ridge Parkway, Monticello, and real-life encounters with the salt of the Earth."

Bikecentennial was the creation of two married couples in their twenties—Greg and June Siple and Dan and Lys Burden—who had met in Ohio as volunteer organizers for bicycle tours. The four friends came up with the Bikecentennial idea in 1972, during "Hemistour," their marathon ride from Anchorage, Alaska to Oaxaca, Mexico. (At Oaxaca, the Siples continued south to Tierra del Fuego, and the Burdens returned to the United States to seek funding and workers to organize the mass coast-to-coast tour.) Despite their affinity for extreme-distance riding, the four didn't consider themselves particularly athletic. What they hoped to demonstrate with Bikecentennial, Dan Burden said at the time, was that "bicycling can be a wonderful intimate way to see the countryside." Their "modest physiques and merely adequate stamina" proved that cycle touring was not just for athletes, he added.

Although the event did not immediately establish bicycle touring as a go-to vacation option for most Americans, it did have a lasting impact. For some of those who rode, hosted, or read about the unexpectedly wholesome wheeled horde in the national press, Bikecentennial may have given them more hope than a politician's speech that better days lay ahead. Along with adding positive, collaborative energy to that anxious summer, the ride encouraged the development of marked on-road bicycle routes—an idea first tried in Florida in the early 1960s—including the creation of long-distance bikeways through California, Washington, Oregon, the Northeast, and North Carolina by 1978. The cyclists' iffier experiences with sharing truck routes may have helped foster support for the development of dedicated cycling paths and rails-to-trails hiking and biking paths as well. And the nonprofit formed to coordinate Bikecentennial never shut down. Now called the Adventure Cycling Association, the Missoula, Montana, group provides route maps and other resources to long-distance cyclists.

Along with the Bikecentennial and the earliest glimmerings of messenger chic, the summer of 1976 saw the start of a third culture of extreme bike riding. These daredevils, a small clique of adrenaline-loving bicycle racers, ironically ended up making cycling less scary for riders nationwide.

On the morning of October 21, 1976, a half-dozen hippies gathered at the high point of a ridge just north of Mount Tamalpais in Marin County, California. It was chilly but clear, and the riders could see for miles, all the way to the San Francisco Bay. At their feet was a rocky, rutted fire road that plunged down the mountainside, losing 1,300 feet of elevation in a span of two miles over a series of blind switchbacks edged by small cliffs. The group of friends had come to settle a question: which of them could bomb down the road the fastest?

Several of the riders were members of a local road racing club, but their delicate European ten-speed bikes would never have made it up to the starting spot that morning, let alone to the bottom of the hill. Instead, the riders used bikes they called "clunkers": weighty old balloon-tired machines such as the 1930s Schwinn Excelsior, hacked to include derailleur gears, steel reinforcement rods, heavy-duty brakes, and wide saddles. The DIY modifications were intended to help both bike and rider survive the bashing downhill run. The group, and others in their orbit, had been riding these Frankenbikes off-road for a couple of years, but this ride would prove historic. It was the first downhill time trial on the machines that would come to be called mountain bikes.

In a magazine article, the race organizer, Charlie Kelly, later described how it felt to ride the course. At the top, where the road is more or less straight, "most of the corners can be taken at full speed, which is a thrilling prospect in light of the fact that it will take you about 200 feet to stop (unless you hit a tree)," he wrote. "A roller-coaster section gives you a new thrill as the bike becomes weightless just when you want the tires on the ground. Into a dip and the bike slides sideways, then corrects itself. . . . Your reflexes and vision improve immeasurably. You are aware of every pebble on the road."

The winning time that first day was 5:12, or an average of about twenty-five miles an hour. The losers demanded a rematch, which led to a series of races that drew more competitors each time. Over the next couple of years, as the new sport of downhill "clunking" gained local popularity, it got harder to find junked balloon-tired bikes to overhaul. Even the sport's originators hunted for bikes, since a decades-old frame would only take so much abuse before failing. In 1977, Kelly hired a fellow rider, a machinist named Joe Breeze, to build him a custom clunker frame. Breeze made that one, plus an extra nine nickel-plated frames that he used as the basis for rugged fat-tired bikes; he sold them for $750 each. He called the bikes "Breezers"; they were the first modern mountain bikes. "We thought in our naivete that Joe Breeze's ten prototype mountain bikes were surely enough to satisfy worldwide demand," Kelly would later recall.

But word of the new sport had started to spread beyond Marin County. In 1978, the national road-racing magazine *VeloNews* reported that "California bikies are mountainside surfing"; *CoEvolution Quarterly* announced the birth of "a new kind of bicycle" developed by "escapist hippies." In early 1979, a San Francisco TV station visited the original course, dubbed "Repack" by its riders, and aired a report that was rebroadcast on CBS affiliates nationwide. The riders in that piece, a pack of two dozen or so lean young men, plus a few women, adhered to a proto-grunge dress code of plaid flannel shirts, faded jeans, hiking boots, leather work gloves, and down vests or jackets. The sandy-haired Charlie Kelly wore a moustache and sideburns; his long scraggly curls were pulled back into a ponytail. Kelly told the reporter how the racecourse had gotten the name "Re-

Joe Breeze, the creator of the first purpose-built mountain bike, raced his prototype—called Breezer #1—down Repack Road in Marin County, California, in late 1977. Now he is the curator of the Marin Museum of Bicycling and Mountain Bike Hall of Fame in Fairfax, California.

pack." "We used to ride down on these coaster brakes," he said. "This hill is so steep and you've got to be on the brakes so much that when you get to the bottom . . . all the grease is gone, it's vaporized. And then you've got to go home and repack your hub."

Another racer, Kelly's former roommate Gary Fisher, had been the first to add gears to his clunker. He squinted into the sun as he spoke to the reporter.

"Now, where did this start?" the interviewer asked.

"It probably started when men started riding bicycles a hundred years ago," Fisher responded. "They had nothing but dirt roads to ride on." But the practice of souping up sturdy old fat-tired bikes had begun much more recently, he added: "It's come a long way since then, and it's *going* to go a long ways."

Later that year, Fisher and Kelly started a company called MountainBikes and sold cycles hand-built from frames made by a fellow Repacker, Tom Ritchey, a gifted machinist. By 1980, there were three local mountain-bike makers; in 1981, a Bay Area importer commissioned a Japanese factory to create the first mass-produced mountain bike, the Specialized Stumpjumper. As it had with the kids' high-riser bike, Schwinn quickly noted the trend and jumped into the game; it released the Sidewinder later that year, though the model's unsophisticated construction meant its off-road capacity was mostly hype. "Let the others stick to those smooth paved roads," one newspaper ad read. "The Sidewinder was born to blaze new trails and go where no ordinary bike can."

Gary Fisher's ballsy prediction was coming true: the mountain bike was on its way. But many of these machines never got close to a mountain. The sleek, racer-style ten-speeds of the early-'70s boom felt too high-maintenance to stay in fashion for long, but the hardy off-road bikes of the 1980s made city streets feel safer. "Their chubby tires rarely go flat and never get stuck in storm grates," the *Baltimore Sun* reported in 1985. "And with their upright handlebars, they allow cyclists to sit higher, the better to see the world with and the better for the world to see them." These cycles, though built for risk takers, were perfect "for the timid who never felt comfortable on racing bikes," the paper added.

And the timid were buying. After the 1970s boom, US bicycle sales had sunk, bottoming out at 6.8 million in 1982, but they now began another surge. In 1985, 11.4 million bikes were sold, and nearly every major manufacturer offered at least one all-terrain model. By 1989, the mountain bike accounted for well over half the US market, and lightweight ten-speeds—by then called "road bikes"—were only a fraction of it. "It's just phenomenal," one Virginia merchant said. "You go to the mountain bike section of the store and it's jammed with people, and the road bike section doesn't have anybody in it." In 1990, there were ninety-three million cyclists in the United States, and the sturdy mountain bike was the ride of choice; even many bike messengers switched to the rugged machines. That year, *Bicycling* magazine asked, "Are Road Bikes Dead?"

They weren't dead, though; they were just resting.

Bikecentennial might well have turned out to be the high-water mark for road biking in the United States if it hadn't been for racers like Connie Carpenter-Phinney and Greg LeMond. To Americans, road racing had long seemed an effete European pursuit. In fact, the main gag of 1979's Oscar-winning coming-of-age film *Breaking Away* is that its protagonist, the doofy nineteen-year-old racer Dave Stoller (played by Dennis Christopher), seems to think he is Italian. American cyclists had a pitiful record in international competition, and at times the US Olympic Committee had seemed ready to drop the sport entirely. At the Tokyo Olympics in 1964, for example, the top US road racer came in seventy-fifth.

But with the renewed interest in adult cycling during the early 1970s had come increased support from the US Olympic Committee to develop amateur bicycle racers. By the early 1980s, that investment had started paying off. At the Los Angeles Olympics in 1984, the five-foot-ten-inch strawberry blonde Carpenter-Phinney broke America's long medal drought by winning the gold in road racing in a photo finish. Two years later, the Nevadan LeMond—also blond, also five-foot-ten—entered the three-week Tour de France; no non-European had ever won. After a grueling public showdown with his mentor turned tormentor, French teammate Bernard Hinault, LeMond won the race and returned to the United States a cult hero. In 1989, he ascended to hero-hero status: after he had come back from a near-fatal hunting accident to win the tour again in 1989, *Sports Illustrated* named him its Sportsman of the Year.

Mountain bikes had overtaken the mass market by then, but road bikes were developing a cachet among some baby boomers—prosperous midcareer yuppies—who bought elite equipment and decked themselves out in the form-fitting, Day-Glo Lycra of the peloton. "I think the clothing has helped increase the popularity of the sport," said a marketing director for the reanimated League of American Wheelmen. "Americans are so trendy they grab onto something like this."

The look escaped the sport: in 1987, Bill Cunningham, the *New York Times* "Street Fashion" photographer, documented a trend toward clingy, racer-style pants that "fit as tightly as anything that isn't skin possibly could." After the microminiskirts of the 1960s and the bralessness of the 1970s, Americans weren't as easily shocked by revealing attire as they had been in the 1890s, but bicycle shorts had a moment of notoriety. One Virginia waitress even sued her employer, a sports bar, for requiring female staffers to wear the skintight pants during night shifts. Her suit accused the bar of "pandering to male patrons in an effort to increase business," the *Washington Post* reported.

During the popularity trough after the 1970s boom, the bicycle morphed in still other ways. Schwinn Sting-Rays didn't die outright; instead, some California kids hacked them into stripped-down, nubby-tired dirt bikes and created the sport of bicycle motocross—BMX—which pitted preteen racers against one another on undulating dirt tracks. In 1974, there were just a handful of BMX tracks, all on the West Coast; by 1978, there were more than three hundred all over the country, and low-performing "look-alike" bikes had taken over the kids' market. In the 1982 film *E.T.*, the boys in the dramatic flying rescue scene are riding BMX bikes. The sport spawned the high-flying acrobatic skateboard-style tricks of BMX freestyle, which in turn led to the heart-stopping televised X Games.

On the other end of the cyclist-age continuum was the recumbent bicycle. It has been known since the days of the safety that riding in a low-slung, reclining posture could reduce wind resistance and increase speed. In fact, the recumbent bicycle was banned from international racing competition in 1934 for this very reason: it was considered cheating. In the mid-1970s, though, some US inventors founded the International Human Powered Vehicle Association and revived the idea of the recumbent bike. By the 1980s, commuter versions had come to market, favored for both their speed and their tipped-back posture, which was easier on aging knees. Then came the so-called hybrid bike, a versatile commuting vehicle that turned down the testosterone on the mountain bike, blending straight handlebars and an upright riding posture with "tires that are stout but not obese, gearing for those whose waist size exceeds the circumference of their quads, and components that are more bullet-resistant than bulletproof," as *Bicycling* magazine reported in 1990. Next came the beach cruiser or "comfort bike," a wide-seated update on the sturdy, balloon-tired tanks of the 1930s.

In the wake of the ten-speed boom of the 1970s, the bicycle had diversified. The packed racing velodromes and stratospheric racers' salaries of the 1920s were long gone, but fixed-gear track bikes lived on as an emblem of urban warrior cool. Balloon-tired clunkers birthed mountain bikes, which transformed placid hiking terrain into a roller coaster for thrill-seekers and also made city and suburban streets feel less threatening to the nervous rider. After US cycle racers started scoring international wins, the road bike arose from its deathbed to embody a pampered, aspirational athleticism not terribly far removed from the attitude of the Ordinary rider. It suddenly seemed as if whatever you might need a bike for, there was a bike for you. And if, like many Americans, you felt you *didn't* need a bike, you could still feel the machine's impact all around you: in the roads, in the cars, in the fitness culture and the women's movement, and even, again, in the scandalously tight pants.

Eleven

ARE WE THERE YET?

America's relationship with the bicycle is an on-again, off-again romance. When a new iteration of the machine first appears, we joyously romp with our darling. After a while, though, we cast it aside in disillusionment or boredom. Years pass. The bike loses weight. It gets a haircut. We run into it on the street. And before you know it, we're right back where we started.

As I write this, the United States seems to be in the throes of yet another dewy-eyed affair. Take bikeshares, for example. These computerized, often solar-powered networks—based on an idea imported from Europe—allow people to easily borrow sturdy three-speed bikes for quick jaunts around town, infusing downtown traffic with a strangely proper-looking assortment of upright, helmetless riders in street clothes. Supporters see the systems as a public good: a way to reduce traffic congestion, carbon emissions, and parking woes while improving public health with a bit of exercise. The country's first automated bikeshare opened in Tulsa, Oklahoma, in 2007, and after several years of small-scale trial programs around the country, the phenomenon blew up. By mid-2015, there were seventy-two public bikeshares operating nationwide in cities like Milwaukee, Salt Lake

City, Chattanooga, San Diego, Seattle, Chicago, and New York, with another eight expected to open by the end of the year. Despite user fees and corporate sponsorships, most of these systems don't break even, but having one is becoming an emblem of the modern American city, advocates say. "If you were to go to a city and they don't have recycling, you'd think, 'Where am I, in the 1970s?'" planning consultant Paul DeMaio told *Slate* in 2013. "It's just one of those amenities that you've come to expect, and I think that's definitely becoming true for bike sharing in the U.S."

Bikeshares have been credited with helping fuel a surge in bicycle commuting. Between 2000 and 2013, the proportion of US commuters who traveled by bike rose nationwide; it doubled in San Francisco, tripled in New Orleans, and quadrupled in Washington, DC. Also feeding the commuting trend is an inclination by local governments to designate street space for cyclists. In 2012, thirty-six of the country's largest cities reported a combined total of nearly 13,000 miles of on-street bicycle lanes, signed routes, and paths. That is 17 percent higher than the bike-lane mileage the same cities had reported just one year earlier. And those numbers don't include the most visible bike lanes: so-called protected lanes or cycle tracks, often painted green, which separate bike riders from car traffic with a curb or other barrier. Between 2012 and 2014, US cities carved out 113 new protected lanes from roadways, more than had been built in this country in the preceding 137 years. The growth of bike lanes involves sort of a feedback loop. Cyclists push for safer routes on city streets; cities respond by striping bike lanes and share-the-road arrows (aka "sharrows"); riders feel safer; formerly hesitant people start riding; more riders push for yet more lanes.

And the bike has once again become a fashion statement. In hipster colonies like Williamsburg, Brooklyn, and hipster nations like Portland, Oregon, the fixie is the stereotypical ride, found locked in heaps in front of coffee bars and indie-music venues. Some argue that the fixed-gear's stripped-down simplicity fits the young cohort's DIY aesthetic; others, that it is a style affectation in line with the tight trousers and lumberjack beards that typify the look. The bike-culture critic Lodovico Pignatti Morano sees the fixie as a radical form of rebellion against urban conformity, "a way to play out a kind of suicide over and over again." While the growth of hipsterdom is difficult to quantify—in part because almost nobody self-identifies as a hipster—the Priceonomics data analysis firm found a work-around: they recently ranked US cities' hipster populations based on the number of fixed-gear bikes offered for sale on Craigslist. (Orange County, California, where freestylers as well as hipsters ride fixed-gears, topped the list with 100 ads.)

The bicycle keeps evolving. In the past decade, a new sport cycle has taken shape: the fatbike, with soft, grippy tires so plump they make a 1930s balloon-tired bike look svelte. These cycles aren't for the road or even for the fire trail. They are designed to traverse soft, slippery terrain like snow or sand. The 25th Infantry Bicycle Corps could have used a few of these. Created in the 1990s to handle Alaska's Anchorage-to-Nome sled-dog trail, "fatties" now feature regularly in outdoor excursions to wintry locales. Said one Minneapolis enthusiast of the cycle's tanklike handling, "It does anything any other bike can do, just slower." More than one hundred makers are currently producing fatbikes, including major manufacturers such as Trek and Specialized. In late 2014, one bicycle dealer in Anchorage, Alaska, estimated that there were ten thousand fatbike riders in the city; a local cross-country skier reported that there were ten fatbikers for every skier on a coastline trail.

Commuter cycles are changing, too. In part because of a steady decline in urban crime since 1990, more middle-class parents are raising kids in walkable, bikable cities, which means that yet another new bike form has caught on—well, two actually: the longtail cargo bike, with a rear platform suitable for hauling a family's worth of groceries; and the bucket bike, or *bakfiets*, a two- or three-wheeler with a wheelbarrow-like compartment that, to judge from the ads, comes preloaded with a set of adorable towheads. These workhorses first appeared on the US market in the late 1990s, when their buyers tended to be outdoorsy types looking to haul surfboards or kayaks, but in recent years they have become a nouveau-yuppie accessory. Dubbed the "new station wagon" by the *Wall Street Journal* in 2013, the cargo bike is now a common sight at upscale urban school drop-offs; one Washington, DC, father told the *New York Times* that more than a dozen families at his kids' elementary school commute that way.

Then, too, there is the electric bicycle, or ebike. At forty pounds and up, these two-wheelers are hefty, but their battery-powered onboard motors make riders feel dazzlingly light, especially when gliding uphill. Ebikes are used widely in Europe and even more widely in China, where half of all bicycles now sold are electric. The idea of adding motors to bicycles isn't new: in the late 1860s, a Massachusetts inventor named Sylvester Roper built a steam-powered pedal velocipede that many regard as the first motorcycle. And the gas-powered motorcycles that followed have a rich history and culture of their own. It is only recently, though, that Americans have begun latching onto ebikes, which are legal on most US surface roads as long as they are built with a speed ceiling of twenty miles per hour. They are pricey, costing an average of $2,500, though they are becoming cheaper as battery technology improves. In 2014, more than 200,000 ebikes were sold in the United States. That is a small fraction of the sixteen million human-powered cycles sold here the same year, but more than double the ebike sales tally from just two years earlier.

Ed Benjamin, the chairman of the Light Electric Vehicle Association, argues that the United States has been slow to adopt the ebike because of snobbery on the part of bicycle industry honchos and bike shop owners, some of whom see the electrical boost as a form of cheating, a perversion of the human-powered cycling ethos. That attitude is fading, though, as the generation that first fell in love with the ten-speed now deals with the aches and pains of aging. "We baby boomers are not as young as we used to be," says Benjamin, who entered the bicycle business as a teenager in 1969. "We find that an electric-assisted bicycle suits us very much. The electric bike extends the riding season by fifteen years."

The categories of fatbike, cargo bike, and electric bike aren't mutually exclusive. Almost every current form of cycle seems to have inspired an e-version, including electric mountain bikes that make the off-road ascent almost as much fun as the descent. There is even a sleek German one-speed called the Coboc: a messenger-style sylph with a battery hidden in the downtube. At $5,900, it is a luxe subversion of the stripped-down track bikes of the 1970s. No Zen survival skills required: along with a top powered speed of 15.5 miles per hour and a range of thirty-seven miles between charges, the Coboc comes with a freewheel and brakes.

All these new bikes, new bike lanes, and new riders are conspicuous. In cities where traffic is perpetually snarled, the sight of them has caused many frustrated motorists to decry a creeping "war on cars." This shadowy conflict is supposedly being waged by lefty politicians who prefer the collectivist benefits of bikes and public transit to the rugged individualism of the private SUV. Bicycle activists, long a reedy minority voice in transportation debates, are now denounced as "an all-powerful enterprise" by opponents such as Dorothy Rabinowitz, a member of the *Wall Street Journal* editorial board, who called bikers "the most important danger in the city" in a 2013 video interview. (She made this claim in the face of statistics provided by her sympathetic interviewer: no pedestrians had been killed by cyclists in New York during the previous four years, when 597 pedestrians were killed by cars and trucks.)

Adult riders—most of whom are also drivers—see the situation differently, of course. With more bike lanes and more company in them, it is starting to feel as if the bike is finally living up to its original promise. It is no longer just a toy for rich men or exclusively for children, not just a liberator for cloistered middle-class women or a tool for armed resistance. In the nation's largest cities, where the live horse has long since vanished and the car is all too plentiful, the bicycle has become a reliable, affordable, socially acceptable mechanical horse, attainable by any worker who wants one. It carries you straight to your destination and waits patiently outside at the hitching post.

And it is true that the bicycle's star is on the rise—but only in the prosperous urban areas where trend spotters tend to hang out. There is no bike boom in the country as a whole. Indeed, since 2000, while bike lanes were being striped and bikeshare stations installed, ridership in the United States *dropped*. Between 2000 and 2013, the number of Americans who said they cycled at least once during the year fell by 6.3 percent, according to an industry report. The number who cycled six or more times fell by 17 percent, to 35.6 million. And the drop-off among children was even starker: in 2000, there were 17.6 million active riders between the ages of seven and seventeen. By 2013, that number was only 10 million—a loss of 43 percent. While sales of adult bikes fell only slightly, from 11.9 million in 2000 to 11.3 million in 2013, sales of kids' bikes tanked. In 2000, 11.6 million children's bicycles were sold in the United States; in 2013, the number was 4.9 million.

So where did all those child riders go? To day care, to sports leagues, to computer and smartphone screens. Older Americans might still regard the bicycle as a quintessential childhood companion, but its heyday in the 1950s and 1960s was part of a demographic fluke: the only time in American history when large numbers of children had such freedom from daytime obligations and such freedom of movement. That brief midcentury moment has become childhood's lost paradise. Since then, a steady increase in two-worker and single-parent households has limited the number of American children who can go straight home or out to the park after school. Indeed, today a parent can get arrested for sending a child to the local park alone. A rapid-fire national media amplifies horrifying but rare crimes against children such as abduction by strangers, raising parental and governmental anxiety. Cell phones seemingly make it compulsory for parents to know their kids' whereabouts at all times. American children, without the adventure of unscheduled roaming, retreat to online role-playing games and house-to-house texting with friends.

It seems that the heightened protectiveness and esteem that middle-class parents began to express for their kids in the 1920s has now, four generations later, intensified into a form of restrictive parenting that even its practitioners bemoan. In April 2014, a freelance writer in an Illinois college town posted a blog entry about her "terrifying" experience of allowing her five-year-old to ride his bike around the block by himself (without incident). In the comments, a self-confessed "helicopter mom" responded that she was struggling with allowing her son the same privilege. "I realized that when I was his age, I lived in a worse neighborhood and played outside by myself all the time," she confessed. "I think about how many hours passed when my Mom had no idea where I was, when I was just a little bit older than him, and

I start to hyperventilate." How strange that the loving impulse that once made the bike a necessary part of childhood may now have helped make solo biking seem too risky for a parent to even contemplate.

For many kids in working-class families, the idea of hopping on a bike never even comes up, says the industry analyst Jay Townley. Today and throughout its history, the US bicycle industry has been dominated by well-off white males, who represent most of the company executives, most of the retailers, and most of the buyers, he says. These big spenders represent a growing share of the bike business, too. While the average price of an adult bicycle has been trending downward relative to inflation, the amount that cycling enthusiasts spend per bike has stayed high. In 2014, hardcore bikies spent more than $1,200 per cycle; the average price of a new adult bike was $400. Some call cycling's appeal "the Lance Armstrong effect"; even after the seven-time Tour de France winner was stripped of his titles in 2012 for doping, the attention and glamour he brought to road racing and high-performance gear lives on among men who can afford the accoutrements.

Meanwhile, racial diversity is increasing among America's children, and many live in households headed by women, in urban neighborhoods where the current zeal for safe bike lanes has yet to penetrate, or else in exurbs whose thrumming arterial roads are designed to discourage pedestrian and bike traffic. Public schools have gotten bigger, drawing pupils from farther away, and schoolbooks have gotten heavier, bulked up with more photographs and more white space. It all makes biking to school a hairy proposition for many young scholars.

In earlier generations, advertisements piqued kids' appetite for bikes, but today few bike ads target middle-income or working-class families. Even though most cycles in the United States are sold through big-box retailers like Walmart and Target, the leaders of bicycle-industry marketing initiatives have resisted collaborating with such down-market vendors on campaigns for their customers. "Bicycles are not yet part of the mainstream culture of our society as they are in Europe, and therefore do not have the relevance they do in Europe and other countries of the world," Townley says. "The bicycle industry needs to reach out and become inclusive, not only of the retailers that sell bicycles in the U.S. but also the broad ethnic fabric and diversity of American culture." Multicultural marketing won't build bike paths next to freeways or move families closer to schools, but it could reintroduce the bike as an aspiration, even if not an immediately viable option.

So what should we make of the urban-adult bike boomlet? Nearly 200 years since the invention of the draisine, 150 years since the birth of the pedal velocipede, and 50 years since the country's last great bike boom, are these fixies and fatbikes, these commuters and ebikers, these cycle tracks and sharrows, the things that will finally make city cycling *normal*, at least for Americans who can arrange (and afford) to live near work, school, and shops? The automobile may have annihilated time and space on the interstate, after all, but in a car-choked city, it is once again the bike that magically shrinks the distance between here and there, allowing riders to percolate through the gridlock while drivers sit and fume. If the bicycle is no longer a suburban kid's birthright, will it become an enduring part of grown-up city life?

Urban planners say that the relationship between the car and the city is changing. Already, on-demand ride services like Uber and Lyft, and car-sharing companies like Car2Go and Zipcar, make it possible for some middle-class urbanites to forgo car ownership altogether. With more telecommuting, online shopping, and home entertainment, even suburban Americans are driving less and buying fewer vehicles. Within the next few years, self-driving cars will appear on the market, and analysts predict that they will eventually be deployed as automated taxis, potentially further reducing the need for private car ownership. But whether these robotic vehicles will make city streets safer for bikes is still up for debate. Some say they will lighten and calm traffic, freeing up asphalt for a dedicated cycle-track system. In a different, darker scenario, though, city streets could fill up with poorly programmed bumper cars that shuttle endlessly, looking for fares and clipping any illogical humans who get in their way. The reality will depend on how corporations and governments respond to the technological and regulatory challenges.

History is full of lofty predictions for the bicycle that didn't come true. But after all this time, maybe making predictions is beside the point. The bicycle's influence is visible throughout American culture: in our roads, cars, and planes; our embrace of mass production and consumption; the clothes women wear and the autonomy they have; even our collective understanding of war. The bike's urban popularity may grow and spread, or cycling may once again fall out of fashion. But if the bike goes away again, it will be back. It is already here to stay.

ACKNOWLEDGMENTS

This book would not exist without the advocacy and support of Mark Crispin Miller, my teacher and friend. The staff of the University of Texas Press, in particular Theresa May and Robert Devens, are due thanks for seeing value in the idea and patiently nudging it through to completion.

Early advisers, including John Plotz and Caleb Crain, set me on a productive course when I had only a fuzzy picture of what I had taken on. David Herlihy gave advice both early and late and saved me from many rabbit holes and rookie mistakes. He and other scholars affiliated with the International Cycling History Conference, including Nick Clayton, Hans-Erhard Lessing, Tom Crouch, and Gary Sanderson, were most generous with their time and expertise.

Writers who kindly agreed to explain and expand on their work included Earl Swift, Andrew Ritchie, Allan Millett, and Susan Shaheen. The analyst Jay Townley went out of his way to provide context and data on the bicycle market. Bernd Lukasch of the Otto Lilienthal Museum located and translated a relevant document for me, and Randall Merris of the International Concertina Association provided a rare monograph about the cycling Elliott family, along with scans of ephemera related to the

Elliotts. I am also grateful to those who spoke to me about their personal experiences with the bicycle during the mid to late twentieth century. Any errors or misapprehensions that persist in this book defy the best efforts of these scholars and civilians to set me straight.

Librarians, one of our nation's greatest undervalued resources, provided crucial assistance via the Internet, e-mail, and snail mail, as well as in person. I am particularly grateful to the staff of the Johns Hopkins University library system, especially Zena Mason and the Interlibrary Loan office. I would also like to acknowledge the unseen army of library workers and volunteers who are scanning out-of-copyright newspapers and books and putting them online. They are creating an amazing resource for anyone curious about our history.

Friends at work, including Jane Clark, Susan Appler, and Bill Horne, helped by tapping their own networks for solutions to various quandaries. Adriana Cordero took time to help me prepare my illustrations. Many friends provided much-needed moral support: Diane Flynn, Mike Dickinson, Ned Washburn, Bob Chesney, Janet Lill, and the men of The Charm Offensive—Chris Lehmann, Geordie Grindle, and Mike Blau—among others.

My colleagues in Salon Orlovsky—Chip Wass, Andrew Talle, Hollis Robbins—saw many chapters in draft form and offered invaluable editorial advice, and my dear friend and fellow Orlovsky Linda DeLibero read and sharpened the whole manuscript. The estimable David Dudley also read the manuscript and gave me much-appreciated advice on thinking through the book's conclusion.

Finally, I would like to thank my family: Marjorie, Sarah, and the rest of the Guroffs and Wehrs, from whom never is heard a discouraging word, and Charlie Barnett, who showed me how to do this.

ABBREVIATIONS

The following abbreviations are used in the notes.

AJO	*American Journal of Obstetrics and Diseases of Women and Children*
ALW	*American Legion Weekly*
AND	*Aberdeen (SD) Daily News*
APS	*American Philosophical Society*
AQ	*American Quarterly*
BDJ	*Boston Daily Journal*
BDT	*Bismarck Daily Tribune*
BEN	*Buffalo Evening News*
BG	*Boston Globe*
BMJ	*Boston Morning Journal*
BMSJ	*Boston Medical and Surgical Journal (BMSJ)*
BP&MA	*Baltimore Patriot and Mercantile Advertiser*
BR	*Binghamton (NY) Republican*
BS	*Baltimore Sun*
BW	*Bicycling World*
BW&MR	*Bicycling World and Motorcycle Review*
CC	*Clinton (NY) Courier*

CDG	*Cincinnati Daily Gazette*
CDT	*Chicago Daily Tribune*
CSM	*Christian Science Monitor*
CT	*Chicago Tribune*
DCDC	*Daily Critic (District of Columbia)*
DIO	*Daily Inter Ocean*
DM	*Daily Missoulian*
DNT	*Duluth News-Tribune*
DSR	*Daily (IA) State Register*
HDC	*Hartford (CT) Daily Courant (HDC)*
ICHC	*Cycle History*, proceedings of International Cycling History conferences: vols. 4, 5, 7, and 15, ed. Rob van der Plas; 8, ed. Nicholas Oddy and van der Plas; 10, ed. Hans-Erhard Lessing, van der Plas, and Andrew Ritchie; 11, ed. Ritchie and van der Plas; 13, ed. Ritchie and Nicholas Clayton; 14, ed. Ron Shepherd; 16, ed. Ritchie; 17, ed. Glen Norcliffe; 22 and 25, ed. Ritchie and Gary Sanderson
ISJ	*Indiana State Journal*
JAMA	*Journal of the American Medical Association*
KCS	*Kansas City Star*
LAH	*Los Angeles Herald*
LAT	*Los Angeles Times*
LAW&GR	*L.A.W. Bulletin and Good Roads*
LAWM	*L.A.W. Magazine*
LHJ	*Ladies' Home Journal*
MC&B	*MotorCycling and Bicycling*
MJ	*Minneapolis Journal*
MT	*Minneapolis Tribune*
NEG&MM	*New-England Galaxy & Masonic Magazine*
NHER	*New Haven Evening Register*
NPG	*National Police Gazette*

NYDA	*New-York Daily Advertiser*
NYEP	*New-York Evening Post*
NYH	*New York Herald*
NYHT	*New York Herald-Tribune*
NYS	*New York Sun*
NYSW	*New York Sunday World*
NYT	*New York Times*
NYTrib	*New-York Tribune*
OBSB	*Official Bulletin and Scrap Book of the League of American Wheelmen*
PI	*Philadelphia Inquirer*
PMD	*Preston (MN) Democrat*
PT	*Philadelphia Tribune*
RG 94	*Records of the Adjutant General's Office,* Record Group 94, National Archives
SDR	*Savannah Daily Republican*
SFC	*San Francisco Chronicle*
SFDEB	*San Francisco Daily Evening Bulletin*
SFEB	*San Francisco Evening Bulletin*
SR	*Springfield (MA) Sunday Republican*
SSR	*Springfield (MA) Sunday Republican*
StLPD	*St. Louis Post-Dispatch*
StLR	*St. Louis Republic*
StLS	*St. Louis Star*
UUSG&TA	*Union, United States Gazette, and True American*
W&CTR	*Wheel and Cycling Trade Review*
WSJ	*Wall Street Journal*
WP	*Washington Post*

NOTES

Introduction

1 *Lane splitting like this is legal:* Metropolitan Police, District Department of Transportation, and Washington Area Bicyclist Association, "Pocket Guide to DC Bike Laws," October 2012, 9.

1 *the main thing that slows cars down:* Traffic studies show that, on average, one cyclist creates a fraction of the congestion created by one car. See, for example, Dianhai Wang, Tianjun Feng, and Chunyan Liang, "Research on Bicycle Conversion Factors," *Transportation Research Part A: Policy and Practice*, October 2008, 1129–1139; Victoria Transport Policy Institute, "Transportation Cost and Benefit Analysis—Congestion Costs," August 29, 2003, 5.5–12; David Cranor, "Standard Responses #3: Response to 'Cyclists Cause Congestion,'" accessed June 16, 2015, www.thewashcycle.com/2011/09/standard-responses-3-response-to-cyclists-cause-congestion.html.

Chapter One: The Birth of the Bike

5 *nearly 10:30 p.m.:* "Tracena," *UUSG&TA*, May 18, 1819. An account of this scene appears in Herlihy, *Bicycle*, 40–42.

5 *the artificial horse:* See, for example, "Tracena," *BP&MA*, February 6, 1819, 3: "These horses are cheap, they are safe, and do not fall without the rider's consent."

5 *fashionable citizens:* Until 1815, the square had been a potter's field, but the addition of walkways and tree plantings starting that year gradually turned it into a "beautiful square" used by "citizens and strangers as a promenade" (Watson, *Annals of Philadelphia,* 351).

5 *a long day of rain: Philadelphia Navy Yard Log/Diary for 1819,* Record Group 181, National Archives and Records Administration.

5 *white picket fence . . . candle-lantern streetlights:* Karie Diethorn, chief curator, Independence National Historical Park, e-mail message to author, March 21, 2012.

5 *misty half-moon:* The moon would enter the last (third) quarter on May 16, 1819.

5 *huge, swinging strides:* Hans-Erhard Lessing, e-mail message to author, March 14, 2012. To see the Toronto artist Alberto de Ciccio riding a reproduction draisine, visit www.youtube.com/watch?v=eKGGOKnmGLk.

5 *The fascinated reporter:* "Tracena," *UUSG&TA,* May 18, 1819.

6 *the first one had appeared in Philadelphia:* Charles Willson Peale to Isaiah Lukens, May 8, 1819, *APS.*

6 *There was a tiller:* Sketch by Charles Willson Peale, 1819, *APS.*

6 *Those who first saw the machine:* Lessing, "What Led to the Invention of the Early Bicycle?," in *ICHC* 11, 33.

6 *A typical draisine could weigh fifty pounds:* Charles Willson Peale to Charles P. Polk, May 16, 1819, *APS.*

6 *twice the weight of the average bicycle:* Most mountain bikes and hybrid bikes weigh twenty-eight to thirty-two pounds; most road bikes, seventeen to twenty-three pounds. Bikes Direct, "What Does It Weigh?," accessed April 5, 2015, http://bikesdirect.com/weights.htm.

6 *The draisine had been invented:* Hadland and Lessing, *Bicycle Design,* 10.

6 *whose well-connected father:* Sören Fink and Hans-Erhard Lessing, "Karl Drais: All about the Beginnings of Individual Mobility," accessed April 4, 2015, www.karldrais.de/?lang=en.

6 *Times were tough in Europe:* Lessing, "Invention of the Early Bicycle?," 33; Hans-Erhard Lessing, "The Two-Wheeled Velocipede: A Solution to the Tambora Freeze of 1816," in *ICHC* 22, 180–182; Hadland and Lessing, *Bicycle Design,* 8–15; Lessing, *Automobilität.*

6 *Drais first demonstrated:* Hadland and Lessing, *Bicycle Design,* 10.

6 *he was selling plans for the devices:* Herlihy, *Bicycle,* 26–27.

7 *"velocipede," constructed from the words:* Lessing suggests that Drais derived the term *vélocipède* from *vélocifère*, the word for a then-new rapid horse-drawn coach (Hadland and Lessing, *Bicycle Design*, 20). The French words *veloce* (swift) and *pied* (foot) have Latin roots.

7 *Crossing the channel to England:* Herlihy, *Bicycle*, 31–38.

7 *In the United States, the draisine:* Ibid., 39.

7 *The maker, James Stewart:* Dunham, "Bicycle Era," 34.

7 *charging twenty-five cents:* "Tracena," *BP&MA*, February 6, 1819, 3.

7 *added evening hours:* "Tracena," *BP&MA*, February 8, 1819, 3.

7 *Philadelphia's Charles Willson Peale:* D. Ward, *Charles Willson Peale*, xvii–xxii.

7 *a mastodon skeleton:* Beth Py-Lieberman, "The Great Hall of American Wonders Opens Today at American Art," July 15, 2011, www.smithsonianmag.com/smithsonian-institution/the-great-hall-of-american-wonders-opens-today-at-american-art-31832317.

7 *only the second fossil reconstruction:* Richard Conniff, "Mammoths and Mastodons: All American Monsters," *Smithsonian*, April 2010, www.smithsonianmag.com/science-nature/mammoths-and-mastodons-all-american-monsters-8898672.

7 *Peale came out of artistic retirement:* "Aged Novelty," *BP&MA*, February 6, 1819, 3.

8 *he found a British illustration:* Charles Willson Peale to his son Rembrandt, May 22, 1819, *APS*. Although the place where he found this illustration, "Aitken's repository," is described as "unidentified" in L. Miller and S. Hart, *Selected Papers*, Karie Diethorn suggests it could refer to (John) Aitken's Musical Repository, a sheet music shop on North Second Street in Philadelphia: "Since Peale had seen in Baltimore the velocipede made by Thomas or James Stewart, and the Stewarts were musical instrument makers, maybe that's the link to John Aitken's shop." Karie Diethorn, e-mail message to author, March 21, 2012.

8 *hiring a blacksmith to make the machine:* Charles Willson Peale to his son Titian, July 20, 1819, *APS*.

8 *Peale deposited the machine:* Charles Willson Peale to his son Rembrandt, May 22, 1819, *APS*.

8 *And the riders were probably:* Charles Willson Peale to Charles P. Polk, May 16, 1819, *APS*.

8 *The young men had liberated:* Charles Willson Peale to his son Titian, July 20, 1819, *APS*; see also Herlihy, *Bicycle*, 40.

8 *flew downhill "like the very devil":* Charles Linnaeus Peale to his brother Titian, May 10, 1819, *APS.*

8 *Among his other activities:* L. Miller and S. Hart, *Selected Papers,* xxxix–xl.

8 *"in a swiftness that dazzles the sight:* Charles Willson Peale to his son Rembrandt, July 24, 1819, *APS.*

8 *the machines bumbled along fine:* "New Patents and Mechanical Inventions," *Monthly Magazine, or British Register,* March 1, 1819, 156; S. Harris, *Horse Gaits,* 36, 49.

9 *"in as short a time as horses": Mississippi State Gazette,* July 24, 1819.

9 *Boston, New Haven:* Herlihy, *Bicycle,* 42–45.

9 *Specimens were spotted: Western Spy,* August 14, 1819, cited in Herlihy, *Bicycle,* 43. Cincinnati's population more than tripled between 1810 and 1820, making it the twelfth-largest city in the United States (Taylor, *Transportation Revolution,* 7).

9 *"breaking through the ice":* See, for example, T. S. Davies, "On the Velocipede, May 1837," reprinted in the *Boneshaker,* Autumn 1985, 9.

9 *"A few lessons are sufficient":* "Experiment," *NYDA,* July 15, 1819, 2.

9 *fewer than a thousand:* According to Lessing, "For the U.S. no production number is known. . . . Students of Harvard and Yale rode velocipedes, but the early clampdown by the authorities didn't leave room for large numbers. I'd guess no more than 500 to 1,000" (e-mail message to author, March 28, 2012). Others place the figure as low as 100. As the British cycle historian Nicholas Clayton notes, "In the U.K. where it was a bigger deal, [Denis] Johnson, the only commercial maker, made barely 350" (e-mail message to author, January 15, 2015).

9 *In July 1819, for example:* R. Chronic, "Dandies & Wooden Horses," *NYEP,* July 29, 1819, 2.

10 *Within months, draisine riding was:* Herlihy, *Bicycle,* 42–45.

10 *Most city streets weren't paved:* This was true even in the 1890s, according to Swift, *Big Roads,* 14.

10 *More than 70 percent of the U.S. population:* Heidler and Heidler, *Daily Life,* 51.

10 *"hardly more than broad paths":* Taylor, *Transportation Revolution,* 15.

10 *in 1813, a cargo wagon:* "Inland Trade," *Baltimore Weekly Register,* March 13, 1813, 32.

10 The *British cycle historian Cally Callomon:* Cally Callomon, e-mail message to author, April 24, 2012.

11 *In May 1820, a wag rewrote:* "Fashionable Amusement," *NEG& MM*, May 12, 1820, 123.

11 *The word "velocipede" stayed in use:* Herlihy, *Bicycle*, 52–65.

11 *these were called "turnpikes":* Zeman, *Greenwood Encyclopedia*, 1:259.

11 *some early turnpikes were built:* Taylor, *Transportation Revolution*, 17.

11 *turnpikes connected only certain cities:* Ibid.

11 *"You can't get there from here":* The punch line comes from the mid-nineteenth-century "Arkansas Traveler" storytelling tradition; in the 1950s, it was transposed to Maine in the popular "Which Way to Millinocket" comedy routine of Marshall Dodge and Robert Bryan, aka "Bert and I." By coincidence, Dodge, who died in 1982, was a longtime bicycle advocate. See, for example, John C. Devlin, "150 Cycle to Fair in Rules Protest," *NYT*, May 18, 1964, 32.

12 *Most trips between East Coast cities:* National Museum of American History, "Transportation History, 1800–1900," accessed April 5, 2015, http://amhistory.si.edu/onthemove/themes/story_48_1.html.

12 *This is why Americans:* C. W. Ernst, "Boston and Transportation," in *Proceedings of the Bostonian Society* (1898), 22.

12 *By 1820, there were fifty:* Heidler and Heidler, *Daily Life*, 85.

12 *That year, one small steamboat:* "Cincinnati, May 17," *City of Washington Gazette*, June 3, 1820, 3.

12 *"is now performed, with the greatest ease":* W. Bullock, "Sketch of a Journey through the Western States of North America, from New Orleans, by the Mississippi, Ohio, City of Cincinnati and Falls of Niagara, to New York, in 1827," in Thwaites, *Early Western Travels*, 128–129.

12 *"Safety" was a relative term:* Taylor, *Transportation Revolution*, 68–69. In 1823, the steamboat *Velocipede* had to stop for two days between New Orleans and Louisville in order to rebuild its flywheel after a passenger was caught by the coattail and crushed to death under it ("Arrived on Friday Evening Last," *Daily National Intelligencer*, March 18, 1823).

12 *The typical American "is devoured":* Chevalier, *Society, Manners, and Politics*, 286.

12 *Starting with the Erie Canal's:* Taylor, *Transportation Revolution*, 33–37.

12 *Too narrow and shallow:* Some canals accommodated steamboats later, but speeds had to be limited to avoid damage to the canals. See, for

example, C&O Canal Association, "Steamboats on the C&O Canal," accessed April 5, 2015, www.candocanal.org/articles/steamboats .html.

13 *In 1827, our English traveler:* Bullock, "Sketch of a Journey," in Thwaites, *Early Western Travels,* 141.

13 *"crowded with boats of considerable size":* Ibid., 151.

13 *Starting with only about 100 miles:* Taylor, *Transportation Revolution,* 32, 52. The cumulative length of built canals in 1840 was 3,326 miles.

13 *the Baltimore and Ohio opened:* Ibid., 77.

13 *Built mainly by private investors:* Ibid., 88.

13 *trains were often twice as fast:* Ibid., 71.

13 *By 1840, there were almost exactly:* Ibid., 79. The cumulative length of built railroads in 1840 was 3,328 miles.

13 *trains seemed to collapse the country's:* For a discussion of this phenomenon, see Schivelbusch, *Railway Journey,* 33–44, 89–112.

13 *"How much such extraordinary dispatch":* Stimson, *History of Express Companies,* 129.

14 *the telegraph, introduced in 1844:* Several inventors, including Samuel Morse, devised electrical telegraph systems in the 1830s. Morse won funding from Congress to build a long-distance demonstration line for his invention, and he successfully sent messages from Washington to Baltimore and back on May 24, 1844; see Smithsonian Institution, "History of the Telegraph," accessed May 9, 2015, http://historywired.si.edu/detail.cfm?ID=324.

14 *In July 1865, a few months after:* Charles E. Pratt, "Pierre Lallement and His Bicycle," *Outing,* October 1, 1883, 7; see also Herlihy, *Bicycle,* 86–87.

14 *one key addition:* Some cycle historians believe that the idea for the pedal velocipede may have derived from an intermediate multi-wheeled device rather than directly from the old draisine. They would object to the description of pedals as an "addition" to the obsolete glider of fifty years before. Still, when the pedal velocipede appeared in the 1860s, it was perceived to be a draisine with pedals added. See, for example, "Notes on the Velocipede," *Scientific American,* January 30, 1869, 67.

14 *a quiet, dark-haired:* Pratt, "Pierre Lallement and His Bicycle," 4.

14 *That fall, Lallement conducted:* Ibid., 7.

14 *Lallement collected himself:* Ibid., 7–8.

15 *Lallement secured a US patent:* Ibid., 8–9.

15 *How this happened is still "murky":* David Herlihy, telephone interview by the author, March 10, 2012; see also Herlihy, *Bicycle*, 88–89. Other cycle historians are less certain than Herlihy that Lallement originated the pedal velocipede. Other claimants include the first French maker—Pierre Michaux—and a Lyon businessman by the name of Raymond Radisson; see Hadland and Lessing, *Bicycle Design*, 45–53. Though I find Herlihy's argument in favor of Lallement convincing, the eminent British cycle historian Nicholas Clayton cautions, "We still do not know who made the first boneshaker [i.e., pedal velocipede], nor in what year" (Clayton to author, January 17, 2015).

15 *the world-famous Hanlon Brothers:* Herlihy, *Bicycle*, 103.

15 *"all agog to fathom":* "The Bicycles of the Rampage," *CDG*, January 12, 1869, 2.

16 *As a reader wrote in a letter:* H.O., "The Philosophy of the Velocipede," *Scientific American*, September 23, 1868, 194.

16 Scientific American *diagnosed:* "The Human Wheel and its Rival—The Velocipede Mania," *Scientific American*, January 9, 1869, 25.

16 *"Space has been a sort of enemy":* "The Future of the Bicycle," *Velocipedist*, February 1869, 2.

Chapter Two: The Need for Speed

17 *Also during that half-century:* For a narrative, see *Appletons' Annual Cyclopaedia 1877*, 386–388.

17 *helped quadruple the country's population:* In 1820, the US population was 9,638,453; in 1870, it was 38,558,371. US Census Bureau, "Population, Housing Units, Area Measurements, and Density: 1790 to 1990," accessed April 5, 2015, www.census.gov/population/www/censusdata/files/table-2.pdf. See also Campbell J. Gibson and Emily Lennon, "Historical Census Statistics on the Foreign-born Population of the United States: 1850–1990," US Bureau of the Census, February 1999, accessed April 16, 2015, https://www.census.gov/population/www/documentation/twps0029/twps0029.html.

17 *"The line of railway":* Stevenson, *Across the Plains*, 42–43. Stevenson immigrated in August 1879, though he did not stay permanently in the United States.

17 *Before 1820, people spent:* Heidler and Heidler, *Daily Life*, 51–61.

18 *sometimes using the labor:* In Augusta, Georgia, for example, a cross-reference of the 1860 manufacturing census with the census of slaveholders shows that slave labor was employed in twenty-four flour mills, thirteen distilleries, and twelve sawmills (William G. Thomas III and Edward L. Ayers, "The Differences Slavery Made: A Close Analysis of Two American Communities," a digital presentation hosted by the University of Virginia, accessed April 16, 2015, www2.vcdh.virginia.edu/AHR).

18 *steamboats and trains made it possible:* Bruchey, *Enterprise*, 148–149.

18 *New labor-saving technologies:* Taylor, *Transportation Revolution*, 224–227.

18 *It was the birth of the wage earner:* Ibid., 250–251.

18 *The end of slavery by 1865:* The US Census of 1860 counted 3,950,343 slaves. These people were progressively freed during the Civil War, 1861–1865; see Census Office, "Map Showing the Distribution of the Slave Population of the Southern States of the United States" (Washington, DC: Department of the Interior, September 9, 1861).

18 *"The people must be amused":* Hone, *Diary*, 2:97.

18 *appearing after croquet:* "American Croquet," *Nation*, August 9, 1866, 113–115.

18 *and before roller-skating:* See, for example, "Parlor Skating," *SFEB*, March 1, 1871, 1. Although the American inventor James Plimpton revolutionized the sport in 1863 by patenting turnable, "rocking action" quad roller skates and opening rinks in New York City and fashionable Newport, Rhode Island, during the Civil War, the resultant roller-skating craze took hold first in Europe and Australia. The US roller-skating boom started in 1870, "once the Plimpton skate reached the masses," according to James Vannurden, director and curator of the National Museum of Roller Skating in Lincoln, Nebraska (Vannurden, e-mail message to author, July 16, 2012).

18 *"Never before in the history":* "The Velocipede Furor," *NYT*, February 19, 1869, 2.

18 *Nationwide, carriage makers:* Ibid.

19 *Makers soon added refinements:* Herlihy, *Bicycle*, 124, 103.

19 *The pedal velocipede had appeared:* See, for example, "General City News," *NYT*, September 4, 1868, 8.

19 *Impresarios converted warehouses:* Many bicycle histories suggest that *roller* rinks were converted into velocipede rinks. In the American ex-

amples I found, though, the rinks converted for the summer of 1869 had been covered *ice* rinks. For example, the Jersey City [Ice] Skating Rink was converted into a bicycle "curriculum" or "velocipedrome" on March 29, 1869; see "Sporting: The Skating Season," *NYS*, October 6, 1868, 1, and *Velocipedist*, April 1869, 3. Exhibitions of both velocipede riding and roller-skating were planned for the rink that summer ("The Jersey City Velocipedrome," *NYT*, March 26, 1869, 5).

19 *"the fiery steed"*: "The Velocipede Mania," *NYT*, January 10, 1869, 3.

19 *"The expert riders of Brooklyn"*: "The Velocipede Furor," *NYT*, February 19, 1869, 2.

20 *Schools expanded their space:* "Velocipedes," *NYT*, January 27, 1869, 8; "Velocipedes," *NYT*, March 8, 1869, 2.

20 *In Nashua, New Hampshire:* "Velocipede Race at Nashua N. H.," *BDJ*, February 12, 1869, 2.

20 *That same month in Des Moines:* "The Velocipede Race," *DSR*, February 26, 1869; "Weather Record for Week Ending Feb. 27, 1869," *DSR*, February 28, 1869, 1; "Gravel!," *DSR*, February 26, 1869, 1.

20 *In 1850, a large crowd: SDR*, January 9, 1850, 3; "Pedestrian Feat," *SDR*, January 10, 1850, 2.

20 *Investors built the first:* This started in the 1830s, according to Vincent, *Mudville's Revenge*, 33–34.

20 *And baseball, descended from:* Michael Aubrecht, "Baseball and the Blue and Gray," July 2004, www.baseball-almanac.com/articles/aubrecht2004b.shtml.

20 *spread "like wildfire"*: "Drift-Wood," *Galaxy*, October 1868, 563.

21 *it was first professionalized:* G. Ward and K. Burns, *Baseball*, 20–21.

21 *ten thousand spectators showed up:* Walter Camp, "Base-Ball for the Spectator," *Century*, October 1889, 831–837.

21 *In 1867, a slight twenty-seven-year-old:* "The Pedestrian Feat," *Harper's Weekly*, November 16, 1867, 725.

21 *"This is a slander"*: "Edward Payson Weston," *DSR*, November 1, 1867, 2.

21 *Wearing a cropped jacket:* "The Pedestrian Feat," 725; "Edward Payson Weston," *CDG*, December 12, 1867, 3.

21 *By 1869, walking 100 miles:* Vincent, *Mudville's Revenge*, 38.

21 *"When the bright pleasant"*: "The Velocipede Mania," *NYT*, January 10, 1869, 3.

22 *Ball fields added: NYH*, April 1, 1869, 9; *Velocipedist*, April 1869, 3.

22 *One such retrofitted park:* "A New Club," *NYH*, April 11, 1869, 8.

22 *wood blocks soaked in creosote:* This material was called Nicolson pavement; it was first installed in Boston in July 1848 (Nicolson, *Nicolson Pavement*, 4).

22 *"one unending mud-hole":* "Gravel!," *DSR*, February 26, 1869, 1.

22 *Machines that went "easily and fast":* "The Bicycle," *BS*, November 7, 1872, 2.

22 *"This was the first series":* "The Velocipede Races at the Union Course, L.I.," *NYT*, April 28, 1869, 7.

22 *The pedal velocipede didn't vanish:* In Detroit, for example, Lyman E. Stowe and a friend rode a pedal velocipede for decades. "Many used to say 'how foolish those old men look,'" Stowe recalled in 1892—at which time he was over fifty and still riding the antiquated device ("They Cling to Their Old Loves," *Bearings*, December 16, 1892, 13).

22 *Velocipede schools closed:* Herlihy, *Bicycle*, 117–122.

22 *Wags began referring:* See, for example, "The Bicycle, and Riding It," *NYT*, January 25, 1880, 6.

22 *"The excitement which followed":* "Velocipede Exhibition," *NYT*, July 28, 1869, 8.

23 *usually as a curiosity:* For example, the National Pedestrian Congress held spring and fall meets featuring walking, running, and velocipede races; see "Pedestrian Congress," *Turf, Field, and Farm*, March 25, 1870, 181. One "main event" held during the fallow years after the 1869 velocipede mania was an 1874 race near White Plains, New York, in which the American Frank Shaw won the "championship of the world" from Henry Naylor of Britain; see "Rational Pastimes," *Forest and Stream*, November 5, 1874, 203.

23 *Bans on sidewalk riding:* Herlihy, *Bicycle*, 120.

23 *"The velocipede mania rages":* "News of the State, All Sorts," *HDC*, May 17, 1873, 4.

23 *"The velocipede idiocy":* "Critic Gossip," *DCDC*, September 17, 1873, 1.

23 *Renewed outbreaks were also noted: Daily Picayune*, April 8, 1871, 2; "The Northwest," *DIO*, April 30, 1874, 1; "Brief Mention," *SFEB*, October 15, 1872, 3; "Latest News Items, *SFDEB*, May 3, 1873, 1.

23 *The lack of a European patent:* Herlihy, e-mail message to publisher, February 18, 2015.

23 *a German mechanic living in Paris:* The mechanic was Eugene Meyer (Vernon Forbes, "Cycles and the Drive for Improvement," in *ICHC* 25, 75); Nicholas Clayton, "Who Invented the Penny-Farthing?," in *ICHC* 7, 37.

23 *This weight-saving innovation:* "Bicycle 'Gear'—What It Means," *Scientific American*, September 19, 1896, 239.

23 *Buyers ordered bicycles:* Dodge, *The Bicycle*, 65.

23 *The Starley Ariel:* Herlihy, *Bicycle*, 161–162; Clayton, "Who Invented the Penny-Farthing?," 38–39.

24 *"One of the more interesting awkwardnesses":* Leonard Larkin, "My Old Bikes," *Strand*, October 1902, 452.

25 *"The machine of the present day":* "Bicycle Riding," *English Mechanic and World of Science*, December 23, 1870, 322.

25 *Big-wheel bikes began to win:* Clayton, "Who Invented the Penny-Farthing?," 35.

25 *"You were perched":* Larkin, "My Old Bikes," 451.

25 *A few high-wheelers:* For example, a Professor Brown rode one in a June 22, 1874, performance of Schumann's European variety company at the Boston Theatre; see "Music and the Drama," *Boston Daily Advertiser*, June 23, 1874, 4; "Early Bicycles," *Bassett's Scrap Book*, April 1913, 18–20.

25 *a few Americans built:* "The First American Bicycle," *Bassett's Scrap Book*, April 1913, 20–24.

25 *That year, a Baltimore importer:* The importer was Timms & Co.; see "The First American Bicycle," 24; Epperson, *Peddling Bicycles to America*, 24; Macy, *Wheels of Change*, 12; Eben Shapiro, "Root Beer: A Flood of Memories, a Sip of Foam," *NYT*, July 22, 1992, C1.

26 *Albert A. Pope, a thirty-three-year-old:* Epperson, *Peddling Bicycles to America*, 22–23.

26 *A portly young man:* "Looking Backward Twenty-Five Years and Beyond," *TBW*, December 18, 1902, 307; "'Papa' Weston Thumbs Back Numbers," *TBW*, December 18, 1902, 311; *McClure's*, September 1893, 316.

26 *"They attracted my attention":* Albert A. Pope, "The Bicycle Industry," in Depew, *One Hundred Years*, 550.

26 *In 1877, Pope hosted:* Epperson, *Peddling Bicycles to America*, 28; "Interview with Colonel Albert A. Pope," *TBW*, May 15, 1880, 222–223.

26 *about twice what a Newton:* The cost of the two horses was $165 (*Ninth Annual Report of the Board of Railroad Commissioners*, 383).

26 *That fall, after he mastered:* Pope, "The Bicycle Industry," 550.

26 *Other American entrepreneurs:* One notable importer was the British expat Frank Weston. He was a silent partner in the Boston firm of Cunningham, Heath & Co., which began importing high-wheel cycles from England in late 1877; see Epperson, *Peddling Bicycles to America*, 28–29.

26 *by getting a jump on production:* Herlihy, *Bicycle*, 190–195.

26 *In 1878, just 50:* Bruce Epperson, "How Many Bikes?," in *ICHC* 11, 49.

27 *"Riding the high-wheel":* Ritchie, *Quest for Speed*, 154–155.

27 *In the United States, along with the telephone:* PBS, "Technology Timeline: 1752–1990," accessed on May 10, 2015, www.pbs.org/wgbh/amex/telephone/timeline/timeline_text.html.

27 *Traditionally, "noon" had always meant:* Corliss, *Day of Two Noons*, 2–4.

27 *clocks didn't even have minute hands:* Dohrn-van Rossum, *History of the Hour*, 272.

27 *In the chaotic years before 1883:* Corliss, *Day of Two Noons*, 4.

28 *"Everyone is familiar":* Frank Leslies, "The Curse of Overwork" *ADN*, August 22, 1888, 2.

28 *a newly identified mental illness:* The diagnosis of neurasthenia was popularized by the Connecticut doctor George Miller Beard starting in 1868; see Jorge Alberto Costa e Silva and Giovanni de Girolamo, "Neurasthenia: History of a Concept" in Sartorius et al, *Psychological Disorders*, 69–70.

28 *also called "Americanitis":* See, for example, "Americanitis," *CT*, September 22, 1895, 34.

28 *thought to be caused by:* Lears, *No Place of Grace*, 50–51.

28 *"In this telegraphic":* "All Sorts of Items," *SFEB*, July 19, 1873, 4.

28 *"An honest investigation":* Richard H. Edmonds, "A Decade of Marvelous Progress," *Engineering*, September 1893, 19.

28 *"History affords nothing":* Ibid., 21.

28 *the nation's first athletic superstars:* The big names included Arthur Augustus "Zimmy" Zimmerman, who created his own shoe and clothing brands in the 1890s; Marshall "Major" Taylor, a record-set-

ting sprinter and one of the first African American professional athletes; and Frank Kramer, who held the national track-racing championship from 1901 through 1917 (Dzierzak, *Evolution of American Bicycle Racing*, 12–15).

28 *One early high-wheel contest:* Ritchie, *Quest for Speed*, 134; "The English and French Champions in Boston," *TBW*, November 15, 1879, 5; Andrew Ritchie, "The Beginnings of Trans-Atlantic Racing," in *ICHC* 8, 136.

29 *"plucky little Frenchman":* "The 60-Hour Professional Race," *TBW*, November 15, 1879, 5–6.

29 *a Chicagoan named Albert Schock: TBW*, October 15, 1886, 578.

29 *lost three and a half pounds:* "An Upper Cut," *DIO*, December 22, 1886, 8; "Racing News," *TBW*, March 19, 1886, 361–362; "Sports Locked Up," *DIO*, December 23, 1886, 3.

29 *one suffered a violent:* "The Bicycle Score," *BDT*, December 25, 1886, 1.

29 *the other fell asleep:* "The Bicycle Tournament," *BDT*, December 24, 1886, 1.

29 *"a vast improvement":* Overman Wheel Company, "A Tip for You," *TBW*, January 7, 1887, 1.

29 *only "on account of":* Gormully & Jeffrey Manufacturing Company, "Read This, Gentlemen!!!," *TBW*, January 14, 1887, 171.

30 *"the question of who sponsored":* Andrew Ritchie, e-mail message to author, April 6, 2015.

30 *Starting with the Boston Bicycle Club:* Ritchie, *Quest for Speed*, 117.

30 *The first of Albert A. Pope's:* Epperson, *Peddling Bicycles to America*, 56.

30 *a laborer might earn $1.30 per day:* Stanley Lebergott, "Wage Trends, 1800–1900," in National Bureau of Economic Research, *Trends in the American Economy*, 462.

30 *"The bicyclers of England":* C. E. Hawley, "Uses of the Bicycle," *Wheelman*, October 1882, 24. Hawley was a consulting engineer for the Pope Manufacturing Co.—makers of Columbia Bicycles—in Hartford.

30 *code of courtly behavior:* Ritchie, *Quest for Speed*, 117–120; "The Clubs Reviewed," *BW*, November 15, 1879, 2.

30 *"From the saddle we perceive":* Hawley, "Uses of the Bicycle," 28.

31 *more expensive by half:* One average price given was $150, at a time when a bicycle cost around $100; see Viator, "Tricycling," *Wheelman*, December 1882, 217.

31 *prone to tipping over:* See, for example, "A Lady on Tricycling," *Evening Telegraph* (Dundee, Scotland), April 17, 1885, 2.

31 *tricycles were considered safer:* Herlihy, *Bicycle*, 206–208.

31 *An English tricycle of 1878:* Ibid., 210–211.

31 *two hundred styles:* Viator, "Tricycling," *Wheelman*, December 1882, 215.

31 *"Certainly no one":* Ibid.

31 *"the same quiet interest":* "The Bicycle in Washington, *BS*, May 1, 1882, Supplement, 2.

32 *roads, which weren't smooth enough:* "A Plea for Modern Tricycles," *LAW&GR*, April 29, 1898, 453.

32 *Women's growing interest in tricycling:* Glen Norcliffe, "The Technological & Social Significance of the Tricycle," in *ICHC* 17, 63.

Chapter Three: The Wheel, the Woman, and the Human Body

33 *On October 28, 1893:* "She Wore Trousers," *NPG*, October 28, 1893, 1, 6; Reel, *National Police Gazette*, 12–14. Allen's maiden name was Lena Ely, and although the *NPG* and some out-of-town papers called her "Angeline," she is referred to as "Angelina" in other press reports; see, for example, "To Journey through Life," *NYT*, January 16, 1884, 3, and "Notes of the Stage," *NYH*, November 4, 1894, 2.

33 *"She rode her wheel":* "She Wore Trousers," 6.

35 *"did not reach within many inches":* "Mrs. Angeline Allen's Bathing Dress," *KCS*, August 30, 1893, 4.

35 *"that's what I wear them for":* "Angeline Allen's Anger," *BMJ*, November 8, 1893, 8.

35 *"The natives watch for her":* "Decidedly Unconventional," *DNT*, November 29, 1893, 4.

35 *"a sort of semi-monster":* Willard, *Wheel within a Wheel*, 13.

35 *particularly men who had aged out:* See, for example, "Safety Machines," *BW*, November 6, 1885, 5.

35 *including models with foot levers:* For example, the 1879 Facile by Beale & Straw of Greenwich, England.

36 *"geared up" bikes with chains:* For example, the 1884 Kangaroo

Dwarf Safety Bicycle by the Premier Bicycle Company of Coventry, England.

36 *a supposedly header-proof version:* The American Star by the H. B. Smith Machine Company of Smithville, New Jersey; see Herlihy, *Bicycle*, 218–220.

36 *geared-up rear-wheel drive:* Henry J. Lawson's 1879 Bicyclette was among the first (Herlihy, *Bicycle*, 217).

36 *the English Rover:* Herlihy, *Bicycle*, 235.

36 *Even today, American bicycles:* Leo Woodland, "It's ALL about the Bike," accessed May 11, 2015, https://www.crazyguyonabike.com/doc/page/?page_id=91585.

36 *The Rover's manufacturer made:* Hadland and Lessing, *Bicycle Design*, 162.

36 *"I looked at nearly all":* "Col. A. A. Pope," *BW*, August 27, 1886, 423.

36 *"Every innovation is":* Ibid.

37 *Pope and other American cycle makers:* Herlihy, *Bicycle*, 241–243.

37 *"In days of old":* Pedals, "Then and Now," *BW*, November 4, 1887, 14. In the child's immigrant accent, the use of "der" for "the" and of "etes" for "ede" in "melosipetes" (i.e., "velocipede") is consistent with German, while the substitution of *m* for *v* in "melosipetes" may represent a misunderstanding of a Yiddish accent, which sometimes sounds *v* as *m* in the middle of a word; see Herman and Herman, *Foreign Dialects*, 366. Thanks to Nadia Nurhussein, author of *Rhetorics of Literacy: The Cultivation of American Dialect Poetry*, for her help with this passage.

38 *"I do not think that":* "Harry Corey Abroad," *BW*, December 2, 1887, 77.

38 *"a clumsy wheelbarrow":* Julius Wilcox, "Ladies' Bicycles," *BW*, March 30, 1888, 368.

38 *makers offered a drop-frame version:* The first commercially available American-made model was by the Smith National Bicycle Company of Washington, DC; see "The Ladies' Dart Bicycle," *BW*, March 30, 1888, 368–369. Drop-frame safeties had been independently developed in England slightly earlier, but they did not catch on immediately, perhaps because of the continued popularity of tricycles there. See Lillias Campbell Davidson, "The Evolution in Feminine Cycling," *W&CTR*, October 26, 1888, 205.

38 *"A sudden desire began to awake":* Davidson, "Evolution in Feminine Cycling," 205.

38 *Devised in Ireland:* H. D. Higman, "The Founding of the Dunlop Tyre Company," in *ICHC* 5, 91. For Dunlop's original goal in creating the tire, see Nick Clayton, "Of Bicycles, Bijker, and Bunkum," *ICHC* 10, 15.

38 *This marvel arrived in the United States:* "The First 'Pneumatic' in America," *W&CTR*, June 20, 1890, 494.

38 *"It permitted travel on streets":* F. A. Egan, "The Evolution of a Sport," *Godey's*, April 1896, 346.

38 *the average weight of a bicycle dropped:* Ibid.

39 *In 1894, while riding a pneumatic-tired:* "Johnson's Wonderful Mile," *NYT*, October 25, 194, 6. The record for one mile on an Ordinary set in 1890 was 2:25⅗: "The Ordinary (High) Bicycle," *New York Clipper Annual for 1893*, 125.

39 *High-wheelers that had sold: Appletons' Annual Cyclopaedia 1895*, 88.

39 *The first safeties, meanwhile:* Herlihy, *Bicycle*, 7.

39 *In 1895, America's three hundred bicycle companies: Appletons' Annual Cyclopaedia 1895*, 86. The economic historian Bruce Epperson has argued that bicycle production numbers during the boom years were inflated; he calculates the true number of bikes produced in the United States in 1895 at 218,600. Evan Friss, in his dissertation, made his own calculations and judged that "the actual numbers are likely in between the two estimates, but probably closer to Epperson's more conservative approximation"; See Bruce Epperson, "How Many Bikes?" in *ICHC* 11, 49; Friss, "The Cycling City," 49.

39 *Even manufacturers were surprised:* "The number of lady riders will be greater than most of us have anticipated," *BW*, March 29, 1889, quoted in Herlihy, *Bicycle*, 244.

39 *"If a pitying Providence":* Mary L. Bisland, "Woman's Cycle," *Godey's*, April 1896, 386.

40 *Starting at puberty:* P. Warner, *When the Girls Came Out to Play*, 74–75; Girard, *Greenwood Encyclopedia*, 4:560–562.

40 *"I 'ran wild'":* Willard, A Wheel Within a Wheel, 10.

40 *newspaper editor Amelia Bloomer:* Bloomer, *Life and Writings*, 65–68.

40 *some women had tailors:* Sally Dillon, "Bicycle Belles: Ladies' Bicycling Fashion in the Mid-1890s," in *ICHC* 14, 94–95.

40 *"The eye of the spectator":* Marguerite Merington, "Woman and the Bicycle," *Scribner's*, June 1895, 703.

40 *posing onstage in scanty attire:* "Real Living Pictures," *NPG*, December 15, 1894, 7.

41 *But while corsets braced women's torsos:* Haller and Haller, *Physician and Sexuality*, 146–174.

41 *this garment was called an "emancipation waist":* Stamper and Condra, *Clothing through American History*, 110.

41 *"bicycle waist":* Sally Simms, "The Bicycle, the Bloomer, and Dress Reform in the 1890s," in Cunningham and Voto, *Dress and Popular Culture*, 131.

41 *One 1896 model:* Gage-Downs Company, "As Graceful as the New Woman," *Munsey's*, June 1896, advertising section.

41 *by 1880, farmers made up:* Rasmussen and Bowers, "History of Agricultural Policy," 2.

41 *married women typically stayed home:* Peiss, *Cheap Amusements*, 5.

41 *Many Americans came to believe:* Barbara Welter, "The Cult of True Womanhood, 1820–1860," *AQ*, Summer 1966, 151–174.

41 *"A true lady walks the streets":* Houghton, *American Etiquette*, 103.

42 *"A single careless act":* Hall, *Social Customs*, 181.

42 *"The world is a new":* Mary L. Bisland, "Woman's Cycle," *Godey's*, April 1896, 386.

42 *"the sufferer can do no better":* Merington, "Woman and the Bicycle," 703.

42 *As for unmarried women:* Garvey, *Adman in the Parlor*, 124.

42 *"New social laws have been enacted":* Joseph B. Bishop, "Social and Economic Influence of the Bicycle," *Forum*, August 1896, 683. At the time, Bishop was the editor of the *New York Evening Post*.

42 *Ellen Gruber Garvey suggests:* Garvey, *Adman in the Parlor*, 209n49.

43 *Moralists warned that skimpy costumes:* Haller and Haller, *Physician and Sexuality*, 179–181.

43 *"Immodest bicycling by young women":* "Anti-Bicycle Crusade," *LAT*, July 2, 1896, 1.

43 *Smith reported that her tours:* "A Moral Crusader," *BS*, July 7, 1896, 8.

43 *Physicians—who at the time shouldered:* Haller and Haller, *Physician and Sexuality*, ix–x; Garvey, *Adman in the Parlor*, 114–115.

43 *"She looked like an innocent child":* E. D. Page, "Woman and the Bicycle," *Brooklyn Medical Journal*, February 1897, 85.

43 *"feelings hitherto unknown to":* T. J. Happel, "The Bicycle from a Medical and Surgical Standpoint," *Memphis Medical Monthly*, Sep-

tember 1898, 398. Curiously, the 1890s also marked the invention of the vibrator to treat a variety of women's complaints. The device, applied to the genitalia by doctors as a medical treatment, brought about a "hysterical paroxysm" that was considered therapeutic rather than harmful. As the historian Rachel P. Maines discovered, some male doctors of that pre-Kinseyan time did not recognize the paroxysm as an orgasm (Maines, *Technology of Orgasm*, 3–10).

43 *Boys faced the same danger:* S. A. K. Strahan, "Bicycle Riding and Perineal Pressure: Their Effect on the Young," *Lancet*, September 20, 1884, 490–491.

43 *many saw physical energy:* De la Peña, *Body Electric*, 4–5.

43 *Overexertion could also cause:* "The Perils of Exercise," *Good Health*, October 1891, 303.

44 *"a sex which is born tired":* W. D. Howells, "By Horse-Car to Boston," *Atlantic Monthly*, January 1870, 116.

44 *"The exertion necessary to riding":* "Women Cyclists," *BS*, July 8, 1896, 10.

44 *"If a halt is not called soon":* "Anti-Bicycle Crusade," *LAT*, July 2, 1896, 1.

44 *Citizens of America's growing cities:* James C. Whorton, "The Hygiene of the Wheel: An Episode in Victorian Sanitary Science," *Bulletin of the History of Medicine*, Spring 1978, 69; W. Harris, *Report of the Commissioner*, 1:549–551.

44 *"For constipation, sleeplessness":* W. Thornton Parker, "A New Remedy," *Wheelman*, October 1883, 59–60.

45 *As a result, many more Americans:* Whorton, "Hygiene of the Wheel," 63.

45 *an estimated two million:* The navy doctor Francis Smith Nash put the number at one million in the early spring of 1896 (Nash, "A Plea for the New Woman and the Bicycle," *AJO*, April 1896, 559). Isaac B. Potter, the president of the League of American Wheelmen, placed the number much higher, at 2.5 million, in September of the same year (Potter, "The Bicycle Outlook," *Century*, September 1896, 789).

45 *Good health was a reflection:* Rosenberg, *Explaining Epidemics*, 12.

45 *It was a doctor's job:* Other traditional balancing treatments, such as emetics and bleeding, began to lose favor in the middle of the nineteenth century but continued in use, particularly in rural areas (ibid., 27).

45 *"No two instances of typhoid fever"*: "Routine Practice," *BMSJ*, January 11, 1883, 43.

45 *To many doctors, advocating*: Rosenberg, *Explaining Epidemics*, 15.

46 *In an 1895 paper on heart disease*: "Cycling and Heart Disease," *Philadelphia Polyclinic*, September 14, 1895, 379.

46 *cycling tended to catch the blame*: See, for example, the story of a seventeen-year-old girl whose overnight death was attributed to "paralysis of the heart, the result of overexertion while learning to ride a bicycle" ("Was Too Much for Her," *PI*, August 14, 1897, 2).

46 *"It might seem almost impossible"*: "Bicycle Accidents," *BMSJ*, July 23, 1896, 95–96.

46 *The bent-over posture of the scorcher*: "The Bicycler Should Sit Erect," *Medical News* (Philadelphia), November 25, 1893, 613.

46 *Repeated stress to the cardiovascular*: "Cycling and Heart Disease," *Philadelphia Polyclinic*, September 14, 1895, 379–380.

46 *Gripping the handlebars too tightly*: "The Bicycle Hand," *Sporting Life*, December 28, 1895, 16.

46 *and a dusty ride*: "Cyclist's Sore Throat," *Southern California Practitioner*, August 1898, 301–302.

46 *at least one New York doctor*: "A Medical Bicycle Specialist," *Medical Record* (New York), November 16, 1895, 702.

46 *Characterized by wide, wild eyes*: A. Shadwell, "The Hidden Dangers of Bicycling," *National Review*, February 1897, 795–796.

47 *drained "every vestige of intelligence"*: "Impress of Wheel on the Face," *WP*, June 28, 1896, 26.

47 *"Once fixed upon the countenance"*: "Facts about the Bicycle Face," *MT*, July 20, 1895, 4.

47 *"Whilst thousands ride immune"*: W. H. Brown, "A Form of Neuralgia Occurring in Cyclists," *British Medical Journal*, February 26, 1898, 553.

47 *"It would not affect my argument"*: Shadwell, "Hidden Dangers of Bicycling," 790.

47 *"The bicycle is inducing multitudes"*: Henry Smith Williams, "The Bicycle in Relation to Health," *Harper's Weekly*, April 11, 1896, 370.

47 *"We have already become accustomed"*: Maurice Thompson, "What We Gain in the Bicycle," *Chautauquan*, August 1897, 550.

47 *The empirical evidence of cycling's health value*: Hallenbeck, "Writing the Bicycle," 190–191.

48 *"The bicycle face, elbow, back":* Francis Smith Nash, "A Plea for the New Woman and the Bicycle," *AJO*, April 1896, 558.

48 *"So long as the cyclist can breathe":* J. West Roosevelt, "A Doctor's View of Bicycling," *Scribner's*, October 1895, 711.

48 *Some went further, citing:* Nash, "Plea for the New Woman," 560.

48 *In Chicago, the demand for morphine:* "Cycling Versus Morphine," *Bulletin of Pharmacy* (Detroit), June 1896, 282.

48 *This shift paralleled a transformation:* Rosenberg, *Explaining Epidemics*, 28–30.

48 *"provided an emotional fault line":* Ibid., 30.

49 *between 1870 and 1900, researchers disproved:* James Trostle, "Early Work in Anthropology and Epidemiology: From Social Medicine to Germ Theory, 1840 to 1920," in James, *Anthropology and Epidemiology*, 48.

49 *this "great leveler":* "The Reign of the Bicycle," *Century*, December 1894, 306.

49 *"In possession of her bicycle":* Mary L. Bisland, "Woman's Cycle," *Godey's*, April 1896, 385.

50 *"I'll tell you what I think of bicycling":* Nelly Bly, "Champion of Her Sex," *NYSW*, February 2, 1896, 10, quoted in Harper, *Life and Work of Susan B. Anthony*, 859.

Chapter Four: Paving the Way for Cars

51 *"The farming communities have been":* "A Mud Blockade," *StLR*, December 25, 1891, 1.

51 *a cold snap on December 28:* "Snow in Iowa," *DIO*, December 29, 1891, 8.

51 *an estimated $1.5 million:* "The Economy of Good Roads," *CC*, March 23, 1892, 1.

51 *"A million voters are disfranchised":* Ibid.

52 *Private turnpikes built in the early 1800s:* Taylor, *Transportation Revolution*, 26–29.

52 *in February 1885:* "Chatfield," *PMD*, February 5, 1885, 3.

52 *Across the nation, roads:* Swift, *Big Roads*, 11.

52 *City halls levied taxes:* McShane, *Down the Asphalt Path*, 63.

52 *male citizens age sixteen to sixty:* Capron, *Report of the Commissioner of Agriculture*, 348.

52 *"The farmers assemble"*: President [Lewis J.] Bates, "Effect of the Bicycle Upon Our Highway Laws," *Wheelman*, October 1882, 43.

52 *"the experienced traveller"*: N. S. Shaler, "The Common Roads," *Scribner's*, October 1889, 477.

53 *In Europe, water-shedding technological*: Reid, *Roads Were Not Built for Cars*, 43–44.

53 *But these developments hadn't reached*: Earl Swift, telephone interview by the author, February 19, 2012; Greene, *Horses at Work*, 228.

53 *In America at the time*: Jerry R. Rogers, "Civil Engineering Education History (1741 to 1893)," in Dennis et al., *American Civil Engineering History*, 71–72.

53 *Smooth, flexible asphalt*: McShane, *Down the Asphalt Path*, 61.

54 *Meanwhile, horse-drawn streetcars*: Brian J. Cudahy, "Mass Transportation in the Cities of America: A Short History and a Current Perspective," accessed April 28, 2015, http://inventors.about.com/library/inventors/blstreetcars.htm.

54 *In 1892, the novelist Rudyard Kipling*: Rudyard Kipling, "New York Described by Rudyard Kipling," *Bush Advocate*, September 3, 1892, 6.

54 *the only self-propelled vehicles*: L. Scott Bailey, "The Other Revolution," in L. S. Bailey, *American Car since 1775*, 42–52; McShane, *Down the Asphalt Path*, 81–85.

54 *"The majority [of Americans]"*: Bates, "Effect of the Bicycle," 41.

55 *In Boston, police stopped*: Charles E. Pratt, "A Sketch of American Bicycling and Its Founder," *Outing*, July 1891, 344.

55 *So cyclists banded together*: McShane, *Down the Asphalt Path*, 116.

55 *A national organization founded in 1880*: Epperson, *Peddling Bicycles to America*, 57, 90.

55 *in 1881, three cyclists*: Ibid., 71–72.

55 *In 1887, New York governor*: Mason, "League of American Wheelmen," 55.

55 *"They are not an obstruction to"*: Desty, *Lawyers' Reports*, 774.

56 *"In Chicago they scurry"*: C.L.C., "Hub of All Wheeldom," *WP*, September 6, 1896, 9.

56 *Unmarked—because the farmers*: Potter, *Cycle Paths*, 64.

56 *"Smooth stretches of road"*: [LAW member] No. 68,146, "The Shenandoah Valley," *LAW&GR*, July 31, 1896, 167.

56 *"for the bicycle is the vehicle"*: Bates, "Effect of the Bicycle," 44.

56 *The dirt roads that had been good enough:* Mason, "League of American Wheelmen," 91.

57 *"they will manage to get":* "The Editor's Table," *Good Roads,* April 1892, 224.

57 *Bicyclist (in disgust):* "Excuse for Bad Roads," *IDS,* July 7, 1892, 7.

57 *In New York's Lower East Side:* Goodman, *Choosing Sides,* 6; Nelson P. Lewis, "From Cobblestones to Asphalt and Brick," *Paving and Municipal Engineering,* April 1896, 234–235.

57 *American farmers owned—and fed:* Potter, *Gospel of Good Roads,* 16.

57 *"A bad road is really":* Ibid., 15.

57 *"The farmer has the same right":* Ibid., 23.

58 *As a result of such advocacy:* Mason, "League of American Wheelmen," 242–244.

58 *LAW representatives monitored:* Ibid., 71.

58 *He enlisted cyclists' help:* Ibid., 140.

58 *In 1893, Pope delivered:* N. S. Shaler, "The Move for Better Highways," *Harper's Weekly,* January 6, 1894, 15.

58 *The so-called monster petition:* Carlton Reid, "The Petition That Paved America," March 21, 2012, www.roadswerenotbuiltforcars.com/the-petition-that-paved-america.

58 *That same year, Congress authorized:* Mason, "League of American Wheelmen," 147.

58 *In 1896, the US Postal Service:* Historically, the Grange took credit for the introduction of rural free delivery, but contemporary reports credit John M. Stahl of the Farmers' National Congress, who rallied support from the Grange, the LAW, and other interested groups (*Appletons' Annual Cyclopaedia 1901,* 341–343).

58 *The catch was that the postmaster:* Heath, *Rural Free Delivery,* 74–75, 125.

58 *When railroads in New York:* "Go Easy, Bicyclists!," *Harper's Weekly,* May 23, 1896, 507.

59 *"Whatever you insist upon having":* Ibid.

59 *an estimated three million:* Frank J. Berto, "The Electric Streetcar and the End of the First American Bicycle Boom," in *ICHC* 17, 91.

59 *"All mankind is a-wheel":* Crane, *Crane: Prose and Poetry,* 859.

59 *In the financial panic that ensued:* David O. Whitten, "The Depression of 1893," EH.Net Encyclopedia, Robert Whaples, ed., August 14, 2001, https://eh.net/encyclopedia/the-depression-of-1893.

59 *"The watchmakers and jewelers"*: "The Bicycle Craze," *ISJ*, June 10, 1896, 6.

60 *Tobacconists, saloon keepers:* Ibid.; "The Bicycle Crowds Out the Accordion," *Nantucket Inquirer and Mirror*, November 13, 1897, 4.

60 *"awakened from a sleep"*: "The Bicycle Craze," *ISJ*, June 10, 1896, 6.

60 *"numberless nooks and corners"*: "The Point of View," *Scribner's*, October 1894, 527.

60 *Wayside inns that had averaged:* "Bicycle Problems and Benefits," *Century*, July 1895, 475; Potter, *Cycle Paths*, 65–67, 89–90.

60 *And as the historian James Longhurst:* Longhurst, *Bike Battles*, 62–79.

60 *St. Paul, Minnesota, for example:* James Longhurst, "The Sidepath Not Taken: Bicycles, Taxes, and the Rhetoric of the Public Good in the 1890s," *Journal of Policy History*, October 2013, 572–574.

60 *True, inventors had been constructing:* The French inventor Nicolas-Joseph Cugnot built a steam-powered artillery tricycle for the French military in 1769 (McShane, *Down the Asphalt Path*, 82–83).

60 *And scientists had started tinkering:* The French inventor Nicéphore Niépce received a patent for a "moss, coal-dust and resin"–fueled internal combustion engine in 1807; see Maison Nicéphore Niépce, "The Pyreolophore," accessed May 13, 2015, www.photo-museum.org/pyreolophore-invention-internal-combustion-engine.

60 *In 1859, the birth of the US:* Peter J. Hugill, "Good Roads and the Automobile in the United States 1880–1929," *Geographical Review*, July 1892, 327. The French physicist who invented the lead-acid battery was Gaston Planté.

61 *And as the historian Clay McShane:* McShane, *Down the Asphalt Path*, 86–101.

61 *Pneumatic tires, differential gears:* Herlihy, *Bicycle*, 300.

61 *The brothers Charles and J. Frank Duryea*: Sidney H. Aronson, "The Sociology of the Bicycle," *Social Forces*, March 1952, 310.

61 *In fact, most early car builders:* Burr, "Markets as Producers and Consumers," 308; Steven Watts, *The People's Tycoon*, 36.

61 *When Pope started manufacturing:* Hounshell, *From the American System*, 3–7, 59–61.

62 *By 1897, US makers:* Contemporary production estimates were as high as two million for 1897, but these were likely inflated (Bruce Epperson, "How Many Bikes?," in *ICHC* 11, 47–48).

62 *innovations that included electric resistance welding:* Hounshell, *From the American System*, 200, 207–208; Martha Moore Trescott, "The Bicycle, a Technical Precursor of the Automobile," in Uselding, *Business and Economic History*, 60–65.

62 *"served as a prototype":* Glen Norcliffe, "Popeism and Fordism: Examining the Roots of Mass Production," *Regional Studies*, May 1997, 272–273. Bruce Epperson has argued that the bicycle industry of the 1890s was not a true mass-production system, but an overheated batch production system (Epperson, *Peddling Bicycles to America*, 235–238).

62 *Henry Ford claimed to have based:* Ford, *My Life and Work*, 81. A modern Albert A. Pope—the great-grandson of Colonel Albert A. Pope—wrote in 1995 that his forebear's Hartford factory had featured "the first electrified continuous production assembly line in America (visited and admired by Henry Ford)," but he provided no date or source for this report (Albert A. Pope, "Colonel Pope and the Founding of the U.S. Cycle Industry," in *ICHC* 5, 97). Other scholars of Pope's factory practice have written about static assembly areas in the plant, but no moving assembly lines before 1913.

62 *Pope himself started producing:* Bruce Epperson, "Failed Colossus: Strategic Error at the Pope Manufacturing Company, 1878–1900, *Technology and Culture*, April 2000, 313.

62 *the first gasoline-powered vehicle:* Reid, *Roads Were Not Built for Cars*, 10.

62 *In 1891 and 1982, though: Horseless Age* magazine set the number of would-be automobile inventors in the U.S. at three hundred, but the inventor Hiram Percy Maxim estimated it at a more conservative fifty (*Horseless Age*, cited in Olson, *Young Henry Ford*, 57; Hiram Percy Maxim, "The Explosive Tricycle and Other Recollections of Horseless Carriage Days," *Harper's Monthly*, November 1936, 611).

62 *the gasoline engine had been around:* L. S. Bailey, *American Car since 1775*, 50–51.

63 *"the bicycle had not yet come":* Maxim, "Explosive Tricycle," 611.

63 *"all the little human":* "A New Generation Discovers the Bike," *NYT*, October 18, 1925, SM2.

63 *Prices for the machines plunged:* Sears, for example, advertised prices as low as $13.95 for a complete bike. Sears, *Consumers Guide 107*, 412–418.

63 *Between 1899 and 1902:* "Cycling's Death Excites Wonder," *CDT*, September 4, 1902, 2.

63 *From its peak of more than 102,600:* Dickerson, *Cycling Handbook*, 20.

63 *"not more than one-hundredth":* "The Death of a Fad," *WP*, December 16, 1906, SM2.

63 *In 1908, a Model T Ford:* Paul Rubenson, "Missing Link: The Case for Bicycle Transportation in the United States in the Early 20th Century," in *ICHC* 16, 80.

63 *And in 1910 there were still nearly:* McShane, *Down the Asphalt Path*, 105.

64 *Nevertheless, by 1900 the bicycle craze:* "Progressive Euchre Now," *NYT*, February 11, 1900, 17; "Ping-Pong Face the Latest," *WP*, March 16, 1902, 21.

64 *"I have tried to discover":* "Cycling's Death Excites Wonder," 2.

64 *Hundreds of thousands of urban workers:* "Workers Who Wheel and What They Gain," *WP*, April 7, 1907, SM3.

64 *"Fashionable society, in one of its whims":* "The Uses of Society Fads," *CDT*, September 16, 1901, 6.

Chapter Five: From Producers to Consumers

65 *Historians of technology:* The "strong programme" for applying sociology to scientific successes and failures is outlined in Barnes, Bloor, and Henry, *Scientific Knowledge*. For an extension of these principles to the history of technology, see Bijker, *Of Bicycles, Bakelites, and Bulbs*.

65 *The air-filled tire, for example:* Pearson, *Rubber Tires*, 34–35.

66 *Lofty journals of politics:* Schneirov, *Dream of a New Social Order*, 27.

66 *"leisurely in habit, literary in tone":* Mott, *History of American Magazines*, 2.

66 *Meanwhile, starting in the late 1860s:* VonHerrlich, "Women's History Trail, 14.1, The Vickery Building," accessed May 16, 2015, http://dll.umaine.edu/historytrail/site14.html; Leiss et al., *Social Communication in Advertising*, 102.

66 *an 1879 drop in postage rates:* Historian, US Postal Service, "Postage Rates for Periodicals: A Narrative History," June 2010, 3, http://about.usps.com/who-we-are/postal-history/periodicals-postage-history.pdf; "The Modern Magazine," *Critic*, May 26, 1894, 365.

67 *But there was no national newspaper:* Schneirov, *Dream of a New Social Order*, 5.

67 *This changed in 1893:* Mott, *History of American Magazines*, 5; Joe Mitchell Chapple, "Flashlights of Famous People," *St. Petersburg (FL) Evening Independent*, May 22, 1924, 20.

67 *With his new venture:* Schneirov, *Dream of a New Social Order*, 77.

67 *In response,* Cosmopolitan*:* Mott, *History of American Magazines*, 4–6; Algernon Tassin, "The Magazine in America," *Bookman*, December 1915, 397.

67 *Within a few years, publishers:* Mott, *History of American Magazines*, 6.

67 *Between 1890 and 1905, the circulation:* Presbrey, *Development of Advertising*, 488.

68 *The March 1896 issue of* Cosmopolitan*:* Mott, *History of American Magazines*, 24.

68 *In 1898, bike ads constituted 10 percent:* Presbrey, *Development of Advertising*, 363.

68 *"To the bicycle manufacturers":* Ibid., 410.

68 *"I never enjoyed summer more":* Pope Manufacturing Company, "My Morning Spin," *LHJ*, November 1892, 20, reprinted in Garvey, *Adman in the Parlor*, 113.

68 *One 1894 ad for Chicago's:* Western Wheel Works, "Crescent Bicycles," *Youth's Companion*, March 22, 1894.

68 *The articles in these magazines:* Garvey, *Adman in the Parlor*, 123–124.

68 *In one overheated 1896 story:* Cleveland Moffett, "A Burglar, a Bicycle, and a Storm," *Godey's*, April 1896, 379.

68 *in another, a young girl defies:* Harry St. Maur, "To Hymen on a Wheel," *Home Magazine*, August 1897, reprinted in the *Scranton Tribune*, August 14, 1897, 10.

70 *"We created the demand for bicycles":* "The Columbia Advertising," *Printers' Ink*, February 9, 1898, 58.

70 *What allowed the change, Leach writes:* Leach, *Land of Desire*, 5–6.

70 *Lower-income workers lost:* Ohmann, *Politics of Letters*, 148.

70 *total personal income, adjusted:* Alexander Klein, "Personal Income of the United States: Estimates for the Period 1880–1910," Warwick Economic Research Papers no. 916 (Coventry: University of Warwick, September 2009), 56.

71 *Instead of cooking up all-purpose soap:* Garvey, *Adman in the Parlor*, 17, 83.

71 *"Some soaps are quick and sharp":* "Pears'," *Scribner's*, December 1891, 134.

71 *"Are you satisfied to move along":* Overman Wheel Co., "Power of Wheels," *Illustrated American*, July 2, 1892, 346.

71 *An 1895 ad for the Stearns brand:* E. C. Stearns & Co., "The Best Bicycle Is None Too Good for You," *Godey's*, June 1895, 679.

71 *"made many a boy useful":* Presbrey, *Development of Advertising*, 412.

71 *Fresh frills for middle-class:* Podesta, *Material Life, 1890s Family*, 2–8.

71 *"If your new house has no bath room":* Mosely Folding Bath Tub Company, "If Your New House Has No Bath Room," *LHJ*, June 1894, 29; Mosely Folding Bath Tub Company, "Mosely Folding Bath Tub," *Texas Medical News*, November 1895, xvii.

72 *"wheeling companionship":* Gormully & Jeffery Mfg. Co., "Wheeling Companionship," *LHJ*, June 1894, 26, 33.

72 *diamond bracelets for dogs:* "Humanizing the Dog," *Munsey's*, June 1897, 471.

72 *"Every day brings some novelty":* "Groveling for Luxury," *Munsey's*, June 1897, 473.

72 *Fashionable cyclists obsessively traded in:* "The Old 'Bikes': What Becomes of Them When Their Best Days Are Past," *LAT*, July 30, 1899, D4.

72 *"Is it true that Bigley":* "Nuggets," *NYT*, April 6, 1898, 6.

72 *In 1899, the economist Thorstein Veblen:* Veblen, *Theory of the Leisure Class*, 68–74.

73 *Because bicycles were a current fad:* Nicholas Oddy, "Cycling in the Drawing Room," in *ICHC* 11, 173–174.

73 *unrelated consumer products:* The invention of BIKE brand jockstraps in the 1870s, on the other hand, was directly related to cycling: a Chicago firm designed them to support the groins of cyclists, aka "bicycle jockeys" (Penn, *It's All about the Bike*, 163).

73 *Since the Civil War, a few dry-goods:* Klaffke, *Spree*, 44.

73 *invaluable for making an impression:* "Women Here and There," *NYT*, September 4, 1898, 14.

73 *"a society preoccupied with consumption":* Leach, *Land of Desire*, xiii.

74 *The first commuter suburbs:* Jackson, *Crabgrass Frontier*, 27–28, 91–92.

74 *Some city dwellers did shuttle:* Glen E. Holt, "The Changing Perception of Urban Pathology: An Essay on the Development of Mass Transit in the United States," in Jackson and Schultz, *Cities in American History*, 327–333.

74 *It is well known that electric trolleys:* See especially S. Warner, *Streetcar Suburbs.*

74 *"a leading factor in the building up":* Sylvester Baxter, "Economic and Social Influences of the Bicycle," *Arena*, October 1892, 580.

75 *Angeline Allen, the Newark rider:* See, for example, "News from New Jersey," *NYHT*, March 29, 1890, 12.

75 *"Man's legs have been lengthened":* "The Bicycle and Real Estate," *LAW&GR*, February 25, 1898, 175–176.

75 *The price of horses dropped:* Latta, *Annual Report of the Secretary*, 64A.

75 *At that point, between the trolley:* Friss, "Cycling City," 71–74. In a contest of speed and endurance, of course, the streetcar would prevail. In 1896, the *New York Times* reported on a patrolman who, taunted by two cycling speeders, hopped on a streetcar, ordered its driver to hit the juice, and apprehended them ("He 'Chalked It Down,'" *NYT*, September 22, 1896, 12).

75 *"Many more persons travel":* Latta, *Annual Report of the Secretary*, 65–66A.

75 *In Springfield, Massachusetts, bike commuters:* Friss, "Cycling City," 86–87.

75 *"In the few minutes which succeed":* "The 6 O'Clock Bicycle Crowd," *SSR*, October 17, 1897, 10.

76 *"will never, of course, come into as common use":* "The Automobile Bicycle," *Literary Digest*, October 14, 1899, 463.

76 *"some other invention:* "The Bicycle's Future," *LAW&GR*, January 21, 1898, 54–55.

76 *In 1901, the* L.A.W. Magazine*:* "Let Us Talk It Over Together," *LAWM*, May 1901, 21.

76 *but the historian Paul Rubenson raises:* Paul Rubenson, "Patents, Profits, and Perceptions: The Single-Tube Tire and the Failure of the American Bicycle, 1897–1933," in *ICHC* 15, 87–97; see also Frank J. Berto, "The Electric Streetcar and the End of the First American Bicycle Boom," in *ICHC* 17, 91.

Chapter Six: The Infinite Highway of the Air

77 *The bachelor brothers who owned:* Ivonette Miller, "Orville and Wilbur Wright: An Intimate Memoir," *Antioch Review*, Summer 1976, 447–450.

77 *When not building or repairing:* William F. Durand, "Biographical Memoir of Orville Wright, 1871–1948," in National Academy of Sciences, *Biographical Memoirs,* 25:259.

77 *Once, when stuck with two old high-wheelers:* F. Kelly, *Wright Brothers,* 41–43.

77 *one calm fall day in 1901:* Wilbur Wright to Octave Chanute, October 6, 1901, in McFarland, *Papers,* 1:123–124.

78 *two pieces of sheet metal:* C. B. Allen, "The Concept of Flight That Worked," *Bee-Hive,* January 1953, 5.

78 *One, a curved piece:* Wilbur Wright to Octave Chanute, October 6, 1901, in McFarland, *Papers,* 1:123.

78 *As one of the brothers pedaled:* Ibid., 1:124.

78 *the redbrick pavement:* Harvey Hylton, Dayton transportation history expert, telephone interview by the author, September 2, 2013.

78 *With their peculiar contraption:* Wright to Chanute, October 6, 1901, in McFarland, *Papers,* 1:123–124.

78 *There was no such thing:* Tom D. Crouch, "Engineers and the Airplane," in Hallion, *Wright Brothers,* 14–15.

78 *That fall, they had returned home dejected:* Crouch, *Bishop's Boys,* 211–212.

78 *"When we left Kitty Hawk":* Wilbur Wright, "Brief and Digest of the Evidence for the Complainant on Final Hearing," *Wright Company v. Herring-Curtiss Company and Glenn H. Curtiss, in Equity No. 400,* Container 88, Wilbur and Orville Wright Papers, Manuscript Division, Library of Congress, Washington, DC, cited in Crouch, *Bishop's Boys,* 213. For the length of the journey from Kitty Hawk to Dayton: Wilbur Wright to Octave Chanute, August 22, 1901, in McFarland, *Papers,* 1:83.

78 *"At this time I made the prediction":* Wright, "Brief and Digest," cited in Crouch, *Bishop's Boys,* 213. Orville Wright remembered Wilbur's statement more dramatically in later years: "On the way home, Wilbur declared his belief: Not within a thousand years would man ever fly!" (F. Kelly, *Wright Brothers,* 72).

78 *The wind required to keep the apparatus aloft:* Wilbur Wright, diary A, July 29, 1901, in McFarland, *Papers,* 1:176.

79 *Growing suspicious of a traditional coefficient:* This was Smeaton's coefficient, derived from the work of the English civil engineer John Smeaton (1724–1792).

79 *The six-foot-long wooden tunnel:* F. Kelly, *Wright Brothers,* 75.

80 *The following summer, the Wrights:* Ibid., 80.

80 *In 1903—convinced that they had:* Ibid., 86; Tom D. Crouch, "Kill Devil Hills, 17 December 1903," *Technology and Culture*, July 1999, 596.

80 *The wings were braced with:* Joe W. McDaniel, "Just the Facts: 1903 Wright Flyer I," accessed May 16, 2015, www.wright-brothers.org/Information_Desk/Just_the_Facts/Airplanes/Flyer_I.htm.

80 *"Isn't it astonishing that all these":* Orville Wright to George A. Spratt, June 7, 1903, in McFarland, *Papers*, 1:313.

80 *In Kitty Hawk on December 17:* Crouch, "Kill Devil Hills, 17 December 1903," 595.

80 *"I don't think I ever saw":* John T. Daniels, quoted in W. O. Saunders, "Then We Quit Laughing," *Collier's*, September 17, 1927, 56.

80 *The first passenger hot-air balloon:* Crouch, *Lighter than Air*, 25–29.

80 *"looked enviously on the birds":* Wilbur Wright, speech to the Aéro-Club de France, November 5, 1908, in McFarland, *Papers*, 2:934.

82 *"And, granting complete success":* Simon Newcomb, "The Outlook for the Flying Machine," *Independent*, October 22, 1903, 2510.

82 *"There be steeds that neither":* "The World on Wheels," *Judge*, May 1894, 1.

82 *Many bikes even had the word:* Charles W. Meinert, "Bicycles in Flight," in *ICHC* 4, 43.

82 *"Darius Green would never have sighed":* Overman Wheel Company, "Darius Green," *Harper's Weekly*, May 4, 1895, 426.

82 *"We are riding upon the wind":* "Bicycle in the Pulpit," *NYH*, May 13, 1895, 4.

82 *"The bicycle no longer satisfies":* "Wanted, An Air Cycle," *NYT*, June 25, 1893, 4.

83 *"Who will stay on the ground":* "The Knell of the Bicycle," *MJ*, July 16, 1895, 4.

83 *"The flying machine problem":* *BR*, June 4, 1886, cited in Crouch, *Dream of Wings*, 229.

83 *The bicycle maker Charles Duryea:* "When Flying Machines Replace Bicycles," *W&CTR*, April 29, 1892, 17. Although the article refers to Duryea as "W. H. Duryea," it is clear from context that the writer meant Charles. This is the same Charles Duryea who, with his brother, built the first automobile in the United States.

83 *Rather than tinker in isolation:* Hiram Maxim and Clement Ader were

two notable examples; see Tom D. Crouch, "Engineers and the Airplane," in Hallion, *Wright Brothers*, 12.

83 *"without question the greatest":* Wilbur Wright, "Otto Lilienthal," *Aero Club of America Bulletin*, September 1912, 21.

83 *Through methodical experimentation, Lilienthal:* Bernd Lukasch, "From Lilienthal to the Wrights," accessed May 16, 2015, www.lilienthal-museum.de/olma/ewright.htm.

83 *"The greater the number is":* Otto Lilienthal, "Practical Experiments for the Development of Human Flight," in Means, *Aeronautical Annual*, 13.

84 *"The admirable wheel of to-day":* James Means, "Wheeling and Flying," in Means, *Aeronautical Annual*, 23.

84 *It was news of his death:* Orville and Wilbur Wright, "The Wright Brothers' Aëroplane," *Century*, September 1908, 642.

84 *"I believe that simple flight":* Wilbur Wright to the Smithsonian Institution, May 30, 1899, in McFarland, *Papers*, 1:4.

84 *Langley had revealed in 1893:* S. P. Langley, "The Internal Work of the Wind," *American Journal of Science*, January 1894, 44; Joseph Le Conte, "New Lights on the Problem of Flying," *Popular Science*, April 1894, 757.

84 *"Whirlwinds go corkscrewing":* Maximilian Foster, "The Sport of Flying," *Outing*, May 1909, 133.

84 *For Langley and like-minded researchers:* Wright and Wright, "The Wright Brothers' Aëroplane," 642–643.

85 *"In the bird we have the last perfection":* Le Conte, "New Lights on the Problem of Flying," 756.

85 *the catapulting of Langley's four-winged:* Langley's ill-fated machine became the subject of a long-standing feud between the Smithsonian and the Wrights after Langley's pals at the Smithsonian named it the first air vehicle "capable" of controlled, powered flight despite its failure to actually fly. The feud was finally resolved in the 1940s, when Langley's successor retracted the claim. Another claimant to the title of "first to fly" is Gustave Whitehead of Bridgeport, Connecticut. Some believe that Whitehead flew on August 14, 1901, more than two years before the Wright brothers' first flight. But if Whitehead did fly, he did not document the event sufficiently to convince many outside Connecticut. See Smithsonian National Air and Space Museum, "Langley Aerodrome A," accessed May 17, 2015, http://airandspace

.si.edu/collections/artifact.cfm?id=A19180001000; Kristin Hussey, "First in Flight? Connecticut Stakes a Claim," *NYT*, April 17, 2015, www.nytimes.com/2015/04/18/nyregion/where-was-modern-flight-invented-connecticut-believes-it-holds-the-answer.html.

85 *"It has been a common aim":* George Kibbe Turner, "The Men Who Learned to Fly," *McClure's*, February 1908, 447, 450–451.

85 *The Wrights studied the movements:* Wilbur Wright to Octave Chanute, May 13, 1900, in McFarland, *Papers*, 1:17.

85 *Wilbur first got the idea:* Smithsonian National Air and Space Museum, "The Breakthrough Concept," accessed May 16, 2015, http://airandspace.si.edu/exhibitions/wright-brothers/online/fly/1899/breakthrough.cfm.

85 *"If you are looking for perfect safety":* Wilbur Wright, "Some Aeronautical Experiments," *Journal of the Western Society of Engineers*, December 1901, reprinted in Smithsonian Institution, *Annual Report of the Board of Regents of the Smithsonian Institution*, 134.

86 *This is why the brothers built:* Wright and Wright, "The Wright Brothers' Aëroplane," 645.

86 *"the bicycle-rider on a slack wire":* Waldemar Kaempffert, "Why Flying-Machines Fly," *HM*, April 1911, 679.

86 *"are often able to remove their hands":* Foster, "Sport of Flying," 136.

86 *Lilienthal was an enthusiastic cyclist:* Runge and Lukasch, *Erfinderleben*, 52 (located and translated with kind help from Bernd Lukasch).

86 *Glenn H. Curtiss, an early Wright competitor:* Glenn H. Curtiss Museum, "Glenn Hammond Curtiss," accessed May 16, 2015, www.glennhcurtissmuseum.org/museum/glenncurtiss.html.

86 *According to Tom D. Crouch:* Tom D. Crouch, "Wheeling and Flying: How the Bicycle Took Wing," in *ICHC* 17, 121.

87 *Einstein rode a bicycle in his youth:* For example, in a September 19, 1900, letter to his girlfriend (later wife) Mileva Maric, he wrote, "When we have scraped together enough money, we can buy bicycles and take a bike tour every couple of weeks" (quoted in Isaacson, *Einstein*, 55). And during a strained vacation to visit family in 1913, Einstein pedaled a bicycle with Maric on the crossbar, a relative later recalled (Krstic, *Mileva and Albert*, 172).

87 *As he once wrote in a letter:* Albert Einstein to Eduard Einstein, February 5, 1930, quoted in Isaacson, *Einstein*, 565. The original German is "Beim Menschen ist es wie biem Velo. Nur wenn er faehrt, kann er bequem die Balance halten."

Chapter Seven: The Cycles of War

89 *Their shirts were blue gingham:* James A. Moss, "Military Purposes," *DM*, June 19, 1897, reprinted on "The 25th Infantry Bicycle Corps," accessed May 5, 2015, http://bicyclecorps.blogspot.com/1997/06/before-trip.html.

89 *had faded their US Army uniforms:* "Across the Continent," *StLS*, July 25, 1897, reprinted on "Following the Lieutenant," accessed May 5, 2015, http://followingthelieutenant.blogspot.com; "Near the End of the Journey," *StLPD*, July 23, 1897, 1–2.

89 *"Their natty blue coats":* Ibid.

89 *As they glided in four-man platoons:* "2200 Miles on Wheels," *StLPD*, July 25, 1897, 7; Roderick A. Hosler, "Hell on Two Wheels: The 25th Infantry Bicycle Corps," *On Point*, Fall 2010, 34–41.

89 *These African American enlisted men:* James A. Moss, "The Army A-Wheel," *LAT*, November 7, 1897, 17.

89 *Six weeks earlier, they had left:* Ibid.; E. H. Boos, "Off for St. Louis," *DM*, June 14, 1897, reprinted on "The 25th Infantry Bicycle Corps," accessed May 5, 2015, http://bicyclecorps.blogspot.com/1997/06/day-1-fort-missoula-to-cottonwood.html.

89 *Each soldier toted about 40 pounds' worth:* "Work of Army Bicycle Corps," *SR*, July 11, 1897, 7.

89 *During their rolling march:* Moss, "The Army A-Wheel," November 7, 1897, 17; James A. Moss, "The Army A-Wheel," *LAT*, November 21, 1897, 22; E. H. Boos, "From Fort to Fort," *DM*, July 17, 1897, reprinted on "The 25th Infantry Bicycle Corps," accessed May 5, 2015, http://bicyclecorps.blogspot.com/1997/06/day-13-custer-battlefield-mt-to-parkman.html; E. H. Boos, "Are Wheeling South," *DM*, July 3, 1897, reprinted on "The 25th Infantry Bicycle Corps," accessed May 5, 2015, http://bicyclecorps.blogspot.com/1997/06/day-1-fort-missoula-to-cottonwood.html.

90 *In Wyoming, they encountered:* "Army Bicyclists in Wyoming," *WP*, June 30, 1897, 9.

90 *in Nebraska, vast, parched expanses:* "Bicycle for War Purposes," *Recreation*, November 1897, 408.

90 *Over one rough patch:* E. H. Boos, "Nebraska Is Reached: Marching On," *DM*, July 17, 1897, reprinted on "The 25th Infantry Bicycle Corps," accessed May 5, 2015, http://bicyclecorps.blogspot.com/1997/06/day-16-arvada-wy-to-moorcroft-wy.html; Moss, "The Army A-Wheel," November 21, 1897, 22.

90 *"We have endured every hardship":* "Near the End of the Journey," *StLPD,* July 23, 1897, 1–2.

90 *"The truth is, I find no pleasure":* Ibid.

90 *The service's standard-issue firearm:* Norwegian Krag-Jørgensen rifles were adopted after an 1892 competition and 1893 contract challenge; see Patrick Feng, "The Krag-Jørgensen Rifle," *On Point: The Online Journal of Army History,* July 2, 2012, http://armyhistoryjournal.com/?p=940.

90 *European soldiers had been issued:* Allan Millett, telephone interview by the author, February 13, 2014.

90 *Even when American arms manufacturers:* N. W. Emmott, "The Devil's Watering Pot," *US Naval Institute Proceedings,* November 1972, 70–71.

90 *By 1890, America's western frontier:* Robert P. Porter, *Extra Census Bulletin,* "Distribution of Population According to Density: 1890," April 20, 1891, 4.

90 *Some lawmakers didn't even:* Millett interview.

91 *"While being the most progressive nation":* "The Adaptation of the Bicycle to Military Uses," *Journal of the Military Service Institution of the United States,* November 1895, 542.

91 *European powers had begun using:* Cromwell Childe, "The Bicycle in Battle," *LAH,* December 16, 1891, 10.

91 *An English colonel first employed:* "A Regiment on Wheels," *Strand,* July 1891, 32; Fitzpatrick, *Bicycle in Wartime,* 44.

91 *By the mid-1890s, the armies of France:* "Adaptation of the Bicycle to Military Uses," 546–549.

91 *some European soldiers pedaled artillery:* "Regiment on Wheels," 36; Riddell, *Manual of Ambulance,* 163–164.

91 *The US Army and some state militias:* Smith, *Social History of the Bicycle,* 228; "Soldiers to Use Bicycles," *WP,* September 20, 1891, 10.

91 *"That the bicycle possesses advantages": Toledo Commercial,* June 23, 1893, cited in L. C. Bailey, *Fort Missoula's Military Cyclists,* 6.

91 *"[The bicycle] will before long":* "Bicycle in the Pulpit," *NYH,* May 13, 1895, 4.

92 *"Should not a modern, up-to-date army":* Lieutenant Moss, "Military Bicycling," *Salt Lake Semi-Weekly Tribune,* June 22, 1897, 10, reprinted on "The 25th Infantry Bicycle Corps," accessed May 5, 2015, http://bicyclecorps.blogspot.com/1997/06/before-trip.html.

92 *The group had averaged fifty miles:* Roderick A. Hosler, "Hell on Two Wheels: The 25th Infantry Bicycle Corps," *On Point*, January 2, 2011, http://armyhistoryjournal.com/?p=396; R. Sheldon, "The Army on the March," *Journal of the United States Infantry Association*, July 1905, 167; Wesley Merritt, "Marching Cavalry," *Journal of the United States Cavalry Association*, March 1888, reprinted in Cozzens, *Eyewitness to the Indian Wars*, 5:88; Everett W. Patterson, "The Ride of the Army Bicycle Corps," *LAW&GR*, August 20, 1897, 282; Terry Burns, "How Fast Could They Travel?," accessed May 23, 2015, www.terryburns.net/How_fast_could_they_travel.htm.

92 *"the most rapid military march on record":* "Across the Continent."

92 *"the greatest march known of":* Moss, "The Army A-Wheel," November 21, 1897, 22.

92 *At the top of that final St. Louis hill:* "Near the End of the Journey," 1–2.

92 *Then they pitched their dingy tents:* "Across the Continent"; "Sunday Morning," *StLPD*, July 25, 1897, reprinted on "The 25th Infantry Bicycle Corps," accessed May 5, 2015, http://bicyclecorps.blogspot.com/1997/07/epilouge-after-trip.html.

92 *The following day, thousands of St. Louis:* "Wheelmen at Forest Park," *St. Louis Globe-Democrat*, July 26, 1897, reprinted on "The 25th Infantry Bicycle Corps," accessed May 5, 2015, http://followingthelieutenant.blogspot.com/2010/07/these-are-some-of-my-favorite-articles.html.

92 *"Now we're happy":* Ibid.

92 *Lieutenant Moss wrote to Washington:* James A. Moss to Adjutant General, July 29, 1897, and note on transmittal folder from Assistant Adjutant General, August 3, 1897, in file 60178, RG 94, NA.

93 *Six months later, Moss again wrote to Washington:* James A. Moss to Adjutant General, February 7, 1898, in file 2166, RG 94, NA.

93 *"The Acting Secretary of War regrets":* Adjutant General to James A. Moss, March 3, 1898, in file 70545, RG 94, NA.

93 *he earned a silver star:* Arlington National Cemetery, "James Alfred Moss," accessed May 18, 2015, www.arlingtoncemetery.net/jamoss.htm.

93 *developed a debilitating case of malaria:* James A. Moss to Adjutant General, August 31, 1898, in file 2166, RG 94, NA.

93 *That October, while still recuperating:* This request and response appear in Charles M. Dollar's scrupulously researched article "Putting the Army on Wheels," in Glasrud, *Buffalo Soldiers in the West*, 253–254. I was not able to find the relevant documents in the cited National Archives file despite several passes through. I was, however, able to confirm that Moss did not command a troop of 100 riot-control soldiers on bicycles in Havana shortly after the war ended, as has been repeatedly asserted by other writers. In the buildup to the war, several state militias seemed to be preparing to send cycle troops to Cuba, and the 25th Infantry Bicycle Corps was reported to be headed there. In the end, no cycle troops seem to have joined that fight, likely because of Cuba's hilly terrain and bad roads. See James A. Moss, Efficiency Report for 1899, in file 2166, RG 94, NA; "The Wheel and Wheelmen," *Bangor Daily Whig and Courier*, May 2, 1898; "Our Boys Start for War," *Springfield Sunday Republican*, April 24, 1898; "Indiana Will Send Bicycle Corps," *Denver Evening Post*, March 14, 1898, 1; "Coming to Vermont," *Argus and Patriot*, June 8, 1898, 4.

93 *"It is an open question which mount":* Howard A. Giddings, "Report of Major Howard A. Giddings, Brigade Inspector, C.N.G.," in Cole, *Report of the Adjutant-General*, 124–125.

94 *Both the French and the Russians built: L'illustration*, translated in "The Bicycle in the Army," *Scientific American Supplement*, October 24, 1896, 17358.

94 *"The lion will be the enemy":* Ibid.

94 *Along with more conventional cavalry, the Brits:* Fitzpatrick, *Bicycle in Wartime*, 51–55.

94 *The Boers' bikes could go where horses:* Ibid., 60–61.

95 *despite the British tactic:* See James Robbins Jewell, "Using Barbaric Methods in South Africa: The British Concentration Camp Policy during the Anglo-Boer War," *Scientia Militaria: South African Journal of Military Studies* 31, no. 1 (2003): 1–18.

95 *When the British finally prevailed:* Fitzpatrick, *Bicycle in Wartime*, 71.

95 *When Imperial German Army troops:* Richard Harding Davis, "The Germans in Brussels," *Scribner's*, November 1914, 569–570.

95 *In one August 25, 1914, battle:* "From Liege to Paris," *Cycling*, February 21, 1918, 151–152.

95 *On September 3, 1914:* Theiss and Regele, *Die Radfahrtruppe*, 26–27. The French cyclists crossed back on September 9, 1914.

96 *The front line moved no more than ten miles:* Robert Cowley, military historian, e-mail to William Horne, May 18, 2015.

96 *One group of New Zealanders:* Fitzpatrick, *Bicycle in Wartime*, 102.

96 *"Horses are slow and quickly become":* "The Use of Three-Speed Bicycles in the War," *BW&MR*, January 19, 1915, 28.

97 *By 1916, British and French engineers:* D. Stevenson, *Cataclysm*, 152–153.

97 *When America joined the fight:* In October 1917, the makers of Pope bicycles announced an order from the US Quartermaster's Department for 10,000 bicycles to be used "mostly for messenger and dispatch work." The following week, *MC&B* reported, "by unofficial but absolutely reliable authority," that the US government would buy 100,000 bicycles for military use within the following six months, but I could find no evidence for this purchase. See Fairfax Downey, "It Wasn't Always Boxcars," *ALW*, September 18, 1925, 10; "Pope Gets Contract for 10,000 War Bikes," *MC&B*, October 29, 1917, 14; "U.S. to Buy 100,000 Bicycles for War," *MC&B*, November 5, 1917, 10.

97 *their users were messengers and supply clerks:* An order in June 1918 reduced the number of riding horses allotted to certain US divisions and increased the number of bicycles allotted, in response to a severe horse shortage. Center of Military History, *United States Army in the World War, 1917–1919*, vol. 1; Center of Military History, *United States Army in the World War, 1917–1919*, 16:341–346.

97 *The cycle "proved to be":* Fitzpatrick, *Bicycle in Wartime*, 105.

97 *Even some of the most storied units:* Ibid., 105–106, 109–110.

97 *"an interesting military experiment:* Clark, *London Cyclist Battalion*, iii–iv, quoted in Fitzpatrick, *Bicycle in Wartime*, 110.

98 *In the US Army in 1925:* Downey, "It Wasn't Always Boxcars," 11.

98 *The terms of the Versailles peace treaty:* United States Holocaust Memorial Museum, "World War I: Treaties and Reparations," accessed May 18, 2015, www.ushmm.org/wlc/en/article.php?ModuleId=10007428.

98 *Germany secretly began rebuilding:* Arthur L. Smith Jr., "General Von Seeckt and the Weimar Republic," *Review of Politics*, July 1958, 347; Theiss and Regele, *Die Radfahrtruppe*. The authors of *Die Radfahrtruppe* were officers in the Austrian military when that book was written. Thiess later became a major general in the Wehrmacht.

98 *that meant rearming openly:* Evans, *Third Reich in Power*, 9–10.

98 *On the morning of March 7:* "Cities on Rhine Are Thrilled by Occupation," *BS*, March 8, 1936, 8.

98 *When Germany invaded Poland:* John Graham Royde-Smith, "Forces and Resources of the European Combatants, 1939," accessed May 23, 2015, www.britannica.com/EBchecked/topic/648813/World-War-II/53533/Forces-and-resources-of-the-European-combatants-1939; Fitzpatrick, *Bicycle in Wartime*, 119.

99 *"With one hand I carried my gun":* Quoted in Ambrose, *D-Day*, 560.

99 *The 400,000 Jews:* United States Holocaust Memorial Museum, "Warsaw," June 20, 2014, www.ushmm.org/wlc/en/article.php?ModuleId=10005069.

99 *"In the beginning a few of them":* Engelking and Leociak, *Warsaw Ghetto*, 109.

99 *These hundreds of bike-based taxis:* Ibid., 120.

99 *A young teenager in northern France:* Chelsea Diana, "Maine Woman Resisted the Nazis on a Beat-Up Old Bicycle," *Portland Press Herald and Maine Sunday Telegram*, June 8, 2014, www.pressherald.com/2014/06/08/maine-woman-resisted-the-nazis-on-a-beat-up-old-bicycle.

99 *In fascist Italy, the Tour de France winner:* McConnon and McConnon, *Road to Valor*, 124–131.

100 *bicycles rigged up to generators:* One example is in the Imperial War Museum of London. War History Online, "Crafty Gadgets and Famous Spies of WWII," accessed May 6, 2015, www.warhistoryonline.com/war-articles/crafty-gadgets-tricks-famous-wwii-spies.html.

100 *In much of occupied France:* "French Bicycles Restricted," *NYT*, May 9, 1942, 5.

100 *They made an exception to the rule:* Michael E. Young, "Soldiers in the Shadows," *Fort Lauderdale Sun-Sentinel*, May 29, 1994; Pascal du 38, "Guillaume Mercader, Chef de Réseau / Résistance du Bessin," accessed December 29, 2011, http://normandie44.canalblog.com/archives/2011/12/29/23066471.html; "Lecture Script of Mr. Guillaume Mercader," July 7, 1987, Bayeux Calvados, France, 5, from the Eisenhower Center World War II Archives and Oral History Collection, University of New Orleans, courtesy of the National WWII Museum, New Orleans.

100 *As a leader of the Resistance:* "D-Day: Secret Maps," *Guardian*, May 28, 1994, B16.

100 *On June 5, 1944, the BBC's:* "Lecture Script of Mr. Guillaume Mercader," 5. This document was translated from French, so the wording is not exact, and I have edited it for clarity. In the document, Mercader says that he rode off "to contact my principal responsible people of an imminent landing." The code phrase, broadcast in French, was "*Les dés sont jetés,*" which is frequently translated as "The dice are on the table" or "The dice are on the carpet."

100 *The saboteurs, many also on bikes:* "War on the Beaches," *History of War*, June 2014, 18.

100 *The folding bicycles that came ashore:* Fitzpatrick, *Bicycle in Wartime*, 127–128.

101 *"Daily we see the highways":* Harold Denny, "Normandy Battle Is Hedge to Hedge," *NYT*, July 6, 1944, 5.

101 *Bicycles had arrived in the Far East:* Amir Moghaddass Esfehani, "The Bicycle and the Chinese People," in *ICHC* 13, 94–102.

101 *Japanese craftsmen soon began:* Allen, *Economic History of Modern Japan*, 79; Edgerton, *Shock of the Old*, 98.

101 *Ravenous for natural resources:* Stanley L. Falk, "'Victory Disease' and the Defeat of Japan," *Army*, February 2014, 53.

101 *In the years before World War II:* Axelrod, *Encyclopedia of World War II*, 470–473; Tsuji, *Singapore*, 183.

101 *In early December 1941:* The invasion occurred on December 8, one hour and twenty minutes before the Pearl Harbor attack on the other side of the international date line, where it was still December 7; see Kratoska, *Japanese Occupation of Malaya*, 36; Tsuji, *Singapore*, 70.

101 *Their goal: to travel six hundred miles:* H. Gordon Bennett, introduction to Tsuji, *Singapore*, vii.

101 *"No more formidable stronghold": London Sunday Observer*, quoted in "Malaya a Terrible Obstacle for Japan," *Straits Times*, November 17, 1941, 9.

102 *Instead, 6,000 soldiers in the Japanese force:* Callahan, *The Worst Disaster*, 245–246.

102 *Riding in groups of sixty or seventy:* U.S. Army Military Intelligence Service, "Notes on Japanese Warfare," Information Bulletin No. 10, March 21, 1942, 14.

102 *More than once, Japanese:* Ibid., 12.

102 *Meanwhile, Japan's tanks trundled south:* Keegan, *Second World War*, 257–258.

102 *One Australian reporter: Bulletin,* January 28, 1942, 23, quoted in Fitzpatrick, *Bicycle in Wartime,* 140.

102 *At night, a company of such tire-less bikes:* Tsuji, *Singapore,* 184.

102 *"a blitzkrieg on bicycles":* Bennett, introduction to Tsuji, *Singapore,* vii.

102 *In just ten weeks:* The retreat to Singapore took sixty-eight days (Fitzpatrick, *Bicycle in Wartime,* 131).

103 *According to legend, the island's:* Keegan, *Second World War,* 259–260.

103 *On February 15, 1942:* Ibid., 261.

103 *"the worst disaster and largest capitulation":* Churchill, *Hinge of Fate,* 81.

103 *Japanese troops occupied British Malaya:* Morgan, *Valley of Death,* 7–8, 113–114.

104 *the Chinese brought in most of their supplies:* Stokesbury, *Short History of the Korean War,* 117–118.

104 *incinerating both landscape and civilians:* See, for example, George Barrett, "Radio Hams in U.S. Discuss Girls, So Shelling of Seoul Is Held Up," *NYT,* February 9, 1951, 1.

104 *it began to seem as if future military victories:* See, for example, Thomas K. Finletter, "Air Power in the Korean Conflict," *Vital Speeches of the Day,* September 15, 1950.

104 *So in 1953, when the French commander:* Morgan, *Valley of Death,* 187–189.

104 *Navarre, an agile, silver-haired:* Ibid., 168, 220.

104 *although China provided some heavy:* Maclear, *Ten Thousand Day War,* 39; Arnold Blumberg, "Pedal Power," *Vietnam,* August 2012, 52.

104 *In the steep jungle terrain:* Morgan, *Valley of Death,* 200.

104 *It was perilous work:* Giap, *People's War,* 202.

105 *Since these porters also had to eat:* Fall, *Viet-Minh Regime,* 84–86.

105 *To feed the troops stationed in Dien Bien Phu:* Morgan, *Valley of Death,* 231, 304; Maclear, *Ten Thousand Day War,* 38.

105 *The military commander of the Vietminh:* Jean Lacouture, preface to Giap, *Banner of People's War,* vii–viii.

105 *"We chose the positions where the enemy":* Giap, *People's War,* 179.

105 *By late 1953, the Vietminh had a force:* Prados, *Blood Road,* 2; Maclear, *Ten Thousand Day War,* 32.

105 *Giap's plan was to surround:* Giap, *People's War,* 196.

105 *a common transportation mode for Vietnamese:* David Arnold and Erich DeWald, "Cycles of Empowerment? The Bicycle and Everyday Technology in Colonial India and Vietnam," *Comparative Studies in Society and History*, October 2011, 974.

105 *In December 1953, Giap:* Maclear, *Ten Thousand Day War*, 31–32; Prados, *Blood Road*, 2.

105 *"We had one day to make preparations":* Maclear, *Ten Thousand Day War*, 32.

106 *tens of thousands of these cargo bikes:* Blumberg, "Pedal Power," 52.

106 *"the colossal human serpent lay coiled":* Do, *Récits sur Dien Bien Phu*, 13. In French: "L'énorme serpent humain s'était ramassé autour de Dien Bien Phu et n'attendait qu'un ordre pour resserrer son étreinte."

106 *Under French fire and under cover of night:* Morgan, *Valley of Death*, 253–256.

106 *And when the Vietminh finally attacked:* Maclear, *Ten Thousand Day War*, 38–41.

106 *Though French and American planes:* Ibid., 305–306.

106 *By May 7, the French were:* Maclear, Ibid., 45.

106 *At a peace conference held in Geneva:* Morgan, *Valley of Death*, 623–625.

108 *In early 1959, the North Vietnamese:* Prados, *Blood Road*, 9.

108 *"We will drive the Americans into the sea":* Elbridge Durbrow, "Despatch from the Ambassador in Vietnam to the Department of State," March 7, 1960, published in US Department of State, *Foreign Relations of the United States, 1958–1960, vol. 1, Vietnam*, Document 112, accessed May 23, 2015, https://history.state.gov/historicaldocuments/frus1958-60v01/d112.

108 *In May of that year, North Vietnam's:* Prados, *Blood Road*, 9–10.

108 *The trail was nicknamed:* The trail's official name was the Truong Son Strategic Supply Route, after the mountain range on Vietnam's western border (ibid., xiii).

108 *As the conflict escalated:* Fitzpatrick, *Bicycle in Wartime*, 173.

108 *"The bicycle convoys of Dien Bien Phu":* Burchett, *Vietnam*, 25–26.

109 *As the war bore on, communist forces:* Plaster, *S.O.G.*, 42.

109 *An insistent barrage of US bombs:* Prados, *Blood Road*, 370–374; "Memorandum of Conversation, Saigon, August 17, 1972," in US Department of State, *Foreign Relations of the United States, 1969–1976, vol. 8, Vietnam, January–October 1972*, Document 242, ac-

cessed July 25, 2014, http://history.state.gov/historicaldocuments/frus1969-76v08/d242.

109 *Every year during the summer monsoon:* William H. Sullivan, "Telegram from the Embassy in Laos to the Department of State," June 9, 1976, 0929Z, in US Department of State, *Foreign Relations of the United States, 1964–1968, vol. 27, Laos*, accessed May 23, 2015, www.state.gov/1997-2001-NOPDFS/about_state/history/vol_xxviii/286_300.html.

109 *"If by some magic weapon":* Harrison E. Salisbury, "North Vietnam Runs on Bicycles," *NYT*, January 7, 1967, 1.

109 *In the southern capital of Saigon:* Reuters, "Three Are Killed in Saigon by Bomb Hidden in Bicycle," *NYT*, June 10, 1965, 3.

109 *One 1963 bicycle bombing rocked:* Associated Press, "Americans Escape Viet Bomb," September 23, 1963.

109 *In 1952, a nationalist warlord:* H. Bruce Franklin, "By the Bombs' Early Light; Or, The Quiet American's War on Terror," *Nation*, February 3, 2003, republished at http://andromeda.rutgers.edu/~hbf/QUIETAM.htm.

109 *And this tactic has endured:* See, for example, "Explosions in Quetta, Peshawar Kill 14, Injure 65," *Daily The Pak Banker*, March 15, 2014.

110 *In the following year, the actress Jane Fonda:* Jane Fonda, "A Vietnam Journal: Rebirth of a Nation," *Rolling Stone*, July 4, 1974, 49.

110 *While most of the bikes used there:* Senate Committee on Foreign Relations, *Harrison E. Salisbury's Trip to North Vietnam*, 11.

110 *"mostly from scrap metal of downed":* Fonda, "Vietnam Journal," 50.

110 *Today, portions of the Ho Chi Minh trail*: Kit Gillet, "Riding Vietnam's Ho Chi Minh Trail," *Guardian*, July 28, 2011, reprinted at www.theguardian.com/travel/2011/jul/28/ho-chi-minh-trail-motorbike.

110 *Giggling schoolchildren often rush:* A typical example: Ed and Clare Wimshurst, "16th–18th Feb—Vietnam—Phon Nha Ke Bang National Park," February 24, 2014, http://cledward.wordpress.com/2014/02/24/16th18th-febvietnamphong-nha-ke-bang-national-park.

110 *In 2015, one American bicycle racer:* The racer is world-champion mountain biker Rebecca Rusch; see Kate Siber, "New Frontier: Mountain Bike the Ho Chi Minh Trail, Vietnam," accessed May 23, 2015, http://adventure.nationalgeographic.com/adventure/trips/bucket-list/2014/mountain-bike-vietnam; Rebecca Rusch, "A Long

Way on the Path Less Traveled," February 24, 2015, www.rebeccarusch.com/a-long-way-on-the-path-less-traveled.

Chapter Eight: The King of the Neighborhood

This chapter is adapted from "Kid Stuff: The Bicycle and American Youth," in *Cycle History 25: Proceedings of the 25th International Cycling History Conference*, edited by Andrew Ritchie and Gary Sanderson (Birmingham, UK: Cycling History, 2015), 88–96. Material used with permission.

111 *On March 26, 1883:* "Barnum Excelling Former Exploits," *NYTrib*, March 27, 1883, 5; "The Record of the Place," *NYT*, April 22, 1880, 1; "At Barnum's Circus," *NYT*, March 27, 1883, 5.

111 *The small children in question:* Viona Elliott Lane, Randall Merris, and Chris Algar, "Tommy Elliott and the Musical Elliotts," in Atlas, *International Concertina Association*, 19, 41–43.

111 *Dressed in tights and spangled costumes:* "Little Ones on Bicycles," *NYT*, March 31, 1883, 2; "At Barnum's Circus," 5.

111 *On these Ordinaries, they rode:* "The Elliott Children," *NYH*, April 5, 1883, 11; "Mr. Barnum Arrested, *NYTrib*, April 3, 1883, 2.

111 *In the audience that afternoon:* W. Miller, *Select Organizations*, 127; "The Elliott Children," *NYH*, 11.

111 *During the Progressive Era:* New York Society for the Prevention of Cruelty to Children, "History," accessed May 23, 2015, nyspcc.org/about/history.

113 *As he watched the Elliotts perform:* The society's concerns about fracture, hernia, and strain were expressed by the SPCC's president, Elbridge T. Gerry, to a reporter for the *New-York Tribune* in "The Child-Performers," *NYTrib*, March 29, 1883, 1. Although Gerry thought that normal bicycle riding was fine for children—just not acrobatic circus riding—Superintendent Jenkins felt otherwise. At Barnum's trial on child cruelty charges, Jenkins stated that he would not allow his own children to cycle or to roller-skate because of the danger (Elliott, *Celebrated Elliott Family*, 50).

113 *"A society claiming to prevent cruelty":* Elliott, *Celebrated Elliott Family*, 46–47.

113 *An agent for the SPCC then went:* "P. T. Barnum under Arrest," *WP*, April 3, 1883, 1.

113 *At the men's trial on April 4:* "The Elliott Children," *NYH*, 11; Elliott, *Celebrated Elliott Family*, 50.

113 *Clearly, he argued, the bicycle:* Elliott, *Celebrated Elliott Family*, 50.

113 *One of them, Dr. Louis A. Sayre:* "The Elliott Children," *NYH*, 11.

113 *The three-judge panel must have:* Court of Special Sessions for New York City Docket Book, April 4, 1883, 8, in New York City Municipal Archives.

114 *"I'll give you $200 per week":* "The Elephants' Fight," *NHER*, April 5, 1883, 3.

114 *But as Robert Turpin convincingly argues:* Turpin, "'Our Best Bet Is the Boy'"; see also Turpin, "'Our Best Bet Is the Boy': Bicycle Marketing Schemes and American Culture after World War" in *ICHC* 22, 159–170.

114 *"essentially a selfish sport for men":* "Cycling Trade History," *NYT*, January 5, 1896, 27.

114 *"We do not think here":* Edmund Boviere, "In Behalf of the Boys," *Outing*, August 1884, 383.

114 *The prevailing snobbism of cycling:* Herlihy, *Bicycle*, 243–250.

115 *While some manufacturers marketed:* In one 1891 ad, the *Youth's Companion* offered a $35 boys' or girls' safety for every twenty subscriptions sold. "The advent of a high-grade Boys' and Girls' Bicycle at a low price was like the advent of a sudden fire on the dry prairies of the West," the ad stated ("Lovell's Boys' or Girls' $35.00 Safety Bicycle," *Youth's Companion*, June 11, 1891, 342). But although children's use of the bicycle did rise during the 1890s as the price of bicycles dropped, kids remained a minority of riders even after the end of the decade-long boom. In 1903, for example, one Indianapolis bicycle dealer reported that there were about twenty thousand registered bicycles in his city and another ten thousand bikes owned either by adults who failed to register or by children under fifteen, who were not required to register ("How to Stop the 'Knocking,'" *BW&MR*, March 12, 1903, 70).

115 *"at no time in American history":* "Play and the History of American Childhood: An Interview with Steven Mintz," *American Journal of Play*, Fall 2010, 149–150.

115 *By the early decades of the twentieth century:* Peter N. Stearns, "Analyzing the Role of Culture in Shaping American Childhood: A Twentieth-Century Case," *European Journal of Developmental Psychology*, 2009, 37–39.

116 *In 1899, as the market for new bicycles collapsed:* Bruce D. Epperson, "'The Finances Stagger These Fellows': The Great American Bicycle Trust, 1899–1903," *International Journal of the History of Sport*, December 2011, 2633–2652.

116 *"Our two oldest veterans":* "With June Come Perfect Days," *OBSB*, June 1917, 84.

116 *In August of that year, the* Bulletin*:* "Our Oldest Members," *OBSB*, August 1917, 120.

116 *Six-day bicycle races continued:* Dzierzak, *Evolution of American Bicycle Racing*, 18–22; Herlihy, *Bicycle*, 381.

116 *People may have preferred:* Burr, "Markets as Producers and Consumers," 336.

116 *Fatal crashes became shockingly common:* Norton, *Fighting Traffic*, 21–24.

117 *In 1933, there were seventeen cars:* "A Bicycle Rampant," *Fortune*, September 1933, 51.

117 *"Play to the kid all the time":* T. J. Sullivan, "'Get After the Boy' Says Farrell," *MC&B*, September 3, 1917, 35, cited in Turpin, "'Our Best Bet Is the Boy,'" 119.

117 *As Robert Turpin argues:* Turpin, "'Our Best Bet Is the Boy,'" 118.

117 *"The selection of a bicycle is":* Iver Johnson's Arms & Cycle Works, "Personal—for Boys Only," *Youth's Companion*, December 9, 1926, 977.

117 *"Dad discovers the reason you've set":* New Departure Manufacturing Company, "So That's Why You Want a Bicycle for Christmas?," *Youth's Companion*, November 1927, 719.

117 *As part of a broader cultural shift:* For more on this shift, see Jacobson, *Raising Consumers*, 56–92.

118 *"They tell me that they would like":* Bertram Reinitz, "City's Cyclists Hold Their Own," *NYT*, October 28, 1928, 140.

118 *"How they did blossom out on it!":* Fairfax Downey, "It Wasn't Always Boxcars," *ALW*, September 18, 1925, 21.

118 *"Give him a bicycle that he will be":* Miami-Made Bicycles, "A Bicycle—*That's* What We'll Get Him for Christmas," *McClure's*, December 1916, 40.

118 *"boyhood without a bicycle is like":* New Departure Manufacturing Company, "This Week Is Yours," *Boys' Life*, May 1922, 45.

118 *"What normal boy wouldn't gladly"*: Lewis Edwin Theiss, "Children, Too, Should Learn to Prepare for a Rainy Day," *American Home*, June 1936, 72.

118 *"Here comes back, freewheeling"*: H. A., "*By-the-Bye* in Wall Street," *WSJ*, August 21, 1933, 6.

119 *"the urge of a weary people"*: "A Bicycle Rampant," *Fortune*, September 1933, 117.

119 *Hans Ohrt, a Los Angeles bicycle merchant:* Hans Ohrt, "Growth of Lightweight Cycling," *Cycling Herald*, November 1941, kindly provided to the author by David Herlihy.

119 *Big names like Joan Crawford:* Herlihy, *Bicycle*, 355.

119 *Bicycle production rose from 249,500:* "The Amazing Return of the 'Bikes,'" *Popular Mechanics*, January 1935, 62; Marshall Sprague, "A Bicycle Army Takes to the Highroad," *NYT*, May 15, 1938, 159.

119 *Like other professional sports:* Nye, *Hearts of Lions*, 24, 125–139.

119 *Despite the new interest in adult cycling:* "Order Trebles Adult Bicycles," *NYT*, March 13, 1942, 38; Turpin, "'Our Best Bet Is the Boy,'" 213.

119 *Makers adopted bulbous frames:* Softer, wider so-called balloon tires for cars were introduced to the American market in 1923, but American bikes continued to have thin tires until the early 1930s, when the balloon tire for bicycles hit the US market. Sears and Montgomery Ward advertised single-tube versions in 1931 and 1932, and Schwinn announced a more practical, double-tube version in 1933. See "Balloon Title Born to the World One Year Ago," *LAT*, May 25, 1924, F10; Shawn Sweeney and Gary Meneghin, "The First American Balloon Tire Bicycle," February 4, 2015, http://thecabe.com/the-first-american-balloon-tire-bicycle; *Fifty Years of Schwinn-Built Bicycles*, 57–59; "Return of Bicycle Arouses Comment of Old-Time Riders," *BS*, August 21, 1933.

119 *"electric blast horn hidden"*: Monark Silver King, Inc., "Now Pay a Little Each Month—and You Can Have the Aluminum Streamlined Silver King," *Boys' Life*, May 1936, 49.

120 *"exclusive instrument panel"*: Westfield Manufacturing Company, *Westfield Columbia-Built Bicycles*, 1941, 2.

120 *By late 1941, when the United States entered:* "Order Trebles Adult Bicycles," 38.

120 *In mid-August of that year, though:* Fitzpatrick, *Bicycle in Wartime*, 161–162.

120 *In September 1945, one month after:* Clayton R. Sutton, "After Lean War Years Industry Hustles to Put Small Fry on Wheels," *WSJ*, September 26, 1945, 1.

120 *The postwar bike industry ramped up:* Turpin, "'Our Best Bet Is the Boy,'" 241; "1950s Monark 'Gene Autry' Girl's Cowboy Bicycle," accessed September 14, 2014, www.legendaryauctions.com/lot–86078.aspx.

120 *American adults, on the other hand:* By 1954, adult cycling was a strange enough activity to occasion an essay in the *Christian Science Monitor*, where the author noted that the children she passed on her way to work had never seen an adult on a bike (Barbara Beecher, "My Cycling in Suburbia," *CSM*, December 18, 1954, 8).

121 *Encouraging this exploration was a new philosophy:* Mintz, *Huck's Raft*, 279–280; Owram, *Born at the Right Time*, 33–41.

121 *"much better that [children] suffer":* Beasley, *Democracy in the Home*, 38.

121 *Then, too, the large number of mothers:* Frank Levy, "Incomes and Income Inequality," in Farley, *State of the Union*, 20; Rose M. Kreider and Diana B. Elliott, "Historical Changes in Stay-at-Home Mothers: 1969–2009," paper presented at the American Sociological Association's 2010 annual meeting, Atlanta, Georgia, 2–3; D'Vera Cohn, "After Decades of Decline, a Rise in Stay-at-Home Mothers," *Pew Social Trends*, April 8, 2014.

121 *The 1950s saw a juvenile delinquency panic:* Mintz, *Huck's Raft*, 293–295.

121 *bike theft fueled by envy:* See, for example, "Youths Riding to Prison on Stolen Bikes," *CT*, June 29, 1943, 24.

121 *"Keep a healthy boy busy and happy":* "Safety Riders Bicycle Club Attracts Youths," *PT*, September 8, 1959, 9. The Bicycle Institute of America, an industry trade group, actively encouraged the formation of such clubs for delinquency prevention; see Turpin, "'Our Best Bet Is the Boy,'" 250–254.

122 *"We have given our children a free ride":* Quoted in Clyde Snyder, "Socialite's Belief in Youth Shaken," *LAT*, August 27, 1967, OC18.

122 *In the early 1960s, youngsters in California:* Dick Degnon, "High Handlebar Fad Draws Official Frowns," *LAT*, January 10, 1960, GB1.

122 *This modification originally allowed newspaper:* Jack McCurdy, "Fad of High Bars on Bikes Stirs Concern," *LAT*, January 10, 1960, SC1.

122 *With the addition of long "banana" seats:* These seats were developed for the US market by Bob Persons of the Persons Majestic Company in the late 1950s, but found no significant market until high-risers came into fashion; see John Brain, "John Brain's History of Kustom Biking," accessed December 4, 2014, http://bikerodnkustom5.homestead.com/brainhistory58.html.

122 *Manufacturers soon copied the trend:* The Huffy Dragster—also called the Penguin for its black-and-white coloring—was being sold in California stores by early March, and the Schwinn Sting-Ray was introduced for model year 1963. See Huffy History . . . and Museum, "1962–1963," accessed May 23, 2015, http://huffyhistory.webs.com/1962-1963; Patrick Sexton, "The Schwinn Stingray," accessed May 23, 2015, http://schwinncruisers.com/bikes/stingray.

122 *"rose up so fantastically tall":* Virginia Grilley, "Bicycle Sea," *CSM*, July 30, 1965, 14.

122 *In 1969, 85 percent of US:* Robert Rosenblatt, "Bicycle Industry Riding High on Ecology Trend," *LAT*, August 15, 1971, G1; Berto, Shepherd, and Henry, *Dancing Chain*, 209.

122 *the awkward form raised safety questions:* In 1970, the National Commission on Product Safety reported that "novel bicycle styles have increased the well-known risks in cycling. . . . The high rise was found to require more skill to operate." A study in the journal *Pediatrics* the following year, though, found no differences "either in injury rate or severity" between high-risers and older styles of kids' bike. See Elizabeth Shelton, "'High Rise' Bikes: Are They Risky?" *WP*, March 5, 1970, G1; National Commission on Product Safety, *Final Report Presented to the President and Congress*, June 1970, 18–19; Julian A. Waller, "Bicycle Ownership, Use, and Injury Patterns Among Elementary School Children," *Pediatrics*, June 1971, 1042.

122 *"Anywhere you go, you can see":* Sarah Booth Conroy, "The Very Best Is a Clean Machine," *WP*, July 18, 1971, D1, D3.

123 *"People would starve, commerce would suffer":* "Bikes Play Big Role in Much of World," *CT*, August 22, 1965, A3.

123 *"by a sizeable margin":* Thierry Sagnier, "Summertime—and the Riding Is Easy," *WP*, July 18, 1971, D4.

124 *no self-respecting adult would ride one:* The British cycle historian Nicholas Clayton remembers visiting a Detroit bicycle collector's showroom in 1980. "There was a notice on the wall explaining to visi-

tors that in Europe, bicycles are actually ridden by adults," he says. "It really struck me in the eye as being a strange thing to say" (Clayton, telephone interview by the author, March 8, 2012).

124 *"What are we to make of these bikes":* Arthur Asa Berger, "The Spyder (Sting-Ray, Screamer) Bike: An American Original," in Lewis, *Side-Saddle on the Golden Calf*, 154–155.

Chapter Nine: The Great American Bicycle Boom

125 *"My husband, my girls":* Molly Mayfield, "Teen-Age Crush," *BS*, July 5, 1966, B5.

125 *"Imagine an old man of 42":* Molly Mayfield, "Father Too 'Old' to Exercise, *BS*, April 11, 1966, B4.

125 *Postwar prosperity and an increasingly car-centric:* While health experts sounded alarm bells about adult obesity in the 1950s, the preferred remedy was a restrictive diet, not regular exercise; see Jesse Berrett, "Feeding the Organization Man: Diet and Masculinity in Postwar America," *Journal of Social History*, Summer 1997, 805–808.

126 *vigorous exercise was bad for adults:* Alan Latham, "The History of a Habit: Jogging as a Palliative to Sedentariness in 1960s America," *Cultural Geographies*, July 4, 2013, 9–10; see, for example, Lydia Lane, "Exercise Is Helpful, but Do Not Overdo It," *LAT*, April 28, 1949, B2.

126 *"After [age] 25 or 30":* Peter J. Steincrohn, "Exercise is 'Slow Suicide' for Some, Specialist Warns," *WP*, July 23, 1950, M1. Steincrohn's many popular health books included *You Don't Have to Exercise: Rest Begins at Forty* (1942).

126 *"In high school, it just wasn't done":* Scott Moore, "Pedals Coming Up Roses on Campus," *LAT*, October 10, 1971, OC2.

126 *"We had bike racks at school":* Glacier John, "70s Bike Boom and 'Breaking Away' Movie," accessed May 30, 2015, bikeforums.net/classic-vintage/98763-70s-bike-boom-breaking-away-movie.html.

126 *"deluxe spring fork balloon model":* Arnold, Schwinn & Co., 1959 Catalogue, 12.

127 *that sophisticated new sensation:* Stephen J. Sansweet, "Sophisticated Cousin of Pinball Machine Entrances the U.S.," *WSJ*, March 18, 1974, 1.

127 *In 1948, to help boost a British economy:* Ross D. Petty, "Peddling Schwinn Bicycles: Marketing Lessons from the Leading Post-WWII US Bicycle Brand," in Branchik, *Marketing History at the Center*, 163–164.

127 *The imports were also among the first:* Berto, Shepherd, and Henry, *Dancing Chain*, 98, 194–195; Nye, *Hearts of Lions*, 148–149.

127 *As these high-tech lightweights found buyers:* "Bicycles from Britain," *Time*, July 5, 1954, 72.

127 *By 1960, US companies were producing:* Petty, "Peddling Schwinn Bicycles," 163–64; "Bicycle Boom Gives No Sign of Weakening," *LAT*, June 11, 1972, F4.

128 *"the bike had a light, springy":* "The Bike's Comeback," *Sunset*, July 1965, 57.

128 *"the difference between driving a tank":* "Bicycle Boom Gives No Sign of Weakening," *LAT*, June 11, 1972, F4.

128 *"This Huffy is one reason":* Huffman Manufacturing Company, "This Huffy Is One Reason you See More Adults on Bicycles Today," *Life*, November 5, 1965, 76.

128 *"So many of us have a Kafkaesque":* "What Kind of Bike D'Ya Ride?," *Forbes*, December 1, 1970, 60; Trevor Jensen, "Eugene A. Sloane: 1916–2008," *CT*, April 1, 2008.

128 *In 1974, an ad for the ten-speed:* AMF Corporation, "Flying Machine," 1974 (publication unknown), offered for sale on eBay.com, December 12, 2014.

128 *In summery locales like Florida:* "The Bike's Comeback," 51.

128 *Unlike the "dead weight":* "Life Guide," *Life*, May 10, 1963, 17.

129 *"You get a chance to notice little things":* Jean Fincher, "Bikes Causing Chain Reaction," *LAT*, August 6, 1966, B1.

129 *"In this age of jet planes and tail fins":* Charles Friedman, "Bicycles Make a Jet-Age Comeback," *NYT*, May 29, 1960, X17.

129 *"Discover the call of far away places":* Arnold, Schwinn & Co., "Schwinn . . . for the Young at Heart," 1968 (publication unknown), offered for sale on eBay.com, December 12, 2014.

129 *"I'd like to put everybody on bicycles":* "Cycling Good for Heart, Expert Says," *LAT*, March 18, 1956, A11.

129 *White flew to the president's bedside:* Robert E. Gilbert, "Eisenhower's 1955 Heart Attack," *Politics and the Life Sciences*, June 24, 2008, 2–21.

130 *White recommended exercise such as cycling:* Kingbay, *Inside Bicycling*,

9; "Dr. White on Wheels," *Life*, November 10, 1961, 71; Herbert Black, "Dr. Paul Dudley White, Heart Pioneer, Dies at 87," *BG*, November 1, 1973, 52.

130 *"Some believe that vigorous exercise":* Paul Dudley White, "Expert Cites Gains in Heart Studies," *CDT*, October 30, 1955, 6.

130 *In Baltimore in 1956, catcalls:* "Bike Riders Irk Drivers," *BS*, August 12, 1956, 34.

130 *"anyone—six to 106":* William Bowerman, *The Joggers Manual*, pamphlet, 1963, quoted in Latham, "History of a Habit," 1.

130 *As the historian Alan Latham has ably documented:* Latham, "History of a Habit," 1–3.

130 *The group published their findings in 1967:* Waldo A. Harris, William Bowerman, Bruce McFadden, and Thomas Kerns, "Jogging: An Adult Exercise Program," *JAMA*, September 4, 1967, 759–761.

131 *"probably the only disadvantage to jogging":* Michael Kilian, "Jogging: The Newest Road to Fitness," *CT*, July 9, 1968, A3.

131 *"pushing 40 or 50 is exercise enough":* Phil Casey, "Some Stand Pat; Some Stand Still," *WP*, April 25, 1969, B2.

131 *"Jogging might be good for you":* Carl Bernstein, "Commuter Cycling Speeds Up," *WP*, June 14, 1970, C1. Bernstein, the famous Watergate reporter, was a cyclist himself, and in that capacity he set a precedent that still stands in DC law. By fighting a September 1970 traffic ticket for running a red light on his bicycle, Bernstein established that the court can't put points on your driver's license based on a cycling infraction (John Kelly, "A Look Back at the Early Days of Bicycling Laws," *WP*, July 21, 2014).

131 *"It's the swiftest way to get uptown":* Judy Klemesrud, "Bicycling: The Individualist's Mode of Transport," *NYT*, May 4, 1970, 50; Bruce Weber, "Morton Gottlieb, a Broadway Producer, Dies at 88," *NYT*, June 27, 2007.

131 *"I think most people are starting to realize":* Sagnier, "Summertime—and the Riding Is Easy," D5.

131 *Although bikers were still a tiny minority:* The federal government did not begin keeping commuting-mode statistics until 1977; in 1980, 0.5 percent of US workers commuted by bicycle. See John Pucher, Ralph Buehler, and Mark Seinen, "Bicycling Renaissance in North America? An Update and Re-Appraisal of Cycling Trends and Policies," *Transportation Research Part A* 45 (2011): 452.

132 *"There is now nearly six times":* Luther L. Terry, "Man Himself Is Now Guinea Pig," *WP*, April 21, 1964, A14.

132 *One 1968 best-seller:* Ehrlich, *Population Bomb.*

132 *During that event, some twenty million:* Elizabeth Kolbert, "In the Air," *New Yorker*, April 27, 2009, 17.

133 *"The alternative to sitting around":* Alan Cartnal, "75 Million Spokesmen Boost Bicycling," *LAT*, June 13, 1971, D1.

133 *the decision of twenty-something Nancy Pearlman:* "Biking Beauties," *LAT*, September 15, 1971, 3.

133 *Others were grander, such as a 1,500-person:* Bob Reiter, "Wheels: The What, the Where, the Who," *LAT*, October 31, 1971, P14; Nancy Pearlman, telephone interview by the author, April 14, 2015.

134 *"If we desire to change the world":* Friends for Bikecology, *Bikecology Overview*, 1971, 11.

134 *a boom that started in the early 1960s:* The distinguished bicycle journalist Frank Berto has argued that the 1970s ten-speed boom resulted from a surge of teenage baby boomers aging out of their high-rise bicycles. He states: "In the late 1960s, millions of American teenagers rode their high-rise bicycles to school because they were 'cool'" (Berto, "The Great American Bicycle Boom" in *ICHC* 10, 136). My research, however, suggests that teenage boomers eschewed the bicycle through the mid-1960s, when adults had already begun riding ten-speeds for exercise or touring. And I was not able to verify Berto's claim that teenagers ever thought the banana-seat high-riser was "cool." One woman who started high school in Cleveland in the late 1960s recalled that between the ages of twelve and fifteen, none of her friends rode bicycles. "If you rode a banana bike in high school there was something seriously wrong with you," she told me (name withheld by request, e-mail to author, December 3, 2014).

134 *Between 1960 and 1970, the number of bikes:* Dougherty and Lawrence, *Bicycle Transportation*, 5.

134 *"No one could have predicted it":* Robert Rosenblatt, "Bicycle Industry Riding High on Ecology Trend," *LAT*, August 15, 1971, G5.

134 *In 1971, Schwinn sold out its entire:* Ted F. Shelsby, "Bicycle Sales Are Booming—But You Can't Get One," *BS*, October 10, 1971, K7.

134 *"If we could have increased our production":* Marilyn Bender, "Bicycle Business Is Booming," *NYT*, August 15, 1971. F1.

134 *European and Japanese importers tried:* Dougherty and Lawrence, *Bicycle Transportation*, 5.

134 *A* Washington Post *reporter named B. D. Colen:* B. D. Colen (misspelled in print as "Cohen"), "Just 10 Blocks and 10 Speeds," *WP*, October 14, 1971, G1.

135 *By 1972, there were 85 million:* Dougherty and Lawrence, *Bicycle Transportation*, 5.

135 *In 1896, the year that "everything was bicycle":* The US population was 209,896,021 in 1972, compared to 70 million in 1896, when there were about two million cyclists. It is worth remembering that even as bicycle prices dropped in the 1890s, a bike was still vastly more expensive, relative to average income, then than in the 1970s. In 1972, the US median income of a man with a full-time job was $10,540, and a ten-speed Schwinn Continental sold for $104.95. See US Census Bureau, "Historical National Population Estimates: July 1, 1900 to July 1, 1999," accessed May 30, 2015, www.census.gov/population/estimates/nation/popclockest.txt; U.S. Census Bureau, "Population, Housing Units, Area Measurements, and Density: 1790 to 1990," accessed April 5, 2015, www.census.gov/population/www/censusdata/files/table-2.pdf; U.S. Department of Commerce, "Money Income in 1972 of Families and Persons in the United States," *Current Population Reports: Consumer Income*, June, 1973, 1; Arnold, Schwinn & Co., 1972 Catalogue, 10–11.

135 *Bicycles outsold cars in the United States:* Monty Hoyt, "More U.S. Families Choosing Bikes as Best Way to Get Around," *CSM*, November 15, 1972, 4; Paul Hodge, "Magnificent Trails Are Planned, But Will Bikers Ever Ride Them?," *WP*, April 22, 1976, MD1.

135 *In 1971, 86 percent of Schwinn's:* Hoyt, "More U.S. Families Choosing Bikes," 4.

135 *"four-and-a-half kids to 300 adults":* Bender, "Bicycle Business Is Booming," F1.

135 *"Most people who looked up at us smiled":* Calvin Trillin, "U.S. Journal: Manhattan," *New Yorker*, December 9, 1971, 126.

135 *Manhattan didn't get its first:* Michael Sterne, "Mid-Manhattan Bikeways a Cyclist's Wish Coming True," *NYT*, August 7, 1978, B1.

135 *In October 1973, Arab oil-producing:* Jill Tennant, "40 Years Later: Legacies of the 1973 Oil Crisis Persist," *World Oil*, October 2013, 121–123.

136 *"The USA energy shortage?":* National Independent Distributor Associates, "The USA Energy Shortage?," *Boys' Life*, May 1974, 21.

136 *At Cal State Fullerton in 1971:* Scott Moore, "Pedals Coming Up Roses on Campus," *LAT*, October 10, 1971, OC2.

136 *At the University of Illinois in Urbana-Champaign:* Michael Sneed, "Bicycles Create Problem at U. of I.," *CT*, December 16, 1973, 3.

136 *"Take a look at the average college campus":* Keith Henderson, "The 10-Speed Dream," *CSM*, March 26, 1975, 14.

136 *"The 'boom' has turned into a 'bust'":* Stuart J. Northrop, "Statement of Bicycle Manufacturers Association of America, Inc.," in Senate Committee on Finance, *Various Revenue and Tariff Bills*, 128.

136 *"Anything with a derailleur could be sold":* Berto, Shepherd, and Henry, *Dancing Chain*, 213.

137 *"a thriving business" nationally:* Peyton Canary, "Bicycle Thievery a Big Business," *LAT*, April 25, 1971, N1.

137 *"America's fastest-growing crime":* Stefan Kanfer, "The Full Circle: In Praise of the Bicycle," *Time*, April 28, 1975, 65.

137 *But after the race riots:* Schulman, *The Seventies*, 56–58; Brian J. L. Berry and Donald C. Dahmann, "Population Redistribution in the United States in the 1970s," *Population and Development Review*, December 1977, 448–450.

137 *in 1975, New York City turned:* Sam Roberts, "Infamous 'Drop Dead' Was Never Said by Ford," *NYT*, December 28, 2006.

137 *The US crime rate doubled:* Borstelmann, *The 1970s*, 169.

137 *On Easter 1974:* "Bike Riders Beware," *WP*, April 20, 1974, D3.

138 *And during a 1980 transit strike:* Barbara Basler, "Muggings Rise on Brooklyn Bridge as More Bicyclists Make Use of It," *NYT*, July 22, 1980, A1, B2.

138 *And the ubiquitous curb cuts:* These cuts were intended for wheelchair users but have proved useful to others as well. Bruce Epperson calls them "America's stealth bikeway program" (*Bicycles in American Highway Planning*, 12).

Chapter Ten: Bike Messengers, Tourists, and Mountain Bikers

139 *"You don't find many landlords":* Tom Buckley, "Mercury on 2 Wheels," *NYT*, August 4, 1976, 23.

139 *His company—one of New York's first:* Dinitia Smith, "Fast Company," *New York*, January 13, 1986, 40.

139 *By 1976, when the* New York Times*:* Buckley, "Mercury on Two Wheels," 23. In 1975 there were five services in New York that used

mainly or exclusively bicycle messengers ("Self-employed," *New Yorker*, December 29, 1975, 16).

139 *"Unlike most of the thousands"*: Buckley, "Mercury on 2 Wheels," 23.

140 *The* New Yorker *called them:* "Self-employed," 16. The lack of fatal accidents did not last, of course. While there is no comprehensive list of messenger traffic deaths, they are significant. In 1999, for example, at least thirty-four cyclists were killed in New York's five boroughs, and most were believed to be messengers (Glenn Collins, "Selling Online, Delivering on Bike," *NYT*, December 24, 1999, B1).

140 *In the mid-1970s, similar services:* Although industry lore names Carl Sparks of San Francisco as having originated the modern bike-messenger service in 1945, this is an error. Sparks founded a delivery service called Sparkie's in 1946 and sold part of it to create another such service, Aero, in 1950, but his primary delivery vehicles then were Harley-Davidson motorcycles, small pickup trucks, and vans. It was only later that Aero became a bicycle messenger service. Cycle-courier services were launched in the early 1970s in Washington, DC; by 1982 they could be found in most large US cities. See Ken Hoover, "Carl Sparks," *SFC*, July 20, 1994, A22; John Saar, "2-Wheeled 'Pony Express' Riders Beat D.C. Traffic," *WP*, July 8, 1973, C1; Herald Staff, "Miami Couriers Try Pedal Power," *Miami Herald*, June 14, 1982, 41.

140 *By 1981 there were six hundred bicycle messengers:* Jack M. Kugelmass, "I'd Rather Be a Messenger," *Natural History*, August 1981, 66–73.

140 *"Like heroes of the West"*: Ibid.

141 *"It's hard. It makes your life harrowing"*: Ibid.

141 *Unfettered by the expectations:* Kidder, *Urban Flow*, 163; Lynette Holloway, "A Leg Up: Messengers Were the Medium," *NYT*, June 16, 1996, 35.

142 *"allowed people with mohawks to earn"*: San Francisco Bike Messengers Association, "Bike Messengering," 1996, reprinted at http://foundsf.org/index.php?title=BIKE_MESSENGERING.

142 *Messengers developed what the anthropologist:* Kidder, *Urban Flow*, 164. The cultural anthropologist Claude Lévi-Strauss introduced the term "social bricolage" in 1962 to describe a pattern of thought that attempts to reuse available materials in order to solve new problems; see Lévi-Strauss, *The Savage Mind*, 16–33.

142 *"phantoms who materialize smug"*: Henry Allen, "Chariots Afire!," *WP*, May 5, 1982, B1.

142 *At those games:* Robert Fachet, "Cycling," *WP*, August 13, 1984, C5. Vails worked as a messenger when not in training ("Riding to the Olympics," *New York Amsterdam News*, April 10, 1982, 50).

142 *Hollywood films like Kevin Bacon's: Quicksilver*, directed by Tom Donnelly (1986).

142 *a comically importunate cyclist*: Although Mars Blackmon is identified in the film as being out of work, many reviewers saw him as a bicycle messenger. Lee's previous project, never completed, was to have been a film about a bicycle courier called *The Messenger* (Lee, *Spike Lee's Gotta Have It*, 38).

142 *And when Lee revived the character:* Patrick Goldstein, "Spike Lee—A Jump Shot into the Big Time," *LAT*, February 12, 1988, G1.

143 *the annual number of bicycle-pedestrian:* In New York in the first ten months of 1985, for example, there were 660 reported injuries to pedestrians caused by bikers, compared to 9,739 caused by cars in the first nine months of the same year (Smith, "Fast Company," 43).

143 *"There is a form of terrorism":* William Morgan, "Terrorists—on Two Wheels," *WP*, May 8, 1987, A22.

143 *more than four thousand commercial bikers:* Michael Fritz, "City's Courier Companies Rush to Beat Competition," *Newsday*, July 14, 1986, 8.

143 *"The problem is not that their actual":* Smith, "Fast Company," 43.

143 *In July 1987, New York mayor:* Alan Finder, "New York to Ban Bicycles on 3 Major Avenues," *NYT*, July 23, 1987.

143 *"What [bike messengers] are doing":* Ibid.

143 *"Our stately pace, perhaps five mph":* Charles Komanoff, "The Bicycle Uprising: Remembering the Midtown Bike Ban 25 Years Later, Part 1," August 7, 2012, www.streetsblog.org/2012/08/07/the-bicycle-uprising-remembering-the-midtown-bike-ban-25-years-later.

144 *The arrival of the office fax:* Judy Temes, "Messenger Firms Scrambling to Survive," *Crain's New York Business*, July 16, 1990, 17.

144 *e-mail attachments in the mid-1990s:* Electronic mail was invented in the 1960s but did not become common until a standard for sharing messages between providers was established after 1989 and a standard for sending attachments was created in 1992. See "E-Mail Searches for a Missing Link," *NYT*, March 12, 1989, F6; Arik Hesseldahl, "Seven Questions for Nathaniel Borenstein, Who Made Email Attachments Easy," accessed January 3, 2015, http://allth-

ingsd.com/20120307/seven-questions-for-nathaniel-borenstein-who-made-email-attachments-easy.

144 *thinned the messenger herd:* In 2011, the New York State Messenger and Courier Association estimated that there were seven hundred bicycle messengers in the New York City area, just one hundred more than a 1981 estimate (J. David Goodman, "The Messenger Goes Hollywood," *NYT*, October 2, 2011, CT4).

144 *"The pedals never stop turning": Premium Rush,* directed by David Koepp (2012).

144 *In fact, UPS began:* United Parcel Service, "1907–1929," accessed December 30, 2014, www.ups.com/content/corp/about/history/1929.html.

144 *And Western Union employed biking:* Gay Talese, "Messenger Boys: A Fading Tintype," *NYT*, December 12, 1959, 45. For an enlightening look at the phenomenon of the telegraph boy in US history, see Downey, *Telegraph Messenger Boys.*

144 *"Without a bicycle in sight":* Sanford L. Jacobs, "Western Union Corp. Launches Jazzy Era of Telegraph Offices," *WSJ*, February 8, 1973, 17. The Western Union office in Los Angeles had three bicycle couriers as late as 1978, but they were regarded as the last of their kind (Lynn Symross, "Endangered Species on Wheels," *LAT*, June 8, 1978, 11).

144 *"For the First Time in History":* "Lads Will Race," *BEN*, Thursday, August 27, 1896.

145 *After World War II, the United States grew:* Alejandro Reuss, "That '70s Crisis," *Dollars & Sense: Real World Economics*, November–December 2009.

145 *When the South Vietnamese capital:* Craig Larson, "Frequent Wind Lifts Evacuees out of South Vietnam," *Marines*, May 1995, 26.

146 *"We have been shaken by a tragic war":* Jimmy Carter, "Our Nation's Past and Future," July 15, 1976, www.presidency.ucsb.edu/ws/?pid=25953.

146 *It was the Bikecentennial:* Dan D'Ambrosio, "Thirty Years and Counting," *Adventure Cyclist*, July 2006, 16; Paul Hodge, "'Bikecentennial' Will Begin along 4,250-Mile Route," *WP*, May 10, 1976, B1.

146 *Signing up solo cost $75:* "The Freewheelers," *Time*, July 5, 1976, 69; Hodge, "'Bikecentennial,'" B1.

146 *scruffy bands of middle-class adventurers:* Forty-five percent of Bikecentennial participants were either students or teachers, and 4 percent were unemployed. Only a few nonwhite people participated; although no data were formally collected, an organizer later noted that only 4 of 4,065 known riders were black (Burgess and Burden, *Bicycle Safety Highway Users Information Report*, 24).

146 *In Prairie City, Oregon:* "Freewheelers," 69.

146 *In Liebenthal, Kansas:* Scott Martin, "America Rides," *Bicycling*, July 1996, 45.

146 *"Not only are the cyclists":* "Freewheelers," 69.

146 *"The Republican National Convention":* Rich Landers, "Trail of Memories," *Spokane Spokesman-Review*, June 2, 1996.

147 *Bikecentennial was the creation:* D'Ambrosio, "Thirty Years and Counting," 12.

147 *"bicycling can be a wonderful intimate":* Hodge, "'Bikecentennial,'" B1.

147 *the development of marked on-road bicycle routes:* The first marked bikeway in the United States opened in Homestead, Florida, on February 24, 1962. See Mary Hornaday, "U.S. Takes to Bicycling—at Last," *CSM*, December 30, 1967, 1; Smith, *Social History of the Bicycle*, 249; Burgess and Burden, *Bicycle Safety Highway Users*, 17.

147 *The cyclists' iffier experiences:* While there was no direct link between the planning for Bikecentennial and such efforts as the Rails-to-Trails Conservancy's founding in 1985, the ride was "very influential" because "it built up the excitement" for bicycle facilities, RTT's cofounder Peter Harnik told me (Peter Harnik, telephone interview by the author, January 5, 2015).

147 *Now called the Adventure Cycling Association:* Adventure Cycling Association, "Resources," accessed May 31, 2015, www.adventurecycling.org/resources.

148 *On the morning of October 21, 1976:* C. Kelly, *Fat Tire Flyer*, 46–47; Frank J. Berto, "Who Invented the Mountain Bike?," in *ICHC* 8, 33.

148 *It was chilly but clear:* US Department of Commerce, National Oceanic and Atmospheric Administration, "Record of Climatological Observations," Kentfield, California, October 1976.

148 *the riders could see for miles:* Joe Breeze, "Repack History," accessed December 19, 2014, http://mmbhof.org/mtn-bike-hall-of-fame/history/repack-history.

148 *At their feet was a rocky, rutted fire road:* C. Kelly and N. Crane, *Richard's Mountain Bike Book*, 22.

148 *The group of friends had come:* Charles Kelly, "Repack Page," accessed December 15, 2014, http://sonic.net/~ckelly/Seekay/repack.htm.

148 *Several of the riders were members:* The Vélo-Club Tamalpais was founded in 1972; see Kelly, "Repack Page; C. Kelly, *Fat Tire Flyer*, 27.

148 *Instead, the riders used bikes:* C. Kelly, *Fat Tire Flyer*, 36.

148 *The DIY modifications were intended:* C. Kelly and N. Crane, *Richard's Mountain Bike Book*, 30–35.

148 *It was the first downhill time trial:* At the time, some adults were turning away from ten-speeds and toward old (unmodified) clunkers in various parts of California, including in Chico, where the old bikes were ridden in an off-road event that occurred several months before this first time trial: the Bidwell Bump, an annual nine-mile race first run on August 29, 1976. See Berto, "Who Invented the Mountain Bike?," 33; Elliott Almond, "New California Fad . . . Clunker Bikes," *WP*, October 8, 1978, L16; Bodfish, "The Very First Off-Road Bike Race (Maybe)," *Mountain Bike*, November–December 1988, 22.

148 *"most of the corners can be taken at full speed":* Charlie Kelly, "Clunkers among the Hills," *Bicycling*, January 1979.

149 *The winning time that first day:* Kelly, "Repack Page."

149 *Even the sport's originators hunted:* Berto, "Who Invented the Mountain Bike?," 35.

149 *In 1977, Kelly hired a fellow rider:* C. Kelly and N. Crane, *Richard's Mountain Bike Book*, 30–49; Berto, "Who Invented the Mountain Bike?," 35.

149 *Breeze made that one:* C. Kelly, *Fat Tire Flyer*, 57.

149 *"We thought in our naivete":* C. Kelly and N. Crane, *Richard's Mountain Bike Book*, 15–16.

149 *"California bikies are mountainside surfing":* Owen Mulholland, "California Bikies Are Mountainside Surfing," *VeloNews*, February 10, 1978, cited in Breeze, "Repack History."

149 *"a new kind of bicycle":* Richard Nilsen, "Clunker Bikes," *CoEvolution Quarterly*, Spring 1978, 114.

149 *In early 1979, a San Francisco:* Breeze, "Repack History."

149 *The riders in that piece:* KPIX, "Klunkers," January 1979, accessed December 20, 2014, https://www.youtube.com/watch?v=SVWP6VaLtvw.

151 *"We used to ride down on these":* Ibid.

151 *"It probably started when men":* Ibid.

151 *Later that year, Fisher and Kelly:* Berto, "Who Invented the Mountain Bike?," 35–36.

151 *three local mountain-bike makers:* The third maker, along with MountainBikes and Joe Breeze, was Mert Lawwill, who manufactured the Pro Cruiser ("Full Bore Cruisers," *Bicycle Motocross Action*, January 1980, 75).

151 *in 1981, a Bay Area importer:* Mike Sinyard of San Jose started Specialized, which is now located in Morgan Hill, California (Maggie Overfelt, "King of the Mountain Bike," *Fortune Small Business*, May 16, 2008).

151 *As it had with the kids' high-riser bike:* Despite Schwinn's recognition of the trend, the company's failure to produce bikes with true off-road features may have contributed to its bankruptcy in 1992; see Museum of Mountain Bike Art & Technology, "Schwinn Bicycles History," accessed June 1, 2015, http://mombat.org/MOMBAT/BikeHistoryPages/Schwinn.html; Crown and Coleman, *No Hands, 122–125.*

151 *"Let the others stick to those smooth":* Arnold, Schwinn & Co., "Introducing the Schwinn Sidewinder," *WP*, November 19, 1981, D4.

151 *"Their chubby tires rarely go flat":* Stephanie Shapiro, "Mountain Biking," *BS*, November 16, 1985, D1.

152 *After the 1970s boom, US sales:* "The Cycle of Change," *WP*, April 25, 1986, D5; Berto, Shepherd, and Henry, *Dancing Chain*, 233.

152 *By 1989, the mountain bike accounted for:* Manufacturers, distributors, and bike shop managers interviewed by *Bicycling* in 1990 estimated that the mountain bike had captured 65 to 80 percent of the market (Scott Martin, "Are Road Bikes Dead?," *Bicycling*, June 1990, 61).

152 *"It's just phenomenal":* Ibid.

152 *In 1990, there were ninety-three million:* T. J. Howard, "Wheel Thrills," *CT*, May 15, 1991, F28; Bill Hale, "First Person," *CT*, July 7, 1985, H38; Thomas Murphy, "Bike Messengers Love to Hate Their Low-Paying Jobs," *LAT*, July 6, 1986, A3.

152 *That year,* Bicycling *magazine asked:* Martin, "Are Road Bikes Dead?," 61.

152 *In fact, the main gag of 1979's: Breaking Away*, directed by Peter Yates (1979).

152 *American cyclists had a pitiful record:* Nye, *Hearts of Lions, 222.*

153 *At the Los Angeles Olympics in 1984:* Ibid., 261–264.

153 *Two years later, the Nevadan LeMond:* Ibid., 278.

153 *After a grueling public showdown:* LeMond had dutifully subjugated his ambition in 1985 to help his teammate Bernard Hinault win the race, and Hinault announced from the podium that he would help LeMond win in 1986. During the 1986 race, though, Hinault gave no quarter. He later claimed he was only pushing LeMond to succeed (ibid., 277–283).

153 *In 1989, he ascended to hero-hero:* E. M. Swift, "Le Grand LeMond," *Sports Illustrated*, December 25, 1989, 54–58.

153 *"I think the clothing has helped":* Rose-Marie Turk, "Clothiers Wheel into the New Field of Cycle Wear," *LAT*, February 20, 1987, F1.

153 *"fit as tightly as anything that isn't skin":* Bill Cunningham, "Now in the Mainstream: Cyclists' Garb," *NYT*, August 23, 1987, 58.

153 *One Virginia waitress even sued:* The bar, Champions, ended up revising its dress code to allow female servers to wear baggy shorts; see Robert F. Howe, "Waitress at Va. Bar Alleges Sexual Harassment in Suit," *WP*, May 8, 1991, B8; "Bar Bows on Shorts Issue," *WP*, May 11, 1991, D4.

154 *Some California kids hacked them:* Scott, "Subcultural Study of Freestyle BMX," 24–28.

154 *In 1974, there were just a handful:* "Bicycle Makers Shift Gears to Catch a Fad," *Business Week*, June 19, 1978, 36–37.

154 *In the 1982 film* E.T.*:* *E.T.: The Extra-Terrestrial*, directed by Stephen Spielberg (1982).

154 *The sport spawned:* Scott, "Subcultural Study of Freestyle BMX," 32–33.

154 *In fact, the recumbent:* Herlihy, *Bicycle*, 388–389.

154 *In the mid-1970s, though, some US:* Herlihy, *Bicycle*, 409–410; Robert Lindsey, "Pedal Pushers Aim at the 60 M.P.H. Barrier," *NYT*, October 28, 1979, E9.

154 *By the 1980s, commuter versions:* Peter Tonge, "The Recumbent Bicycle—a Different Way to Get Around," *CSM*, August 20, 1980, 18; Kevin Sullivan, "Laid-Back Bikers Love This Cycle," *WP*, July 12, 1992, B1.

154 *"tires that are stout but not obese":* Martin, "Are Road Bikes Dead?," 64.

155 *Next came the beach cruiser:* Sal Ruibal, "Peddling in a New Direction: Makers Look for Antidote to Sales Slump," *USA Today*, September 17, 1996, 3C.

Chapter 11: Are We There Yet?

157 *These computerized, often solar-powered:* Tom Vanderbilt, "The Best Bike-Sharing Program in the United States," *Slate,* January 7, 2013.

157 *Supporters see the systems as:* Elliot Fishman, Simon Washington, and Narelle Haworth, "Bike Share: A Synthesis of the Literature," *Transport Reviews,* March 2013, 150.

157 *The country's first automated bikeshare:* Susan A. Shaheen, Elliot W. Martin, Adam P. Cohen, and Rachel S. Finison, "Public Bikesharing in North America: Early Operator and User Understanding," Mineta Transportation Institute report, June 2012, 13.

157 *By mid-2015, there were seventy-two:* Susan Shaheen, telephone interview by the author, June 15, 2015; Russell Meddin, "The Bike-Sharing World Map," accessed June 6, 2015, www.bikesharingmap.com.

158 *Despite user fees and corporate sponsorships:* Matthew Christensen and Susan Shaheen, "Can Bikeshare Systems Ever Stand on Their Own Two Wheels?," The Conversation, February 17, 2014, https://theconversation.com/can-bikeshare-systems-ever-stand-on-their-own-two-wheels-22981.

158 *"If you were to go to a city":* Vanderbilt, "Best Bike-Sharing Program." DeMaio is the founder of the bikeshare consultancy MetroBike LLC.

158 *Between 2000 and 2013, the proportion:* League of American Bicyclists, "Where We Ride: Analysis of Bicycle Commuting in American Cities," December 6, 2014, 13–14; League of American Bicyclists, "The Growth of Bike Commuting" (chart), accessed June 7, 2015, http://bikeleague.org/sites/default/files/Bike_Commuting_Growth_2015_final.pdf. The rate went from 2.0 to 3.8 percent in San Francisco; 1.2 to 3.6 percent in New Orleans, and 1.2 to 4.5 percent in Washington, DC.

158 *In 2012, thirty-six of the country's largest:* These figures are calculated from Alliance for Biking and Walking, *2012 Benchmarking Report*, 99, and Alliance for Biking and Walking, *2014 Benchmarking Report*, 152, 247. The 2012 report is based on a survey conducted in 2010–2011, while the 2014 report is based on a survey conducted in 2011–2012. The total miles in 2010–2011 for the thirty-six cities were 11,025, compared to 12,931 in 2011–2012. I excluded cities for which no data was available in any category on either report.

158 *And those numbers don't include:* Alliance for Biking and Walking, *2014 Benchmarking Report*, 152.

158 *Between 2012 and 2014, US cities:* Joe Lindsey, "The Secret to Safer Cities," *Bicycling*, July 2015, 34. From 1874 to 2011, 78 protected lanes were added, compared to 113 between 2012 and 2014.

158 *Cyclists push for safer routes:* Ralph Buehler and John Pucher, "Cycling to Work in 90 Large American Cities: New Evidence on the Role of Bike Paths and Lanes," *Transportation*, July 6, 2011, 410–411.

159 *Some argue that the fixed-gear's:* J. R. Thorpe, "The Symbolic Meaning of 6 Hipster Trends, from Beards to Fixies (Kind of Fascinating, but Whatever)," Bustle.com, March 18, 2015.

159 *The bike-culture critic Lodovico Pignatti Morano:* Lodovico Pignatti Morano, e-mail message to author, June 15, 2015.

159 *almost nobody self-identifies as a hipster:* For a discussion of the unique stigma of this consumer label, see Zeynep Arsel and Craig J. Thompson, "Demythologizing Consumption Practices: How Consumers Protect Their Field-Dependent Identity Investments from Devaluing Marketplace Myths," *Journal of Consumer Research*, February 2011, 791–793.

159 *the Priceonomics data analysis firm found:* Rohin Dhar, "The Fixie Bike Index," Priceonomics, January 17, 2012, http://priceonomics.com/post/16013457968/the-fixie-bike-index.

159 *Created in the 1990s to handle Alaska's:* Adam Fisher, "Rollin' Large," *Bicycling*, January 7, 2014, www.bicycling.com/bikes-gear/rollin-large.

159 *"It does anything any other bike can do":* Ibid.

159 *More than one hundred makers are currently producing:* Gary Sjoquist, advocacy director, Quality Bicycle Products, e-mail message to author, June 15, 2015.

159 *In late 2014, one bicycle dealer:* Craig Medred, "Despite Expense, Popularity of Fatbikes Continues to Soar in Alaska," *Alaska Dispatch News*, November 4, 2014, www.adn.com/article/20141104/despite-expense-popularity-fatbikes-continues-soar-alaska.

159 *In part because of a steady decline:* Daniel B. Wood, "U.S. Crime Rate at Lowest Point in Decades," *CSM*, January 9, 2012; Lucy Westcott, "More Americans Moving to Cities," *Wire*, March 27, 2014, www.thewire.com/national/2014/03/more-americans-moving-to-cities-reversing-the-suburban-exodus/359714.

160 *These workhorses first appeared:* Laura Moser, "No Longer a Novelty, a Cargo Bike Built for All," *NYT*, April 23, 2015, D-9.

160 *Dubbed the "new station wagon":* Tom Vanderbilt, "Cargo Bikes: The New Station Wagon," *WSJ*, July 5, 2013, www.wsj.com/articles/SB10001424127887324328204578572011343756542.

160 *one Washington, DC, father:* Moser, "No Longer a Novelty."

160 *Ebikes are used widely in Europe:* Ed Benjamin, chairman of the Light Electric Vehicle Association, telephone interview by the author, June 10, 2015.

160 *in the late 1860s, a Massachusetts inventor:* Allan Girdler, "First Fired, First Forgotten," *Cycle World*, February 1998, 63. This object is in the collection of the Smithsonian Institution, which estimates that it was built around 1869.

160 *They are pricey, costing an average:* Marc Sani, "E-Bikes Finding Traction in U.S. Market," *Bicycle Retailer and Industry News*, April 9, 2014, www.bicycleretailer.com/north-america/2014/04/09/e-bikes-finding-traction-us-market#.VXyBzSiWekY.

160 *In 2014, more than 200,000 ebikes:* The number was 270,000, according to Frank E. Jamerson with Ed Benjamin, "Electric Bikes Worldwide Reports: 2014 Update to 2013 Edition," 2. Navigant Research estimated 2014 sales at a more conservative 200,000 (Ryan Citron, research analyst, Navigant Research, telephone interview by the author, June 12, 2015).

160 *That is a small fraction of:* National Bicycle Dealers Association, "2013—The NBDA Statpak," accessed June 13, 2015, http://nbda.com/articles/industry-overview-2013-pg34.htm.

160 *more than double the ebike sales tally:* The total for 2013 was 100,000 according to Jamerson, "Electric Bikes Worldwide Reports," 2.

161 *Ed Benjamin, chairman of the Light Electric Vehicle Association:* Benjamin interview.

161 *"We baby boomers are not as young":* Ibid.

161 *There is even a sleek German one-speed:* Darren Quick, "Coboc Impersonates Non-Electric Bike to Take Gold Award at Eurobike," Gizmag, August 30, 2013, www.gizmag.com/coboc-ecycle-gold-award-eurobike/28876.

161 *This shadowy conflict is supposedly:* Franklyn Cater, "Motorists to Urban Planners: Stay in Your Lane," NPR.org, July 18, 2012; Stephen Moore, "The War against the Car," *WSJ*, November 11, 2005, A10.

161 *"an all-powerful enterprise":* Dorothy Rabinowitz, "Opinion: Death by Bicycle," *WSJ*, May 31, 2013, www.wsj.com/video/opinion-death-by-bicycle/C6D8BBCE-B405-4D3C-A381-4CA50BDD8D4D.html.

162 *statistics provided by her sympathetic interviewer:* Ibid.; Nicole Gelinas, City Journal, "Bike Share's Promise and Peril," May 30, 2013, www.city-journal.org/2013/eon0530ng.html.

162 *Indeed, since 2000:* Gluskin Townley Group, "National Bicycle Dealers Association (NBDA) U.S. Bicycle Overview Report, 2013," section A, 4–5.

162 *And the drop-off among children:* Ibid., section A, 6.

162 *While sales of adult bikes fell:* National Bicycle Dealers Association, "A Look at the Bicycle Industry's Vital Statistics," accessed January 18, 2014, nbda.com/articles/industry-overview-2013-pg34.htm.

163 *the only time in American history when large:* Howard P. Chudacoff, "Child's Play: A Brief History of American Childhood," *Antiques*, July 1, 2014, 121; Chudacoff, *Children at Play*, 158–162.

163 *Since then, a steady increase in two-worker:* Ibid.

163 *Indeed, today a parent can get arrested:* Conor Friedersdorf, "Working Mom Arrested for Letting Her 9-Year-Old Play Alone at Park," *Atlantic*, July 15, 2014.

163 *In April 2014, a freelance writer:* Amy Hatch, "The Terrifying Time My Kid Went around the Block Alone," *BabyCenter Blog*, April 7, 2014, http://blogs.babycenter.com/mom_stories/04072014-kids-ride-bikes-alone.

163 *In the comments, a self-confessed:* Ibid.; the comment is by Laura E.

164 *For many kids in working-class families:* Jay Townley, e-mail message to author, January 5, 2015.

164 *While the average price of an adult bicycle:* Jay Townley, e-mail message to author, June 16, 2015. In 2000, according to Townley, the average new adult bicycle cost $393. The average amount spent on a bike by the most active segment of the bicycle market, dubbed "enthusiasts" in Townley's research, was $946. In 2014, the average price of an adult bike rose only slightly, to $400.25; if it had kept up with inflation, it would have risen to $540.29. Meanwhile, enthusiasts spent $1,231.37 in 2014, just a little less than the $1,300.54 they would have needed to spend in order to keep up with inflation (Bureau of Labor Statistics, "CPI Inflation Calculator," accessed July 16, 2015, http://data.bls.gov/cgi-bin/cpicalc.pl).

164 *"the Lance Armstrong effect":* Andre Mayer, "How Lance Armstrong Transformed North American Culture," CBC.com, October 12, 2012, www.cbc.ca/news/world/how-lance-armstrong-transformed-north-american-culture-1.1234593.

164 *Public schools have gotten bigger:* Safe Routes to School National Partnership, "School Siting: Location Affects the Potential to Walk or Bike," accessed June 14, 2015, http://saferoutespartnership.org/state/bestpractices/schoolsiting; Eric A. Morris, "The Vanishing Walk to School," Freakonomics, September 19, 2011, http://freakonomics.com/2011/09/19/the-vanishing-walk-to-school/?sc=1#comments.

165 *"Bicycles are not yet part of the mainstream":* Townley, e-mail to the author, January 5, 2015.

165 *With more telecommuting, online shopping:* Kerry Cardoza, "Millennials Lead Trend in Less Car-Ownership, Driving," Medill Reports Chicago, June 5, 2014, http://newsarchive.medill.northwestern.edu/chicago/news-231073.html; Brad Tuttle, "8 Ways the American Consumer May Have Already Peaked," *Time*, September 25, 2014, http://time.com/money/3426697/american-consumers-have-peaked; Tony Dutzik, Jeff Inglis, and Phineas Baxandall, "Millennials in Motion: Changing Travel Habits of Young Americans and the Implications for Public Policy," U.S. PIRG Education Fund Frontier Group report, October 2014, 3–4.

166 *Some say they'll lighten and calm traffic:* Susan Shaheen, telephone interview by the author, June 15, 2015.

166 *The reality will depend on how corporations:* Ibid.

BIBLIOGRAPHY

Adventure Cycling Association. "Resources." Retrieved from adventurecycling.org.

Allen, C. B. "The Concept of Flight That Worked." *Bee-Hive*, January 1953.

Allen, George Cyril. *A Short Economic History of Modern Japan, 1867–1937*. London: Routledge, 2003. Orig. pub. 1946.

Allen, Henry. "Chariots Afire!" *Washington Post*, May 5, 1982.

Alliance for Biking and Walking. *Bicycling and Walking in the United States: 2012 Benchmarking Report*. Washington, DC: Alliance for Biking and Walking, 2012.

———. *Bicycling and Walking in the United States: 2014 Benchmarking Report*. Washington, DC: Alliance for Biking and Walking, 2014.

Almond, Elliott. "New California Fad . . . Clunker Bikes." *Washington Post*, October 8, 1978.

Ambrose, Stephen E. *D-Day, June 6, 1944: The Climactic Battle of World War II*. New York: Touchstone, 1995.

AMF Corporation. "Flying Machine." 1974.

Annual Report of the Board of Regents of the Smithsonian Institution. Washington, DC: Government Printing Office, 1903.

Appletons' Annual Cyclopaedia and Register of Important Events of the Year 1877. New York: Appleton, 1886.

Appletons' Annual Cyclopaedia and Register of Important Events of the Year 1895. New York: Appleton, 1896.

Appletons' Annual Cyclopaedia and Register of Important Events of the Year 1901. New York: Appleton, 1902.

Arlington National Cemetery. "James Alfred Moss." Retrieved from arlingtoncemetery.net.

Arnold, David, and Erich DeWald. "Cycles of Empowerment? The Bicycle and Everyday Technology in Colonial India and Vietnam." *Comparative Studies in Society and History* 53, no. 4 (October 2011): 971–996.

Arnold, Schwinn & Co. *Cycling '72*. Catalogue, 1972.

———. "Introducing the Schwinn Sidewinder." *Washington Post*, November 19, 1981.

———. "Schwinn . . . for the Young at Heart." 1968.

———. *Schwinn: "The World's Finest Bicycles."* Catalogue, 1959.

Aronson, Sidney H. "The Sociology of the Bicycle." *Social Forces* 30, no. 3 (March 1952): 305–312.

Arsel, Zeynep, and Craig J. Thompson. "Demythologizing Consumption Practices: How Consumers Protect Their Field-Dependent Identity Investments from Devaluing Marketplace Myths." *Journal of Consumer Research* 37 (February 2011): 791–806.

Associated Press. "Americans Escape Viet Bomb." September 23, 1963.

Atlas, Allan, ed. *Papers of the International Concertina Association*, vol. 5. New York: Center for the Study of Free-Reed Instruments, 2008.

Aubrecht, Michael. "Baseball and the Blue and Gray." Retrieved from baseball-almanac.com.

Automobile Quarterly. The American Car since 1775: The Most Complete Survey of the American Automobile Ever Published. New York: Automobile Quarterly, 1971.

Axelrod, Alan. *Encyclopedia of World War II*. New York: Facts on File, 2007.

Bailey, Linda C. *Fort Missoula's Military Cyclists: The Story of the 25th U.S. Infantry Bicycle Corps*. Fort Missoula, MT: The Friends of the Historical Museum at Fort Missoula, February 1997.

Bailey, L. Scott. "The Other Revolution." In *Automobile Quarterly, The American Car since 1775*, 10–93. New York: Automobile Quarterly, 1971.

Baltimore Patriot and Mercantile Advertiser. "Aged Novelty." February 6, 1819.

———. "Tracena." February 6, 1819.

———. "Tracena." February 8, 1819.

Baltimore Sun. "The Bicycle." November 7, 1872.

———. "The Bicycle in Washington." May 1, 1882.
———. "Bike Riders Irk Drivers." August 12, 1956.
———. "Cities on Rhine Are Thrilled by Occupation." March 8, 1936.
———. "A Moral Crusader." July 7, 1896.
———. "Return of Bicycle Arouses Comment of Old-Time Riders." August 21, 1933.
———. "Women Cyclists." July 8, 1896.
Baltimore Weekly Register. "Inland Trade." March 13, 1813.
Bangor (ME) Daily Whig and Courier. "The Wheel and Wheelmen." May 2, 1898.
Barnes, Barry, David Bloor, and John Henry. *Scientific Knowledge: A Sociological Analysis*. Chicago: University of Chicago Press, 1996.
Barrett, George. "Radio Hams in U.S. Discuss Girls, So Shelling of Seoul Is Held Up." *New York Times*, February 9, 1951.
Basler, Barbara. "Muggings Rise on Brooklyn Bridge as More Bicyclists Make Use of It." *New York Times*, July 22, 1980.
Bassett's Scrap Book. "Early Bicycles." April 1913.
———. "The First American Bicycle." April 1913.
Bates, [Lewis J.]. "Effect of the Bicycle Upon Our Highway Laws." *Wheelman*, October 1882.
Baxter, Sylvester. "Economic and Social Influences of the Bicycle." *Arena*, October 1892.
Bearings. "They Cling to Their Old Loves." December 16, 1892.
Beasley, Christine. *Democracy in the Home*. New York: Association Press, 1954.
Beecher, Barbara. "My Cycling in Suburbia." *Christian Science Monitor*, December 18, 1954.
Bender, Marilyn. "Bicycle Business is Booming." *New York Times*, August 15, 1971.
Bennett, H. Gordon. Introduction to *Singapore: The Japanese Version*, by Masanobu Tsuji, vii–viii. New York: St. Martin's, 1960.
Berger, Arthur Asa. "The Spyder (Sting-Ray, Screamer) Bike: An American Original." In *Side-Saddle on the Golden Calf*, edited by George H. Lewis, 154–157. Pacific Palisades, CA: Goodyear Publishing, 1972.
Bernstein, Carl. "Commuter Cycling Speeds Up." *Washington Post*, June 14, 1970.
Berrett, Jesse. "Feeding the Organization Man: Diet and Masculinity in Postwar America." *Journal of Social History* 30, no. 4 (Summer 1997): 805–825.

Berry, Brian J. L., and Donald C. Dahmann. "Population Redistribution in the United States in the 1970s." *Population and Development Review* 3, no. 4 (December 1977): 443–471.

Berto, Frank J. "The Electric Streetcar and the End of the First American Bicycle Boom." In *Cycle History 17: Proceedings of the 17th International Cycling History Conference*, edited by Glen Norcliffe, 91–100. San Francisco: Cycle Publishing, 2007.

———. "The Great American Bicycle Boom." In *Cycle History 10: Proceedings of the 10th International Cycling History Conference*, edited by Hans-Erhard Lessing, Rob van der Plas, and Andrew Ritchie, 133–141. San Francisco: Van der Plas Publications, 1999.

———. "Who Invented the Mountain Bike?" In *Cycle History 8: Proceedings of the 8th International Cycling History Conference*, edited by Nicholas Oddy and Rob van der Plas, 25–48. San Francisco: Van der Plas, 1998.

Berto, Frank, Ron Shepherd, and Raymond Henry. *The Dancing Chain: History and Development of the Derailleur Bicycle*. San Francisco: Van der Plas, 2000.

Bicycle Motocross Action. "Full Bore Cruisers." January 1980.

Bicycling World. "The Clubs Reviewed." November 15, 1879.

———. "Col. A. A. Pope." August 27, 1886.

———. "The English and French Champions in Boston." November 15, 1879.

———. "Harry Corey Abroad." December 2, 1887.

———. "The Ladies' Dart Bicycle." March 30, 1888.

———. "Looking Backward Twenty-Five Years and Beyond." December 18, 1902.

———. "'Papa' Weston Thumbs Back Numbers." December 18, 1902.

———. "Racing News." March 19, 1886.

———. "Racing News." October 15, 1886.

———. "Safety Machines." November 6, 1885.

———. "The 60-Hour Professional Race." November 15, 1879.

Bicycling World and Motorcycle Review. "How to Stop the 'Knocking.'" March 12, 1903.

———. "The Use of Three-Speed Bicycles in the War." January 19, 1915.

Bijker, Wiebe E. *Of Bicycles, Bakelites, and Bulbs: Toward a Theory of Sociotechnical Change*. Cambridge, MA: MIT Press, 1995.

Bikes Direct. "What Does It Weigh?" Retrieved from bikesdirect.com.

Bishop, Joseph B. "Social and Economic Influence of the Bicycle." *Forum*, August 1896.

Bisland, Mary L. "Woman's Cycle." *Godey's*, April 1896.

Bismarck Daily Tribune, "The Bicycle Score." December 25, 1886.

———. "The Bicycle Tournament." December 24, 1886.

Black, Herbert. "Dr. Paul Dudley White, Heart Pioneer, Dies at 87." *Boston Globe*, November 1, 1973.

Bloomer, D. C. *Life and Writings of Amelia Bloomer*. Boston: Arena, 1895.

Blumberg, Arnold. "Pedal Power." *Vietnam*, August 2012.

Bly, Nelly. "Champion of Her Sex." *New York Sunday World*, February 2, 1896.

Bodfish. "The Very First Off-Road Bike Race (Maybe)." *Mountain Bike*, November–December 1988.

Boos, E. H. "Are Wheeling South." *Daily Missoulian*, July 3, 1897.

———. "From Fort to Fort." *Daily Missoulian*, July 17, 1897.

———. "Nebraska Is Reached: Marching On." *Daily Missoulian*, July 17, 1897.

———. "Off for St. Louis." *Daily Missoulian*, June 14, 1897.

Borstelmann, Thomas. *The 1970s: A New Global History from Civil Rights to Economic Inequality*. Princeton, NJ: Princeton University Press, 2012.

Boston Daily Advertiser. "Music and the Drama." June 23, 1874.

Boston Daily Journal. "Velocipede Race at Nashua N.H." February 12, 1869.

Boston Medical and Surgical Journal. "Bicycle Accidents." Vol. 135, no. 4 (July 23, 1896): 95–96.

———. "Routine Practice." Vol. 108, no. 2 (January 11, 1883): 42–43.

Boston Morning Journal. "Angeline Allen's Anger." November 8, 1893.

Boviere, Edmund. "In Behalf of the Boys." *Outing*, August 188.

Bowerman, William. *The Joggers Manual*. 1963.

Brain, John. "John Brain's History of Kustom Biking." Retrieved from bikerodnkustom5.homestead.com.

Branchik, Blaine J., ed. *Marketing History at the Center: Proceedings of the 13th Biennial Conference on Historical Analysis and Research in Marketing (CHARM)*. Durham, N.C: Duke University, 2007.

Breeze, Joe. "Repack History." Retrieved from mmbhof.org.

———. With Charlie Kelly and Otis Guy. "Response to Berto's 'Who Invented the Mountain Bike?'" In *Cycle History 8: Proceedings of the 8th International Cycling History Conference*, edited by Nicholas Oddy and Rob van der Plas, 157–160. San Francisco: Van der Plas, 1998.

Brown, W. H. "A Form of Neuralgia Occurring in Cyclists." *British Medical Journal* 1, no. 1939 (February 26, 1898): 553.

Bruchey, Stuart Weems. *Enterprise: The Dynamic Economy of a Free People*. Cambridge, MA: President and Fellows of Harvard University, 1990.

Buckley, Tom. "Mercury on 2 Wheels." *New York Times*, August 4, 1976.

Buehler, Ralph, and John Pucher. "Cycling to Work in 90 Large American Cities: New Evidence on the Role of Bike Paths and Lanes." *Transportation* 39 (March 2012): 409–432.

Buffalo Evening News. "Lads Will Race." August 27, 1896.

Bullock, W. "Sketch of a Journey through the Western States of North America, from New Orleans, by the Mississippi, Ohio, City of Cincinnati and Falls of Niagara, to New York, in 1827." In *Early Western Travels, 1748–1846*, edited by Reuben Gold Thwaites, 19:119–154. Cleveland: Clark, 1905.

Burchett, Wilfred G. *Vietnam: Inside Story of the Guerrilla War*. New York: International Publishers, 1965.

Burgess, Bruce, and Dan Burden. *Bicycle Safety Highway Users Information Report*. Washington, DC: Department of Transportation, National Highway Traffic Safety Administration, January 1978.

Burns, Terry. "How Fast Could They Travel?" Retrieved from terryburns.net.

Burr, Thomas Cameron. "Markets as Producers and Consumers: The French and U.S. National Bicycle Markets, 1875–1910." PhD diss., University of California, Davis, 2005.

Business Week. "Bicycle Makers Shift Gears to Catch a Fad." June 19, 1978.

Callahan, Raymond. *The Worst Disaster: The Fall of Singapore*. Newark: University of Delaware Press, 1977.

Camp, Walter. "Base-Ball For The Spectator." *Century*, October 1889.

Campbell Davidson, Lillias. "The Evolution in Feminine Cycling." *Wheel and Cycling Trade Review*, October 26, 1888.

Canary, Peyton. "Bicycle Thievery a Big Business." *Los Angeles Times*, April 25, 1971.

Capron, Horace. *Report of the Commissioner of Agriculture for the Year 1868*. Washington, DC: Government Printing Office, 1869.

Cardoza, Kerry. "Millennials Lead Trend in Less Car-Ownership, Driving." Retrieved from newsarchive.medill.northwestern.edu.

Carter, Jimmy. "Our Nation's Past and Future." Retrieved from presidency.ucsb.edu.

Cartnal, Alan. "75 Million Spokesmen Boost Bicycling." *Los Angeles Times*, June 13, 1971.

Casey, Phil. "Some Stand Pat; Some Stand Still." *Washington Post*, April 25, 1969.

Cater, Franklyn. "Motorists to Urban Planners: Stay in Your Lane." Retrieved from npr.org.

Center of Military History. *United States Army in the World War, 1917–1919*, vol. 1: *Organization of the American Expeditionary Forces*. Washington, DC: US Army, 1988.

———. *United States Army in the World War, 1917–1919*, vol. 16: *General Orders, GHQ, AEF*. Washington, DC: US Army, 1992.

Century. "Bicycle Problems and Benefits." July 1895.

———. "The Reign of the Bicycle." December 1894.

Chapple, Joe Mitchell. "Flashlights of Famous People." *St. Petersburg (FL) Evening Independent*, May 22, 1924.

Chevalier, Michael. *Society, Manners, and Politics in the United States: Being a Series of Letters on North America*. Boston: Weeks, Jordan, 1839.

Chicago Daily Tribune. "Cycling's Death Excites Wonder." September 4, 1902.

———. "The Uses of Society Fads." September 16, 1901.

Chicago Tribune. "Americanitis." September 22, 1895.

———. "Bikes Play Big Role in Much of World." August 22, 1965.

———. "Youths Riding to Prison on Stolen Bikes." June 29, 1943.

Childe, Cromwell. "The Bicycle in Battle." *Los Angeles Herald*, December 16, 1891.

Christensen, Matthew, and Susan Shaheen. "Can Bikeshare Systems Ever Stand on Their Own Two Wheels?" Retrieved from theconversation.com.

Chronic, R. "Dandies & Wooden Horses." *New-York Evening Post*, July 29, 1819.

Chudacoff, Howard P. *Children at Play: An American History*. New York: New York University Press, 2007.

——— "Child's Play: A Brief History of American Childhood." *Antiques*, July 1, 2014.

Churchill, Winston. *The Hinge of Fate*. New York: Mariner Books, 1985. Orig. pub. 1950.

Cincinnati Daily Gazette. "The Bicycles of the Rampage." January 12, 1869.

———. "Edward Payson Weston." December 12, 1867.

City of Washington Gazette. "Cincinnati, May 17." June 3, 1820.

Clark, A. S., ed. *The London Cyclist Battalion: A Chronicle of Events Connected with the 26th Middlesex (Cyclist) V.R.C., and the 25th (C. of L.) Cyclist Battalion, the London Regiment, and Military Cycling in General*. London: Forster, Groom, 1932.

Clayton, Nicholas. "Of Bicycles, Bijker, and Bunkum." In *Cycle History 10: Proceedings of the 10th International Cycling History Conference*, edited by Hans-Erhard Lessing, Rob van der Plas, and Andrew Ritchie, 11–24. San Francisco: Van der Plas, 1999.

———. "Who Invented the Penny-Farthing?" In *Cycle History [7]: Proceedings of the 7th International Cycle History Conference*, edited by Rob Van der Plas, 31–42. San Francisco: Rob van der Plas, 1997.

C.L.C. "Hub of All Wheeldom." *Washington Post*, September 6, 1896.

Clinton (NY) Courier. "The Economy of Good Roads." March 23, 1892.

C&O Canal Association. "Steamboats on the C&O Canal." Retrieved from candocanal.org.

Cohn, D'Vera. "After Decades of Decline, a Rise in Stay-at-Home Mothers." *Pew Social Trends*, April 8, 2014.

Cole, George M. *Report of the Adjutant-General, State of Connecticut, to the Commander-in-Chief, for the Year Ended September 30, 1901*. Bridgeport, CT: Marigold–Foster Printing Company, 1901.

Colen, B. D. "Just 10 Blocks and 10 Speeds." *Washington Post*, October 14, 1971. [The author's surname is misspelled in print as "Cohen."]

Collins, Glenn. "Selling Online, Delivering on Bike." *New York Times*, December 24, 1999.

Collins, Mary. *American Idle: A Journey through Our Sedentary Culture*. Sterling, VA: Capital, 2009.

Conniff, Richard. "Mammoths and Mastodons: All American Monsters." *Smithsonian*, April 2010.

Conroy, Sarah Booth. "The Very Best Is a Clean Machine." *Washington Post*, July 18, 1971.

Corliss, Carlton. *The Day of Two Noons*. Washington, DC: Association of American Railroads, 1952.

Costa e Silva, Jorge Alberto, and Giovanni de Girolamo, "Neurasthenia: History of a Concept." In *Psychological Disorders in General Medical Settings*, edited by N. Sartorius, D. Goldberg, G. de Girolamo, J. Costa e Silva, Y. Lecrubier, and U. Wittchen, 69–81. Toronto: Hogrefe und Huber, 1990.

Cozzens, Peter, ed. *Eyewitness to the Indian Wars, 1865–1890, vol. 5*. Mechanicsburg, PA: Stackpole, 2005.

Crane, Stephen. *Crane: Prose and Poetry*. New York: Penguin Putnam, 1984.

Cranor, David. "Standard Responses #3: Response to 'Cyclists Cause Congestion.'" Retrieved from thewashcycle.com.

Critic. "The Modern Magazine." May 26, 1894.

Crouch, Tom D. *The Bishop's Boys: A Life of Wilbur and Orville Wright*. New York: Norton, 1989.

———. *A Dream of Wings: Americans and the Airplane, 1875–1905*. New York: Norton, 1981.

———. "Engineers and the Airplane: Aeronautics in the Pre-Wright Era." In *The Wright Brothers: Heirs of Prometheus*, edited by Richard P. Hallion, 3–19. Washington, DC: National Air and Space Museum, 1978.

———. "Kill Devil Hills, 17 December 1903." *Technology and Culture* 40, no. 3 (July 1999): 595–598.

———. *Lighter than Air: An Illustrated History of Balloons and Airships*. Baltimore: Johns Hopkins University Press, 2009.

———. "Wheeling and Flying: How the Bicycle Took Wing." In *Cycle History 22: Proceedings of the 22nd International Cycling History Conference*, edited by Andrew Ritchie and Gary Sanderson, 113–122. Cheltenham, UK: Cycling History, 2012.

Crown, Judith, and Glenn Coleman. *No Hands: The Rise and Fall of the Schwinn Bicycle Company, an American Institution*. New York: Holt, 1996.

Cudahy, Brian J. "Mass Transportation in the Cities of America: A Short History and a Current Perspective." Retrieved from inventors.about.com.

Cunningham, Bill. "Now in the Mainstream: Cyclists' Garb." *New York Times*, August 23, *1987*.

Cunningham, Patricia A., and Susan Voto Lab, eds. *Dress and Popular Culture*. Bowling Green, Ohio: Bowling Green State University Popular Press, 1991.

Cycling. "From Liege to Paris." February 21, 1918.

Daily Inter Ocean. "The Northwest." *April* 30, 1874.

———. "Snow in Iowa." December 29, *1891*.

———. "Sports Locked Up." December 23, 1886.

———. "An Upper Cut." December 22, *1886*.

Daily Iowa State Register. "Edward *Payson* Weston." November 1, 1867.
———. "Gravel!" February 26, *1869*.
———. "The Velocipede Race." February 26, 1869.
———. "Weather Record for Week Ending Feb. 27, 1869." February 28, 1869.
Daily National Intelligencer. "Arrived on Friday Evening Last." March 18, 1823.
Daily the Pak Banker. "Explosions in *Quetta*, Peshawar Kill 14, Injure 65." March 15, 2014.
D'Ambrosio, Dan. "Thirty *Years* and Counting." *Adventure Cyclist*, July 2006.
Davies, T. S. "On the Velocipede, May 1837." *Boneshaker*, Autumn 1985.
Davis, Richard Harding. "The Germans in Brussels." *Scribner's*, November 1914.
Degnon, Dick. "High Handlebar Fad Draws Official Frowns." *Los Angeles Times*, January 10, 1960.
De la Peña, Carolyn Thomas. *The Body Electric: How Strange Machines Built the Modern American*. New York: New York University Press, 2003.
Dennis, Bernard G., Jr., Robert J. Kapsch, Robert J., Robert LoContee, Robert, Bruce W. Mattheiss, Bruce W., and Steven M. Pennington, Steven M., eds. *American Civil Engineering History: The Pioneering Years*. Washington, DC: American Society of Civil Engineers, 2003.
Denny, Harold. "Normandy Battle Is Hedge to Hedge." *New York Times*, July 6, 1944.
Denver Evening Post. "Indiana Will Send Bicycle Corps." March 14, 1898.
Depew, Chauncey M. *One Hundred Years of* American *Commerce*. New York: Haynes, 1895.
Desty, Robert, ed. *Lawyers' Reports, Annotated, book 8*. Rochester, NY: Lawyers' Co-Operative Publishing Company, 1890.
Detroit *Bulletin of Pharmacy*. "Cycling Versus Morphine." Vol. 10, no. 6 (June 1896): 282.
Devlin, John C. "150 Cycle to Fair in Rules Protest." *New York Times*, May 18, 1964.
Dhar, Rohin. "The Fixie Bike Index." Retrieved from priceonomics.com.
Diana, Chelsea. "Maine Woman Resisted the Nazis on a Beat-Up Old Bicycle." *Portland Press Herald and Maine Sunday Telegram*, June 8, 2014.
Dickerson, Miriam, ed. *Cycling Handbook*. Chicago: League of American Wheelmen, 1947.

Dillon, Sally. "Bicycle Belles: Ladies' Bicycling Fashion in the Mid-1890s." In *Cycling History 14: Proceedings of the 14th International Cycling History Conference*, edited by Ron Shepherd, 92–103. Dickson, Australia: Canberra Bicycle Museum, 2003.

District of Columbia Daily Critic. "Critic Gossip." September 17, 1873.

Do, Tran. *Récits sur Dien Bien Phu*. Hanoi: Éditions en Langues Étrangéres, 1962.

Dodge, Pryor. *The Bicycle*. New York: Flammarion, 1996.

Dohrn-van Rossum, Gerhard. *History of the Hour: Clocks and Modern Temporal Orders*. Chicago: University of Chicago Press, 1996.

Dollar, Charles M. "Putting the Army on Wheels." In *Buffalo Soldiers in the West*, edited by Bruce A. Glasrud, 242–256. College Station: Texas A&M University Press, 2007.

Dougherty, Nina, and William Lawrence. *Bicycle Transportation*. Washington, DC: US Environmental Protection Agency, December 1974.

Downey, Fairfax. "It Wasn't Always Boxcars." *American Legion Weekly*, September 18, 1925.

Downey, Gregory J. *Telegraph Messenger Boys: Labor, Technology, and Geography, 1850–1950*. New York: Routledge, 2002.

Duluth News-Tribune. "Decidedly Unconventional." November 29, 1893.

Dundee (Scotland) Evening Telegraph. "A Lady on Tricycling." April 17, 1885.

Dunham, Norman L. "The Bicycle Era in American History." PhD diss., Harvard University, 1956.

Durand, William F. "Biographical Memoir of Orville Wright, 1871–1948." In National Academy of Sciences, *Biographical Memoirs*, 25:255–274. Washington, DC: National Academy of Sciences, 1948.

Dutzik, Tony, Jeff Inglis, and Phineas Baxandall. *Millennials in Motion: Changing Travel Habits of Young Americans and the Implications for Public Policy*. US PIRG Education Fund Frontier Group, October 2014.

Dzierzak, Lou. *The Evolution of American Bicycle Racing*. Guilford, CT: Globe Pequot, 2007.

E. C. Stearns & Co. "The Best Bicycle Is None Too Good For You." *Godey's*, June 1895.

Edgerton, David. *The Shock of the Old: Technology and Global History since 1900*. New York: Oxford University Press, 2007.

Edmonds, Richard H. "A Decade of Marvelous Progress." *Engineering*, September 1893.

Egan, F. A. "The Evolution of a Sport." *Godey's*, April 1896.

Ehrlich, Paul R. *The Population Bomb*. New York: Ballantine, 1968.

Elliott, J. B. *Life and Career of the Celebrated Elliott Family*. Undated monograph.

Emmott, N. W. "The Devil's Watering Pot." *United States Naval Institute Proceedings*, September 1972.

Engelking, Barbara, and Jacek Leociak. *The Warsaw Ghetto: A Guide to the Perished City*. Translated by Emma Harris. New Haven, CT: Yale University Press, 2009.

English Mechanic and World of Science. "Bicycle Riding." December 23, 1870.

Epperson, Bruce D. *Bicycles in American Highway Planning: The Critical Years of Policy-Making, 1969–1991*. Jefferson, NC: McFarland, 2014.

———. "Failed Colossus: Strategic Error at the Pope Manufacturing Company, 1878–1900." *Technology and Culture* 41, no. 2 (April 2000): 300–320.

———. "'The Finances Stagger These Fellows': The Great American Bicycle Trust, 1899–1903." *International Journal of the History of Sport* 28, no. 18 (December 2011): 2633–2652.

———. "How Many Bikes?" In *Cycle History 11: Proceedings, 11th International Cycling History Conference*, edited by Andrew Ritchie and Rob van der Plas, 42–50. San Francisco: Van der Plas, 2001.

———. *Peddling Bicycles to America: The Rise of an Industry*. Jefferson, NC: McFarland, 2010.

Ernst, C. W. "Boston and Transportation." In *Proceedings of the Bostonian Society*, vol. 4, *1898–1902*, 18–31. Boston: Old State House, 1898.

Esfehani, Amir Moghaddass. "The Bicycle and the Chinese People." In *Cycle History [13]: Proceedings of the 13th International Cycle History Conference*, edited by Andrew Ritchie and Nicholas Clayton, 94–102. San Francisco: Rob van der Plas, 2003.

Evans, Richard J. *The Third Reich in Power*. New York: Penguin, 2005.

Fachet, Robert. "Cycling." *Washington Post*, August 13, 1984.

Falk, Stanley L. "'Victory Disease' and the Defeat of Japan." *Army*, February 2014.

Fall, Bernard B. *The Viet-Minh Regime: Government and Administration in the Democratic Republic of Vietnam*. New York: Institute of Pacific Relations, 1956.

Farley, Reynolds, ed. *State of the Union: America in the 1990s, vol. 1*. New York: Russell Sage Foundation, 1995.

Feng, Patrick. "The Krag-Jørgensen Rifle." Retrieved from armyhistoryjournal.com.

Fifty Years of Schwinn-Built Bicycles: The Story of the Bicycle and Its Contribution to Our Way of Life. Chicago: Arnold, Schwinn, 1945.

Fincher, Jean. "Bikes Causing Chain Reaction." *Los Angeles Times*, August 6, 1966.

Finder, Alan. "New York to Ban Bicycles on 3 Major Avenues." *New York Times*, July 23, 1987.

Fink, Sören, and Hans-Erhard Lessing. "Karl Drais: All about the Beginnings of Individual Mobility." Retrieved from www.karldrais.de.

Finletter, Thomas K. "Air Power in the Korean Conflict." *Vital Speeches of the Day*, September 15, 1950.

Fisher, Adam. "Rollin' Large." *Bicycling*, January 7, 2014.

Fishman, Elliot, Simon Washington, and Narelle Haworth. "Bike Share: A Synthesis of the Literature." *Transport Reviews* 33, no. 2 (March 2013): 148–165.

Fitzpatrick, Jim. *The Bicycle in Wartime: An Illustrated History*. Dulles, VA: Brassey's, 1998.

Fonda, Jane. "A Vietnam Journal: Rebirth of a Nation." *Rolling Stone*, July 4, 1974.

Forbes. "What Kind of Bike D'Ya Ride?" December 1, 1970.

Forbes, Vernon. "Cycles and the Drive for Improvement." In *Cycle History 25: Proceedings of the 25th International Cycling History Conference*, edited by Andrew Ritchie and Gary Sanderson, 70–75. Birmingham, UK: Cycling History, 2015.

Ford, Henry. *My Life and Work*. Garden City, NY: Garden City Publishing, 1922.

Forest and Stream. "Rational Pastimes." November 5, 1874.

Fortune. "A Bicycle Rampant." September 1933.

Foster, Maximilian. "The Sport of Flying." *Outing*, May 1909.

Fox, Richard Wightman, and T. J. Jackson Lears, eds. *The Culture of Consumption: Critical Essays in American History, 1880–1980*. New York: Pantheon, 1983.

Franklin, H. Bruce. "By the Bombs' Early Light; Or, The Quiet American's War on Terror." *Nation*, February 3, 2003.

Friedersdorf, Conor. "Working Mom Arrested for Letting Her 9-Year-Old Play Alone at Park." *Atlantic*, July 15, 2014.

Friedman, Charles. "Bicycles Make a Jet-Age Comeback." *New York Times*, May 29, 1960.

Friends for Bikecology. *Bikecology Overview*. 1971.

Friss, Evan. "The Cycling City: Bicycles and the Transformation of Urban America." PhD diss., City University of New York, 2011.

Fritz, Michael. "City's Courier Companies Rush to Beat Competition." *Newsday*, July 14, 1986.

Furness, Zack. *One Less Car: Bicycling and the Politics of Automobility*. Philadelphia: Temple University Press, 2010.

Gage-Downs Company. "As Graceful as the New Woman." *Munsey's*, June 1896.

Galaxy. "Drift-Wood." October 1868.

Galison, Peter. *Einstein's Clocks, Poincaré's Maps: Empires of Time*. New York: Norton, 2003.

Garvey, Ellen Gruber. *The Adman in the Parlor: Magazines and the Gendering of Consumer Culture, 1880s to 1910s*. New York: Oxford University Press, 1996.

Gelinas, Nicole. "Bike Share's Promise and Peril." Retrieved from city-journal.org.

Giap, Vo Nguyen. *Banner of People's War, the Party's Military Line*. New York: Praeger, 1970.

———. *People's War, People's Army*. Hanoi: Foreign Languages Publishing House, 1974.

Gibson, Campbell J., and Emily Lennon. "Historical Census Statistics on the Foreign-born Population of the United States: 1850–1990." Retrieved from census.gov.

Giddings, Howard A. "Report of Major Howard A. Giddings, Brigade Inspector, C.N.G." In George M. Cole, *Report of the Adjutant-General, State of Connecticut, to the Commander-in-Chief, For the Year Ended September 30, 1901*, 122–125. Bridgeport, CT: Marigold–Foster Printing Company, 1901.

Gilbert, Robert E. "Eisenhower's 1955 Heart Attack." *Politics and the Life Sciences* 27, no. 1 (June 24, 2008): 2–21.

Gillet, Kit. "Riding Vietnam's Ho Chi Minh Trail." *Guardian*, July 28, 2011.

Girard, Jolyon P., ed. *The Greenwood Encyclopedia of Daily Life in America*, vol. 4. Westport, CT: Greenwood, 2006.

Girdler, Allan. "First Fired, First Forgotten." *Cycle World*, February 1998.

Glacier John. "70s Bike Boom and 'Breaking Away' Movie." Retrieved from bikeforums.net.

Glenn H. Curtiss Museum. "Glenn Hammond Curtiss." Retrieved from glennhcurtissmuseum.org.

Gluskin Townley Group. "National Bicycle Dealers Association (NBDA) U.S. Bicycle Overview Report." 2013.

Goldstein, Patrick. "Spike Lee—A Jump Shot into the Big Time." *Los Angeles Times*, February 12, 1988.

Good Health. "The Perils of Exercise." October 1891.

Goodman, Cary. *Choosing Sides: Playground and Street Life on the Lower East Side*. New York: Schocken, 1979.

Goodman, J. David. "The Messenger Goes Hollywood." *New York Times*, October 2, 2011.

Good Roads. "The Editor's Table." April 1892.

Gormully & Jeffery Manufacturing Company. "Read This, Gentlemen!!!" *Bicycling World*, January 14, 1887.

———. "Wheeling Companionship." *Ladies' Home Journal*, June 1894.

Greene, Ann Norton. *Horses at Work: Harnessing Power in Industrial America*. Cambridge, MA: Harvard University Press, 2008.

Grilley, Virginia. "Bicycle Sea." *Christian Science Monitor*, July 30, 1965.

Guardian. "D-Day: Secret Maps." May 28, 1994.

H.A. "*By-the-Bye* in Wall Street." *Wall Street Journal*, August 21, 1933.

Hadland, Tony, and Hans-Erhard Lessing. *Bicycle Design: An Illustrated History*. Cambridge, MA: MIT Press, 2014.

Hale, Bill. "First Person." *Chicago Tribune*, July 7, 1985.

Hall, Florence Howe. *Social Customs*. Boston: Estes and Lauriat, 1887.

Hallenbeck, Sarah Overbaugh. "Writing the Bicycle: Women, Rhetoric, and Technology in Late Nineteenth-Century America." PhD diss., University of North Carolina, Chapel Hill, 2009.

Haller, John S., Jr., and Robin Haller. *The Physician and Sexuality in Victorian America*. New York: Norton, 1974.

Hallion, Richard P., ed. *The Wright Brothers: Heirs of Prometheus*. Washington, DC: National Air and Space Museum, 1978.

Happel, T. J. "The Bicycle from a Medical and Surgical Standpoint." *Memphis Medical Monthly* 18, no. 9 (September 1898): 394–402.

Harper, Ida Husted. *The Life and Work of Susan B. Anthony*. Indianapolis: Bowen-Merrill, 1898.

Harper's Weekly. "Go Easy, Bicyclists!" May 23, 1896.

———. "The Pedestrian Feat." November 16, 1867.

Harris, Susan E. *Horse Gaits, Balance, and Movement*. Hoboken, NJ: Howell Book House, 1993.

Harris, Waldo A., William Bowerman, Bruce McFadden, and Thomas Kerns. "Jogging: An Adult Exercise Program." *Journal of the American Medical Association* 201, no. 10 (September 4, 1967): 759–761.

Harris, William T. *Report of the Commissioner of Education for the Year 1897–98*. Washington, DC: Government Printing Office, 1899.

Hartford (CT) Daily Courant. "News of the State, All Sorts." May 17, 1873.

Hatch, Amy. "The Terrifying Time My Kid Went around the Block Alone." Retrieved from blogs.babycenter.com.

Hawley, C. E. "Uses of the Bicycle." *Wheelman*, October 1882.

Heath, Perry S. *Rural Free Delivery: Its History and Development*. Washington, DC: Government Printing Office, 1899.

Heidler, David S., and Jeanne T. Heidler. *Daily Life in the Early American Republic, 1790–1820*. Westport, CT: Greenwood, 2004.

Henderson, Keith. "The 10-Speed Dream." *Christian Science Monitor*, March 26, 1975.

Herlihy, David V. *Bicycle: The History*. New Haven, CT: Yale University Press, 2004.

———. *The Lost Cyclist: The Epic Tale of an American Adventurer and His Mysterious Disappearance*. New York: Mariner, 2011.

Herman, Lewis, and Marguerite Shalette Herman. *Foreign Dialects: A Manual for Actors, Directors, and Writers*. London: Routledge, 1997.

Hesseldahl, Arik. "Seven Questions for Nathaniel Borenstein, Who Made Email Attachments Easy." Retrieved from allthingsd.com.

Higgins, Mike. "Following the Lieutenant." Retrieved from followingthelieutenant.blogspot.com.

———. "The 25th Infantry Bicycle Corps." Retrieved from bicyclecorps.blogspot.com.

Higman, H. D. "The Founding of the Dunlop Tyre Company." In *Cycle History [5]: Proceedings of the 5th International Cycle History Conference*, edited by Rob van der Plas, 91–94. San Francisco: Bicycle Books, 1995.

History of War. "War on the Beaches." June 2014.

H.O. "The Philosophy of the Velocipede." *Scientific American*, September 23, 1868.

Hobsbawm, Eric. "Mass-Producing Traditions: Europe, 1870–1914." In *The Invention of Tradition*, ed. Eric Hobsbawm and Eric Ranger, 263–307. Cambridge: Cambridge University Press, 1992.

Hodge, Paul. "'Bikecentennial' Will Begin along 4,250-Mile Route." *Washington Post*, May 10, 1976.

———. "Magnificent Trails Are Planned, but Will Bikers Ever Ride Them?" *Washington Post*, April 22, 1976.

Holloway, Lynette. "A Leg Up: Messengers Were the Medium." *New York Times*, June 16, 1996.

Holt, Glen E. "The Changing Perception of Urban Pathology: An Essay on the Development of Mass Transit in the United States." In *Cities in American History*, edited by Kenneth T. Jackson and Stanley K. Schultz, 324–343. New York: Knopf, 1972.

Hone, Philip. *The Diary of Philip Hone, 1828–1851*. New York: Dodd, Mead, 1889.

Hoover, Ken. "Carl Sparks." *San Francisco Chronicle*, July 20, 1994.

Hornaday, Mary. "U.S. Takes to Bicycling—at Last." *Christian Science Monitor*, December 30, 1967.

Hosler, Roderick A. "Hell on Two Wheels: The 25th Infantry Bicycle Corps." Retrieved from armyhistoryjournal.com.

Houghton, Walter R. *American Etiquette and Rules of Politeness*. Chicago: Rand McNally, 1889.

Hounshell, David A. *From the American System to Mass Production, 1800–1932: The Development of Manufacturing Technology in the United States*. Baltimore: Johns Hopkins University Press, 1984.

Howard, T. J. "Wheel Thrills." *Chicago Tribune*, May 15, 1991.

Howe, Robert F. "Waitress at Va. Bar Alleges Sexual Harassment in Suit." *Washington Post*, May 8, 1991.

Howells, W. D. "By Horse-Car to Boston." *Atlantic Monthly*, January 1870.

Hoyt, Monty. "More U.S. Families Choosing Bikes as Best Way to Get Around." *Christian Science Monitor*, November 15, 1972.

Huffman Manufacturing Company. "This Huffy Is One Reason you See More Adults on Bicycles Today." *Life*, November 5, 1965.

Huffy History . . . and Museum. "1962–1963." Retrieved from huffyhistory.webs.com.

Hugill, Peter J. "Good Roads and the Automobile in the United States 1880–1929." *Geographical Review* 72, no. 3 (July 1982): 327–349.

Hussey, Kristin. "First in Flight? Connecticut Stakes a Claim." *New York Times*, April 17, 2015.

Idaho Daily Statesman. "Excuse for Bad Roads." July 7, 1892.

Indiana State Journal. "The Bicycle Craze." June 10, 1896.

Isaacson, Walter. *Einstein: His Life and Universe*. New York: Simon and Schuster, 2007.

Iver Johnson's Arms & Cycle Works. "Personal—for Boys Only." *Youth's Companion*, December 9, 1926.

Jackson, Kenneth. *Crabgrass Frontier: The Suburbanization of the United States*. New York: Oxford University Press, 1985.

Jacobs, Sanford L. "Western Union Corp. Launches Jazzy Era of Telegraph Offices." *Wall Street Journal*, February 8, 1973.

Jacobson, Lisa. *Raising Consumers: Children and the American Mass Market in the Early Twentieth Century*. New York: Columbia University Press, 2004.

Jamerson, Frank E. "2014 Update to 2013 Edition." With Ed Benjamin. *Electric Bikes Worldwide Reports*. February 2014.

James, Craig R., ed. *Anthropology and Epidemiology*. Dordrecht: Reidel, 1986.

Jensen, Trevor. "Eugene A. Sloane: 1916–2008." *Chicago Tribune*, April 1, 2008.

Jewell, James Robbins. "Using Barbaric Methods in South Africa: The British Concentration Camp Policy during the Anglo-Boer War." *Scientia Militaria: South African Journal of Military Studies* 31, no. 1 (2003): 1–18.

Joselit, Jenna Weissman. *A Perfect Fit: Clothes, Character, and the Promise of America*. New York: Metropolitan, 2001.

Journal of the Military Service Institution of the United States. "The Adaptation of the Bicycle to Military Uses." November 1895.

Judge. "The World on Wheels." May 1894.

Kaempffert, Waldemar. "Why Flying-Machines Fly." *Harper's Monthly*, April 1911.

Kanfer, Stefan. "The Full Circle: In Praise of the Bicycle." *Time*, April 28, 1975.

Kansas City Star. "Mrs. Angeline Allen's Bathing Dress." August 30, 1893.

Keegan, John. *The Second World War*. New York: Viking Penguin, 1990.

Kelly, Charles, and Nick Crane. *Richard's Mountain Bike Book*. New York: Ballantine, 1988.

Kelly, Charlie. "Clunkers among the Hills." *Bicycling*, January 1979.

———. *Fat Tire Flyer: Repack and the Birth of Mountain Biking*. Boulder, CO: Velo Press, 2014.

———. "Repack Page." Retrieved from sonic.net.

Kelly, Fred C. *The Wright Brothers: A Biography Authorized by Orville Wright*. New York: Harcourt, Brace, 1943.

Kelly, John. "A Look Back at the Early Days of Bicycling Laws." *Washington Post*, July 21, 2014.

Kern, Stephen. *The Culture of Time and Space, 1880–1918*. Cambridge, MA: Harvard University Press, 2003.

Kidder, Jeffrey L. *Urban Flow: Bike Messengers in the City*. Ithaca, NY: Cornell University Press, 2011.

Kilian, Michael. "Jogging: The Newest Road to Fitness." *Chicago Tribune*, July 9, 1968.

Kingbay, Keith. *Inside Bicycling*. Chicago: Regnery, 1976.

Kipling, Rudyard. "New York Described by Rudyard Kipling." *Bush Advocate*, September 3, 1892.

Klaffke, Pamela. *Spree: A Cultural History of Shopping*. Vancouver: Arsenal Pulp Press, 2003.

Klein, Alexander. "Personal Income of the United States: Estimates for the Period 1880–1910." Warwick Economic Research Papers no. 916. Coventry, UK: University of Warwick, 2009.

Klemesrud, Judy. "Bicycling: The Individualist's Mode of Transport." *New York Times*, May 4, 1970.

Kolbert, Elizabeth. "In the Air." *New Yorker*, April 27, 2009.

Komanoff, Charles. "The Bicycle Uprising: Remembering the Midtown Bike Ban 25 Years Later, Part 1." Retrieved from streetsblog.org.

KPIX. "Klunkers." Retrieved from youtube.com.

Kratoska, Paul H. *The Japanese Occupation of Malaya: A Social and Economic History*. London: Hurst, 1998.

Kreider, Rose M., and Diana B. Elliott. "Historical Changes in Stay-at-Home Mothers: 1969–2009." Paper presented at the American Sociological Association annual meetings, 2010.

Krstic, Dord. *Mileva and Albert Einstein: Their Love and Scientific Collaboration*. Radovljica, Slovenia: Didakta, 2004.

Kugelmass, Jack M. "I'd Rather Be a Messenger." *Natural History*, August 1981, 66–73.

Lacouture, Jean. Preface to Vo Nguyen Giap, *In Banner of People's War: The Party's Military Line*, vii–x. New York: Praeger, 1970.

Landers, Rich. "Trail of Memories." *Spokane Spokesman-Review*, June 2, 1996.

Lane, Lydia. "Exercise Is Helpful, but Do Not Overdo It." *Los Angeles Times*, April 28, 1949.

Lane, Viona Elliott, Randall Merris, and Chris Algar. "Tommy Elliott and the Musical Elliotts." In *Papers of the International Concertina Association*, edited by Allan Atlas, 5:16–49. New York: Center for the Study of Free-Reed Instruments, 2008.

Langley, S. P. "The Internal Work of the Wind." *American Journal of Science* 47 (January 1894): 41–63.

Larkin, Leonard. "My Old Bikes." *Strand*, October 1902.

Larson, Craig. "Frequent Wind Lifts Evacuees out of South Vietnam." *Marines*, May 1995.

Latham, Alan. "The History of a Habit: Jogging as a Palliative to Sedentariness in 1960s America." *Cultural Geographies* 22, no. 1 (January 2015): 103–126.

Latta, James W. *Annual Report of the Secretary of Internal Affairs of the Commonwealth of Pennsylvania for the Year Ending November 30, 1897*. Harrisburg, PA: Wm. Stanley Ray, 1898.

L.A.W. Bulletin and Good Roads. "The Bicycle and Real Estate." February 25, 1898.

———. "The Bicycle's Future." January 21, 1898.

———. "A Plea for Modern Tricycles." April 29, 1898.

L.A.W. Magazine. "Let Us Talk It Over Together." May 1901.

[L.A.W. Member] No. 68,146. "The Shenandoah Valley." *L.A.W. Bulletin and Good Roads*, July 31, 1896.

Leach, William. *Land of Desire: Merchants, Power, and the Rise of a New American Culture*. New York: Vintage, 1993.

League of American Bicyclists. "The Growth of Bike Commuting." Retrieved from bikeleague.org.

———. "Where We Ride: Analysis of Bicycle Commuting in American Cities." October 6, 2014.

Lears, T. J. Jackson. *Fables of Abundance: A Cultural History of Advertising in America*. New York: Basic Books, 1994.

———. *No Place of Grace: Antimodernism and the Transformation of American Culture, 1880–1920*. Chicago: University of Chicago Press, 1981.

———. *Rebirth of a Nation: The Making of Modern America, 1877–1920*. New York: HarperCollins, 2009.

Lebergott, Stanley. "Wage Trends, 1800–1900." In National Bureau of Economic Research, *Trends in the American Economy in the Nineteenth Century*, 449–499. Princeton, NJ: Princeton University Press, 1960.

Le Conte, Joseph. "New Lights on the Problem of Flying." *Popular Science*, April 1894.

Lee, Spike. *Spike Lee's Gotta Have It: Inside Guerrilla Filmmaking*. New York: Simon and Schuster, 1987.

Leiss, William, Stephen Kline, Sut Jhally, and Jacqueline Botterill. *Social Communication in Advertising: Consumption in the Mediated Marketplace*. New York: Routledge, 2005.

Leslies, Frank. "The Curse of Overwork." *Aberdeen (SD) Daily News*, August 22, 1888.

Lessing, Hans-Erhard. *Automobilität: Karl Drais und die unglaublichen Anfänge*. Leipzig: Maxime-Verlag, 2003.

———. "The Two-Wheeled Velocipede: A Solution to the Tambora Freeze of 1816." In *Cycle History 22: Proceedings of the 22nd International Cycling History Conference*, edited by Andrew Ritchie and Gary Sanderson, 180–188. Cheltenham, UK: Cycling History, 2012.

———. "What Led to the Invention of the Early Bicycle?" In *Cycle History 11: Proceedings, 11th International Cycling History Conference*, edited by Andrew Ritchie and Rob van der Plas, 28–36. San Francisco: Van der Plas, 2001.

Lessing, Hans-Erhard, Rob van der Plas, and Andrew Ritchie, eds. *Cycle History 10: Proceedings of the 10th International Cycling History Conference*. San Francisco: Van der Plas Publications, 1999.

Lévi-Strauss, Claude. *The Savage Mind*. Chicago: University of Chicago Press, 1966.

Levy, Frank. "Incomes and Income Inequality." In *State of the Union: America in the 1990s, vol. 1*, edited by Reynolds Farley, 1–57. New York: Russell Sage Foundation, 1995.

Lewis, George H., ed. *Side-Saddle on the Golden Calf*. Pacific Palisades, CA: Goodyear Publishing, 1972.

Lewis, Nelson P. "From Cobblestones to Asphalt and Brick." *Paving and Municipal Engineering*, April 1896.

Life. "Dr. White on Wheels." November 10, 1961.

———. "Life Guide." May 10, 1963.

Lilienthal, Otto. "Practical Experiments for the Development of Human Flight." In *The Aeronautical Annual*, edited by James Means, 7–20. Boston: Clarke, 1896.

Lindsey, Joe. "The Secret to Safer Cities." *Bicycling*, July 2015.

Lindsey, Robert. "Pedal Pushers Aim at the 60 M.P.H. Barrier." *New York Times*, October 28, 1979.

Literary Digest. "The Automobile Bicycle." October 14, 1899.

Longhurst, James. *Bike Battles: A History of Sharing the American Road*. Seattle: University of Washington Press, 2015.

———. "The Sidepath Not Taken: Bicycles, Taxes, and the Rhetoric of the Public Good in the 1890s." *Journal of Policy History* 25, no. 4 (October 2013): 557–586.

Los Angeles Times. "Anti-Bicycle Crusade." July 2, 1896.

———. "Balloon Title Born to World One Year Ago." May 25, 1924.

———. "Bicycle Boom Gives No Sign of Weakening." June 11, 1972.

———. "Biking Beauties." September 15, 1971.

———. "Cycling Good for Heart, Expert Says." March 18, 1956.

———. "The Old 'Bikes': What Becomes of Them When Their Best Days Are Past." July 30, 1899.

Lukasch, Bernd. "From Lilienthal to the Wrights." Retrieved from lilienthal-museum.de.

Maclear, Michael. *The Ten Thousand Day War: Vietnam, 1945–1975*. New York: St. Martin's, 1981.

Macy, Sue. *Wheels of Change: How Women Rode the Bicycle to Freedom (with a Few Flat Tires along the Way)*. Washington, DC: National Geographic, 2011.

Maines, Rachel P. *The Technology of Orgasm: "Hysteria," the Vibrator, and Women's Sexual Satisfaction*. Baltimore: Johns Hopkins University Press, 1999.

Maison Nicéphore Niépce. "The Pyreolophore." Retrieved from photomuseum.org.

Mapes, Jeff. *Pedaling Revolution: How Cyclists Are Changing American Cities*. Corvallis: Oregon State University Press, 2009.

Martin, Scott. "America Rides." *Bicycling*, July 1996.

———. "Are Road Bikes Dead?" *Bicycling*, June 1990.

Mason, Philip Parker. "The League of American Wheelmen and the Good-Roads Movement, 1880–1905." PhD diss., University of Michigan, 1957.

Maxim, Hiram Percy. "The Explosive Tricycle and Other Recollections of Horseless Carriage Days." *Harper's Monthly*, November 1936.

May, Elaine Tyler. *Homeward Bound: American Families in the Cold War Era*. New York: Basic Books, 1999.

Mayer, Andre. "How Lance Armstrong Transformed North American Culture." Retrieved from cbc.ca.

Mayfield, Molly. "Father Too 'Old' to Exercise." *Baltimore Sun*, April 11, 1966.

———. "Teen-Age Crush." *Baltimore Sun*, July 5, 1966.

McClure's. "Colonel Albert A. Pope." September 1893.

McConnon, Aili, and Andres McConnon. *Road to Valor: A True Story of World War II Italy, the Nazis, and the Cyclist Who Inspired a Nation*. New York: Crown, 2012.

McCurdy, Jack. "Fad of High Bars on Bikes Stirs Concern." *Los Angeles Times*, January 10, 1960.

McDaniel, Joe W. "Just the Facts: 1903 Wright Flyer I." Retrieved from wright-brothers.org.

McFarland, Marvin W., ed. *The Papers of Wilbur and Orville Wright*. 2 vols. New York: McGraw-Hill, 1953.

McShane, Clay. *Down the Asphalt Path: The Automobile and the American City*. New York: Columbia University Press, 1994.

Means, James. "Wheeling and Flying." In *The Aeronautical Annual*, edited by James Means, 23–25. Boston: Clarke, 1896.

Meddin, Russell. "The Bike-Sharing World Map." Retrieved from bike-sharingmap.com.

Medred, Craig. "Despite Expense, Popularity of Fatbikes Continues to Soar in Alaska." *Alaska Dispatch News*, November 4, 2014.

Meinert, Charles W. "Bicycles in Flight." In *Cycle History 4: Proceedings of the 4th International Cycling History Conference*, edited by Rob van der Plas, 43–47. San Francisco: Bicycle Books, 1994.

Mercader, Guillaume. "Lecture Script of Mr. Guillaume Mercader." July 7, 1987. From the Eisenhower Center World War II Archives and Oral History Collection, University of New Orleans, courtesy of the National WWII Museum, New Orleans, Louisiana.

Merington, Marguerite. "Woman and the Bicycle." *Scribner's*, June 1895.

Merritt, Wesley. "Marching Cavalry." *Journal of the United States Cavalry Association*, March 1888.

Metropolitan Police, District Department of Transportation, and Washington Area Bicyclist Association. "Pocket Guide to DC Bike Laws." Pamphlet, October 2012.

Miami Herald. "Miami Couriers Try Pedal Power." June 14, 1982.

Miami-Made Bicycles. "A Bicycle—*That's* What We'll Get Him for Christmas." *McClure's*, December 1916.

Miller, Ivonette. "Orville and Wilbur Wright: An Intimate Memoir." *Antioch Review* 34, no. 4 (Summer 1976): 447–450.

Miller, Lillian, and Sidney Hart, eds. *The Selected Papers of Charles Willson Peale and His Family*. Vol. 5. New Haven, CT: Yale University Press, 2000.

Miller, William Van Rensselaer. *Select Organizations in the United States*. New York: Knickerbocker, 1896.

Minneapolis Journal. "The Knell of the Bicycle." July 16, 1895.

Minneapolis Tribune. "Facts about the Bicycle Face." July 20, 1895.

Mintz, Steven. *Huck's Raft: A History of American Childhood*. Cambridge, MA: Harvard University Press, 2006.

———. "Play and the History of American Childhood: An Interview with Steven Mintz." *American Journal of Play* 3, no. 2 (Fall 2010): 143–156.

Mississippi State Gazette. "By an Advertisement in the Philadelphia Papers." July 24, 1819.

Moffett, Cleveland. "A Burglar, a Bicycle, and a Storm." *Godey's*, April 1896.

Monark Silver King, Inc. "Now Pay a Little Each Month—and You Can Have the Aluminum Streamlined Silver King." *Boys' Life*, May 1936.

Monthly Magazine, or British Register. "New Patents and Mechanical Inventions." March 1, 1819.

Montpelier (VT) *Argus and Patriot*. "Coming to Vermont." June 8, 1898.

Moore, Scott. "Pedals Coming Up Roses on Campus." *Los Angeles Times*, October 10, 1971.

Moore, Stephen. "The War against the Car." *Wall Street Journal*, November 11, 2005.

Morgan, Ted. *Valley of Death: The Tragedy at Dien Bien Phu That Led America into the Vietnam War*. New York: Random House, 2010.

Morgan, William. "Terrorists—on Two Wheels." *Washington Post*, May 8, 1987.

Morris, Eric A. "The Vanishing Walk to School." Retrieved from freakonomics.com.

Mosely Folding Bath Tub Company. "If Your New House Has No Bath Room." *Ladies' Home Journal*, June 1894.

———. "Mosely Folding Bath Tub." *Texas Medical News* 5, no. 1 (November 1895): xvii.

Moser, Laura. "No Longer a Novelty, a Cargo Bike Built for All." *New York Times*, April 23, 2015.

Moss, James A. "The Army A-Wheel." *Los Angeles Times*, November 7, 1897.
———. "The Army A-Wheel." *Los Angeles Times*, November 21, 1897.
———. "Military Bicycling." *Salt Lake Semi-*Weekly *Tribune*, June 22, 1897.
———. "Military Purposes." *Daily Missoulian*, June 19, 1897.
MotorCycling and Bicycling. "Pope Gets Contract for 10,000 War Bikes." October 29, 1917.
———. "U.S. to Buy 100,000 Bicycles for War." November 5, 1917.
Mott, Frank Luther. *A History of American Magazines, 1885–1905*. Cambridge, MA: Belknap, 1957.
Mulholland, Owen. "California Bikies Are Mountainside Surfing." *VeloNews*, February 10, 1978.
Munsey's. "Groveling for Luxury." June 1897.
———. "Humanizing the Dog." June 1897.
Murphy, Thomas. "Bike Messengers Love to Hate Their Low-Paying Jobs." *Los Angeles Times*, July 6, 1986.
Museum of Mountain Bike Art and Technology. "Schwinn Bicycles History." Retrieved from mombat.org.
Nantucket Inquirer and Mirror. "The Bicycle Crowds Out the Accordion." November 13, 1897.
Nash, Francis Smith. "A Plea for the New Woman and the Bicycle." *American Journal of Obstetrics and Diseases of Women and Children* 33, no. 4 (April 1896): 556–560.
Nation. "American Croquet." August 9, 1866.
National Bicycle Dealers Association. "A Look at the Bicycle Industry's Vital Statistics." Retrieved from nbda.com.
———. "2013—The NBDA Statpak." Retrieved from nbda.com.
National Bureau of Economic Research. *Trends in the American Economy in the Nineteenth Century*. Princeton, NJ: Princeton University Press, 1960.
National Commission on Product Safety. *Final Report Presented to the President and Congress*, June 1970.
National Independent Distributor Associates. "The USA Energy Shortage?" *Boys' Life*, May 1974.
National Museum of American History. "Transportation History, 1800–1900." Retrieved from amhistory.si.edu.
National Police Gazette. "Real Living Pictures." December 15, 1894.
———. "She Wore Trousers." October 28, 1893.

Nevins, Allan. *The Emergence of Modern America, 1865–1878*. New York: Macmillan, 1927.

Newcomb, Simon. "The Outlook for the Flying Machine." *Independent*, October 22, 1903.

New Departure Manufacturing Company. "So That's Why You Want a Bicycle for Christmas?" *Youth's Companion*, November 1927.

———. "This Week Is Yours." *Boys' Life*, May 1922.

New-England Galaxy and Masonic Magazine. "Fashionable Amusement." May 12, 1820.

New Haven (CT) Evening Register. "The Elephants' Fight." April 5, 1883.

New Orleans Daily Picayune. "St. Charles." April 8, 1871.

New York Amsterdam News. "Riding to the Olympics." April 10, 1982.

The New York Clipper Annual for 1893. New York: Frank Queen, 1892.

New-York Daily Advertiser. "Experiment." July 15, 1819.

New Yorker. "Self-employed." December 29, 1975.

New York Herald. "Bicycle in the Pulpit." May 13, 1895.

———. "The Elliott Children." April 5, 1883.

———. "Inauguration of Cammeyer's Amphicyclotheatron at the Union Grounds, Brooklyn." April 1, 1869.

———. "A New Club." April 11, 1869.

———. "Notes of the Stage." November 4, 1894.

New York Herald-Tribune. "News from New Jersey." March 29, 1890.

New York Medical Record. "A Medical Bicycle Specialist." *Vol.* 48, no. 20 (November 16, 1895): 702.

New York Society for the Prevention of Cruelty to Children. "History." Retrieved from nyspcc.org.

New York Sun. "Sporting: The Skating Season." October 6, 1868.

New York Times. "At Barnum's Circus." March 27, 1883.

———. "The Bicycle, and Riding It." January 25, 1880.

———. "Cycling Trade History." January 5, 1896.

———. "E-Mail Searches for a Missing Link." March 12, 1989.

———. "French Bicycles Restricted." May 9, 1942.

———. "General City News." September 4, 1868.

———. "He 'Chalked It Down,'" September 22, 1896.

———. "The Jersey City Velocipedrome." March 26, 1869.

———. "Johnson's Wonderful Mile." October 25, 1894.

———. "Little Ones on Bicycles." March 31, 1883.

———. "A New Generation Discovers the Bike." October 18, 1925.

———. "Nuggets." April 6, 1898.

———. "Order Trebles Adult Bicycles." March 13, 1942.
———. "Progressive Euchre Now." February 11, 1900.
———. "The Record of the Place." April 22, 1880
———. "To Journey through Life." January 16, 1884.
———. "Velocipede Exhibition." July 28, 1869.
———. "The Velocipede Furor." February 19, 1869.
———. "The Velocipede Mania." January 10, 1869.
———. "The Velocipede Races at the Union Course, L.I." April 28, 1869.
———. "Velocipedes." January 27, 1869.
———. "Velocipedes." March 8, 1869.
———. "Wanted: An Air Cycle." June 25, 1893.
———. "Women Here and There." September 4, 1898.
New-York Tribune. "Barnum Excelling Former Exploits." March 27, 1883.
———. "The Child-Performers." *New-York Tribune*, March 29, 1883.
———. "Mr. Barnum Arrested." April 3, 1883.
Nicolson, Samuel. *The Nicolson Pavement*. Boston: Dutton and Son, 1859.
Nilsen, Richard. "Clunker Bikes." *CoEvolution Quarterly*, Spring 1978.
Ninth Annual Report of the Board of Railroad Commissioners. Boston: Rand, Avery, 1878.
Norcliffe, Glen, ed. *Cycle History 17: Proceedings of the 17th International Cycling History Conference*. San Francisco: Cycle Publishing, 2007.
———. "Popeism and Fordism: Examining the Roots of Mass Production." *Regional Studies* 31, no. 3 (May 1997): 267–280.
———. *The Ride to Modernity: The Bicycle in Canada, 1869–1900*. Toronto: University of Toronto Press, 2001.
———. "The Technological and Social Significance of the Tricycle." In *Cycle History 17: Proceedings of the 17th International Cycling History Conference*, edited by Glen Norcliffe, 59–68. San Francisco: Cycle Publishing, 2007.
Norton, Peter D. *Fighting Traffic: The Dawn of the Motor Age in the American City*. Cambridge, MA: MIT Press, 2008.
Nye, Peter. *Hearts of Lions: The History of American Bicycle Racing*. New York: Norton, 1988.
———. *The Six-Day Bicycle Races*. With Jeff Groman and Mark Tyson. San Francisco: Van der Plas Publications / Cycle Publishing, 2006.
Oddy, Nicholas. "Cycling in the Drawing Room." In *Cycle History 11: Proceedings, 11th International Cycling History Conference*, edited by Andrew Ritchie and Rob van der Plas, 169–176. San Francisco: Van der Plas, 2001.

Oddy, Nicholas, and Rob van der Plas, eds. *Cycle History 8: Proceedings of the 8th International Cycling History Conference*. San Francisco: Van der Plas, 1998.

Official Bulletin and Scrap Book of the League of American Wheelmen. "Our Oldest Members." August 1917.

———. "With June Come Perfect Days." June 1917.

Ohmann, Richard. *Politics of Letters*. Middletown, CT: Wesleyan University Press, 1987.

Ohrt, Hans. "Growth of Lightweight Cycling." *Cycling Herald*, November 1941.

Oliver, Smith Hempstone, and Donald H. Berkebile. *Wheels and Wheeling: The Smithsonian Collection*. Washington, DC: Smithsonian Institution Press, 1974.

Olson, Sidney. *Young Henry Ford*. Detroit: Wayne State University Press, 1997.

Overfelt, Maggie. "King of the Mountain Bike." *Fortune Small Business*, May 16, 2008.

Overman Wheel Company. "Darius Green." *Harper's Weekly*, May 4, 1895.

———. "Power of Wheels." *Illustrated American*, July 2, 1892.

———. "A Tip for You." *Bicycling World*, January 7, 1887.

Owram, Doug. *Born at the Right Time: A History of the Baby-Boom Generation*. Toronto: University of Toronto Press, 1996.

Page, E. D. "Woman and the Bicycle." *Brooklyn Medical Journal* 11, no. 2 (February 1897): 81–87.

Parker, W. Thornton. "A New Remedy." *Wheelman*, October 1883.

Pascal du 38. "Guillaume Mercader: Chef de Réseau / Résistance du Bessin." Retrieved from normandie44.canalblog.com.

Patterson, Everett W. "The Ride of the Army Bicycle Corps." *L.A.W. Bulletin and Good Roads*, August 20, 1897.

PBS. "Technology Timeline: 1752–1990." Retrieved from pbs.org.

Pearson, Henry C. *Rubber Tires and All about Them*. New York: India Rubber Publishing Company, 1906.

Pedals. "Then and Now." *Bicycling World*, November 4, 1887.

Peiss, Kathy. *Cheap Amusements: Leisure in Turn-of-the-Century New York*. Philadelphia: Temple University Press, 1986.

Penn, Robert. *It's All about the Bike: The Pursuit of Happiness on Two Wheels*. London and New York: Bloomsbury, 2010.

Perry, David B. *Bike Cult: The Ultimate Guide to Human-Powered Vehicles*. New York: Four Walls Eight Windows, 1995.

Petty, Ross D. "Peddling Schwinn Bicycles: Marketing Lessons from the Leading Post-WWII US Bicycle Brand." In *Marketing History at the Center: Proceedings of the 13th Biennial Conference on Historical Analysis and Research in Marketing (CHARM)*, edited by Blaine J. Branchik, 162–171. Durham, NC: Duke University Press, 2007.

Philadelphia Inquirer. "Was Too Much for Her." August 14, 1897.

Philadelphia Medical News. "The Bicycler Should Sit Erect." Vol. 63, no. 22 (November 25, 1893): 613.

Philadelphia Polyclinic. "Cycling and Heart Disease." Vol. 4, no. 37 (September 14, 1895): 379–381.

Philadelphia Tribune. "Safety Riders Bicycle Club Attracts Youths." September 8, 1959.

Plaster, John L. *S.O.G.: The Secret Wars of America's Commandos in Vietnam*. New York: Simon and Schuster, 1997.

Podesta, Melita. *Material Life, 1890s Family*. New England Economic Adventure educational brochure. Boston: Federal Reserve Bank of Boston, October 2004.

Pope, Albert A. "Colonel Pope and the Founding of the U.S. Cycle Industry." In *Cycle History [5]: Proceedings of the 5th International Cycle History Conference*, edited by Rob van der Plas, 95–98. San Francisco: Bicycle Books, 1995. [This Albert A. Pope is the great-grandson of the industrialist of the same name.]

Pope, Albert A. "The Bicycle Industry." In *One Hundred Years of American Commerce*, edited by Chauncey M. Depew, 549–553. New York: Haynes, 1895. [This Albert A. Pope was a well-known industrialist.]

———. "Interview with Colonel Albert A. Pope." *Bicycling World*, May 15, 1880.

Pope Manufacturing Company. "My Morning Spin." *Ladies' Home Journal*, November 1892.

Popular Mechanics. "The Amazing Return of the 'Bikes.'" January 1935.

Porter, Robert P. "Distribution of Population According to Density: 1890." *Extra Census Bulletin*, April 20, 1891.

Potter, Isaac B. "The Bicycle Outlook." *Century*, September 1896.

———. *Cycle Paths*. Boston: League of American Wheelmen, 1898.

———. *The Gospel of Good Roads: A Letter to the American Farmer*. New York: League of American Wheelmen, 1891.

Prados, John. *The Blood Road: The Ho Chi Minh Trail and the Vietnam War*. New York: Wiley, 1999.

Pratt, Charles E. "Pierre Lallement and His Bicycle." *Outing*, October 1, 1883.

———. "A Sketch of American Bicycling and its Founder." *Outing*, July 1891.

Presbrey, Frank. *The History and Development of Advertising*. Garden City, NY: Doubleday, Doran, 1929.

Preston (MN) Democrat. "Chatfield." February 5, 1885.

Printers' Ink. "The Columbia Advertising." February 9, 1898.

Proceedings of the Bostonian Society at the Annual Meeting, January 11, 1898. Boston: Old State House, 1898.

Pucher, John, and Ralph Buehler, ed. *City Cycling*. Cambridge, MA: MIT Press, 2012.

Pucher, John, Ralph Buehler, and Mark Seinen. "Bicycling Renaissance in North America? An Update and Re-Appraisal of Cycling Trends and Policies." *Transportation Research Part A*, 45, no. 6 (July 2011): 451–475.

Py-Lieberman, Beth. "The Great Hall of American Wonders Opens Today at American Art." Retrieved from smithsonianmag.com.

Quick, Darren. "Coboc Impersonates Non-Electric Bike to Take Gold Award at Eurobike." Retrieved from gizmag.com.

Rabinowitz, Dorothy. "Opinion: Death by Bicycle." Video interview. *Wall Street Journal*, May 31, 2013.Rasmussen, Wayne D. and Douglas E. Bowers. "A History of Agricultural Policy: Chronological Outline." US Department of Agriculture, Economic Research Service white paper. April 1992.

Recreation. "Bicycle for War Purposes." November 1897.

Reel, Guy. *The National Police Gazette and the Making of the Modern American Man, 1879–1906*. New York: Palgrave Macmillan, 2006.

Reid, Carlton. "The Petition That Paved America." Retrieved from roadswerenotbuiltforcars.com.

———. *Roads Were Not Built for Cars: How Cyclists Were the First to Push for Good Roads and Became the Pioneers of Motoring*. Redondo Beach, CA: Red Kite, 2014.

Reinitz, Bertram. "City's Cyclists Hold Their Own." *New York Times*, October 28, 1928.

Reiter, Bob. "Wheels: The What, the Where, the Who." *Los Angeles Times*, October 31, 1971.

Reuss, Alejandro. "That '70s Crisis." *Dollars and Sense: Real World Economics*, November–December 2009.

Reuters. "Three Are Killed in Saigon by Bomb Hidden in Bicycle." June 10, 1965.

Riddell, J. Scott. *A Manual of Ambulance*. London: Charles Griffin, 1897.

Ritchie, Andrew. "The Beginnings of Trans-Atlantic Racing." In *Cycle History 8: Proceedings of the 8th International Cycling History Conference*, edited by Nicholas Oddy and Rob van der Plas, 131–142. San Francisco: Van der Plas, 1998.

———, ed. *Cycle History 16: Proceedings of the 16th International Cycling History Conference*. San Francisco: Van der Plas Publications, 2006.

———. *King of the Road: An Illustrated History of Cycling*. Berkeley, CA: Ten Speed Press, 1975.

———. *Quest for Speed: A History of Early Bicycle Racing, 1868–1903*. El Cerrito, Calif., 2011.

Ritchie, Andrew, and Nicholas Clayton, ed. *Cycle History [13]: Proceedings of the 13th International Cycle History Conference*. San Francisco: Rob van der Plas, 2003.

Ritchie, Andrew, and Gary Sanderson, ed. *Cycle History 22: Proceedings of the 22nd International Cycling History Conference*. Cheltenham, UK: Cycling History, 2012.

———. *Cycle History 25: Proceedings of the 25th International Cycling History Conference*. Birmingham, UK: Cycling History, 2015.

Ritchie, Andrew, and Rob van der Plas, ed. *Cycle History 11: Proceedings, 11th International Cycling History Conference*. San Francisco: Van der Plas, 2001.

Roberts, Sam. "Infamous 'Drop Dead' Was Never Said by Ford." *New York Times*, December 28, 2006.

Rogers, Jerry R. "Civil Engineering Education History (1741 to 1893)." In *American Civil Engineering History: The Pioneering Years*, edited by Bernard G. Dennis Jr., Robert J. Kapsch, Robert LoConte, Bruce W. Mattheiss, and Steven M. Pennington, 69–73. Washington, DC: American Society of Civil Engineers, 2003.

Roosevelt, J. West. "A Doctor's View of Bicycling." *Scribner's*, October 1895.

Rosenberg, Charles. *Explaining Epidemics, and Other Studies in the History of Medicine*. Cambridge: Cambridge University Press, 1992.

Rosenblatt, Robert. "Bicycle Industry Riding High on Ecology Trend." *Los Angeles Times*, August 15, 1971.

Roth, Harold. *Bike Factory*. New York: Pantheon Books, 1985.

Royde-Smith, John Graham. "Forces and Resources of the European Combatants, 1939." Retrieved from britannica.com.

Rubenson, Paul. "Missing Link: The Case for Bicycle Transportation in the United States in the Early 20th Century." In *Cycle History 16: Proceedings of the 16th International Cycling History Conference*, edited by Andrew Ritchie, 73–84. San Francisco: Van der Plas, 2006.

———. "Patents, Profits and Perceptions: The Single-Tube Tire and the Failure of the American Bicycle, 1897–1933." In *Cycle History 15: Proceedings of the 15th International Cycling History Conference*, edited by Rob van der Plas, 87–97. San Francisco: Van der Plas, 2005.

Ruibal, Sal. "Peddling in a New Direction: Makers Look for Antidote to Sales Slump." *USA Today*, September 17, 1996.

Runge, Manuela, and Lukasch, Bernd. *Erfinderleben: Die Brüder Otto und Gustav Lilienthal*. Berlin: Berlin-Verlag, 2005.

Rusch, Rebecca. "A Long Way on the Path Less Traveled." Retrieved from rebeccarusch.com.

Saar, John. "2-Wheeled 'Pony Express' Riders Beat D.C. Traffic." *Washington Post*, July 8, 1973.

Safe Routes to School National Partnership. "School Siting: Location Affects the Potential to Walk or Bike." Retrieved from saferoutespartnership.org.

Sagnier, Thierry. "Summertime—and the Riding Is Easy." *Washington Post*, July 18, 1971.

Salisbury, Harrison E. "North Vietnam Runs on Bicycles." *New York Times*, January 7, 1967.

San Francisco Bike Messengers Association. "Bike Messengering." Retrieved from foundsf.org.

San Francisco Daily Evening *Bulletin*. "Latest News Items," May 3, 1873.

San Francisco Evening Bulletin. "All Sorts of Items." July 19, 1873.

———."Brief Mention." October 15, 1872.

———. "Parlor Skating." March 1, 1871.

Sani, Marc. "E-Bikes Finding Traction in U.S. Market." *Bicycle Retailer and Industry News*, April 9, 2014.

Sansweet, Stephen J. "Sophisticated Cousin of Pinball Machine Entrances the U.S." *Wall Street Journal*, March 18, 1974.

Sartorius, N., D. Goldberg, D., G. de Girolamo, G., J. Costa e Silva, J., Y. Lecrubier, Y., and U. Wittchen, U., eds. *Psychological Disorders in General Medical Settings*. Toronto: Hogrefe und Huber, 1990.

Saunders, W. O. "Then We Quit Laughing." *Collier's*, September 17, 1927.
Savannah Daily Republican. "Pedestrian Feat." January 10, 1850.
———. "Sporting." January 9, 1850.
Schivelbusch, Wolfgang. *The Railway Journey: The Industrialization of Time and Space in the Nineteenth Century*. Berkeley: University of California Press, 1986.
Schneirov, Matthew. *The Dream of a New Social Order: Popular Magazines in America, 1893–1914*. New York: Columbia University Press, 1994.
Schulman, Bruce J. *The Seventies: The Great Shift in American Culture, Society, and Politics*. New York: Da Capo, 2002.
Scientific American. "Bicycle 'Gear'—What It Means." September 19, 1896.
———. "The Human Wheel and Its Rival—The Velocipede Mania." January 9, 1869.
———. "Notes on the Velocipede." January 30, 1869.
Scientific American Supplement. "The Bicycle in the Army." October 24, 1896.
Scott, Shane. "A Subcultural Study of Freestyle BMX: The Effects of Commodification and Rationalization on Edgework." M.A. thesis, University of Louisville, 2013.
Scribner's. "Pears.'" December 1891.
———. "The Point of View." October 1894.
Sears, Roebuck and Company. *Consumers Guide No. 107*. Chicago: Sears, Roebuck, September 1898.
Sexton, Patrick. "The Schwinn Stingray." Retrieved from schwinncruisers.com.
Shadwell, A. "The Hidden Dangers of Bicycling." *National Review*, February 1897.
Shaheen, Susan A., Elliot W. Martin, Adam P. Cohen, and Rachel S. Finison. "Public Bikesharing in North America: Early Operator and User Understanding." Mineta Transportation Institute report, June 2012.
Shaler, N. S. *American Highways: A Popular Account of their Conditions and of the Means by Which They May Be Bettered*. New York: Century, 1896.
———. "The Common Roads." *Scribner's*, October 1889.
———. "The Move for Better Highways." *Harper's Weekly*, January 6, 1894.
Shapiro, Eben. "Root Beer: A Flood of Memories, a Sip of Foam." *New York Times*, July 22, 1992.

Shapiro, Stephanie. "Mountain Biking." *Baltimore Sun*, November 16, 1985.

Sheldon, R. "The Army on the March." *Journal of the United States Infantry Association*, July 1905.

Shelsby, Ted F. "Bicycle Sales Are Booming—But You Can't Get One." *Baltimore Sun*, October 10, 1971.

Shelton, Elizabeth. "'High Rise' Bikes: Are They Risky?" *Washington Post*, March 5, 1970.

Shepherd, Ron, ed. *Cycling History 14: Proceedings of the 14th International Cycling History Conference*. Dickson, Australia: Canberra Bicycle Museum, 2003.

Siber, Kate. "New Frontier: Mountain Bike the Ho Chi Minh Trail, Vietnam." Retrieved from adventure.nationalgeographic.com.

Simms, Sally. "The Bicycle, the Bloomer, and Dress Reform in the 1890s." In *Dress and Popular Culture*, edited by Patricia A. Cunningham and Susan Voso Lab, 125–145. Bowling Green, Ohio: Bowling Green State University Popular Press, 1991.

Smith, Arthur L., Jr., "General Von Seeckt and the Weimar Republic." *Review of Politics* 20, no. 3 (July 1958): 347–357.

Smith, Dinitia. "Fast Company." *New York*, January 13, 1986.

Smith, Robert A. *A Social History of the Bicycle*. New York: American Heritage Press, 1972.

Smithsonian Institution. "History of the Telegraph." Retrieved from historywired.si.edu.

Smithsonian National Air and Space Museum. "The Breakthrough Concept." Retrieved from airandspace.si.edu.

———. "Langley Aerodrome A." Retrieved from airandspace.si.edu.

Sneed, Michael. "Bicycles Create Problem at U. of I." *Chicago Tribune*, December 16, 1973.

Snyder, Clyde. "Socialite's Belief in Youth Shaken." *Los Angeles Times*, August 27, 1967.

Southern California Practitioner. "Cyclist's Sore Throat." Vol. 13, no. 8 (August 1898): 301–302.

Sporting Life. "The Bicycle Hand." December 28, 1895.

Sprague, Marshall. "A Bicycle Army Takes to the Highroad." *New York Times*, May 15, 1938.

Springfield (MA) Sunday Republican. "Our Boys Start for War." April 24, 1898.

———. "The 6 O'Clock Bicycle Crowd." October 17, 1897.

———. "Work of Army Bicycle Corps." July 11, 1897.

Stamper, Anita A., and Jill Condra. *Clothing through American History: The Civil War through the Gilded Age, 1861–1899*. Santa Barbara, CA: Greenwood, 2011.

Stearns, Peter N. "Analyzing the Role of Culture in Shaping American Childhood: A Twentieth-Century Case." *European Journal of Developmental Psychology* 6, no. 1 (January 2009): 34–52.

Steincrohn, Peter J. "Exercise Is 'Slow Suicide' for Some, Specialist Warns." *Washington Post*, July 23, 1950.

Sterne, Michael. "Mid-Manhattan Bikeways a Cyclist's Wish Coming True." *New York Times*, August 7, 1978.

Stevenson, David. *Cataclysm: The First World War as Political Tragedy*. New York: Basic Books, 2004.

Stevenson, Robert Louis. *Across the Plains, with Other Memories and Essays*. New York: Charles Scribner's Sons, 1906.

Stimson, Alexander Lovett. *History of Express Companies and American Railroads*. New York, 1859.

St. Louis Globe-Democrat. "Wheelmen at Forest Park." July 26, 1897.

St. Louis Post-Dispatch. "Near the End of the Journey." July 23, 1897.

———. "Sunday Morning." July 25, 1897.

———. "2200 Miles on Wheels." July 25, 1897.

St. Louis Republic. "A Mud Blockade." December 25, 1891.

St. Louis Star. "Across the Continent." July 25, 1897.

St. Maur, Harry. "To Hymen on a Wheel." *Home Magazine*, August 1897.

Stokesbury, James L. *A Short History of the Korean War*. New York: Morrow, 1988.

Strahan, S. A. K. "Bicycle Riding and Perineal Pressure: Their Effect on the Young." *Lancet* 124, no. 3186 (September 20, 1884): 490–491.

Straits Times. "Malaya a Terrible Obstacle for Japan." November 17, 1941.

Strand. "A Regiment on Wheels." July 1891.

Street, Roger. *The Pedestrian Hobby-Horse at the Dawn of Cycling*. Dorset, UK: Artesius, 1998.

Sullivan, Kevin. "Laid-Back Bikers Love This Cycle." *Washington Post*, July 12, 1992.

Sullivan, T. J. "'Get After the Boy' Says Farrell." *MotorCycling and Bicycling*, September 3, 1917.

Sunset. "The Bike's Comeback." July 1965.

Sutton, Clayton R. "After Lean War Years Industry Hustles to Put Small Fry on Wheels." *Wall Street Journal*, September 26, 1945.

Sweeney, Shawn, and Gary Meneghin. "The First American Balloon Tire Bicycle." Retrieved from thecabe.com.

Swift, Earl. *The Big Roads: The Untold Story of the Engineers, Visionaries, and Trailblazers who Created the American Superhighways*. Boston: Houghton Mifflin Harcourt, 2011.

Swift, E. M. "Le Grand LeMond." *Sports Illustrated*, December 25, 1989.

Symross, Lynn. "Endangered Species on Wheels." *Los Angeles Times*, June 8, 1978.

Talese, Gay. "Messenger Boys: A Fading Tintype." *New York Times*, December 12, 1959.

Tassin, Algernon. "The Magazine In America." *Bookman*, December 1915.

Taylor, George Rogers. *The Transportation Revolution, 1815–1860*. New York: Holt, Rinehart and Winston, 1951.

Temes, Judy. "Messenger Firms Scrambling to Survive." *Crain's New York Business*, July 16, 1990.

Tennant, Jill. "40 Years Later: Legacies of the 1973 Oil Crisis Persist." *World Oil*, October 2013.

Terry, Luther L. "Man Himself Is Now Guinea Pig." *Washington Post*, April 21, 1964.

Theiss, Lewis Edwin. "Children, Too, Should Learn to Prepare for a Rainy Day." *American Home*, June 1936.

Theiss, Rudolf, and Oskar Regele. *Die Radfahrtruppe: Nach Kriegserfahrungen Bearbeitet*. Berlin: R. Eisenschmidt, 1925.

Thomas, William G., III, and Edward L. Ayers. "The Differences Slavery Made: A Close Analysis of Two American Communities." Retrieved from vcdh.virginia.edu.

Thompson, Maurice. "What We Gain in the Bicycle." *Chautauquan*, August 1897.

Thorpe, J. R. "The Symbolic Meaning of 6 Hipster Trends, from Beards to Fixies (Kind of Fascinating, but Whatever)." Retrieved from bustle.com.

Thwaites, Reuben Gold, ed. *Early Western Travels, 1748–1846*. Cleveland: Clark, 1905.

Time. "Bicycles from Britain." July 5, 1954.

———. "The Freewheelers." July 5, 1976.

Todd, Jan. *Physical Culture and the Body Beautiful: Purposive Exercise in the Lives of American Women, 1800–1870*. Macon, GA: Mercer University Press, 1998.

Tonge, Peter. "The Recumbent Bicycle—a Different Way to Get Around." *Christian Science Monitor*, August 20, 1980.

Trescott, Martha Moore. "The Bicycle, a Technical Precursor of the Automobile." In *Business and Economic History*, edited by Paul Uselding, 51–75. Urbana: University of Illinois Press, 1976.

Trillin, Calvin. "U.S. Journal: Manhattan." *New Yorker*, December 9, 1971.

Trostle, James. "Early Work in Anthropology and Epidemiology: From Social Medicine to Germ Theory, 1840 to 1920." In *Anthropology and Epidemiology*, edited by Craig R. James, 35–57. Dordrecht, Holland: Reidel, 1986.

Tsuji, Masanobu. *Singapore: The Japanese Version*. Translated by Margaret E. Lake. New York: St. Martin's, 1960.

Turf, Field, and Farm. "Pedestrian Congress." March 25, 1870.

Turk, Rose-Marie. "Clothiers Wheel Into the New Field of Cycle Wear." *Los Angeles Times*, February 20, 1987.

Turner, George Kibbe. "The Men Who Learned to Fly." *McClure's*, February 1908.

Turpin, Robert J. "'Our Best Bet Is the Boy': Bicycle Marketing Schemes and American Culture after World War." In *Cycle History 22: Proceedings of the 22nd International Cycling History Conference*, edited by Andrew Ritchie and Gary Sanderson, 159–170. Cheltenham, UK: Cycling History, 2012.

———. "'Our Best Bet Is the Boy': A Cultural History of Bicycle Marketing and Consumption in the United States, 1880–1960." PhD diss., University of Kentucky, 2013.

Tuttle, Brad. "8 Ways the American Consumer May Have Already Peaked." *Time*, September 25, 2014.

Union, United States Gazette, and True American. "Tracena." May 18, 1819.

United Parcel Service. "1907–1929." Retrieved from ups.com.

US Army Military Intelligence Service. *Notes on Japanese Warfare: Information Bulletin No. 10*, March 21, 1942.

US Bureau of the Census. "Historical National Population Estimates: July 1, 1900 to July 1, 1999." Retrieved from census.gov.

———. "Map Showing the Distribution of the Slave Population of the Southern States of the United States." Washington, DC: Department of the Interior, September 9, 1861.

———. "Population, Housing Units, Area Measurements, and Density: 1790 to 1990." Retrieved from census.gov.

US Congress. Senate. Committee on Finance. Stuart J. Northrop, "Statement of Bicycle Manufacturers Association of America, Inc." In *Various Revenue and Tariff Bills: Testimony to Be Received Tuesday, August 24, 1976, and Departmental Comments*, 126–134. 94th Cong., 2nd sess. Washington, DC: Government Printing Office, 1976.

———. Committee on Foreign Relations. *Harrison E. Salisbury's Trip to North Vietnam: Hearing before the Committee on Foreign Relations*. 90th Cong., 1st sess., February 2, 1967. Washington, DC: Government Printing Office, 1967.

US Department of Commerce. "Money Income in 1972 of Families and Persons in the United States." *Current Population Reports: Consumer Income*, June 1973.

———. National Oceanic and Atmospheric Administration. "Record of Climatological Observations." Kentfield, California, October 1976.

US Department of State. *Foreign Relations of the United States, 1958–1960*, vol. 1, *Vietnam*. Retrieved from state.gov.

———. *Foreign Relations of the United States, 1964–1968*, vol. 27, *Laos*. Retrieved from state.gov.

———. *Foreign Relations of the United States, 1969–1976*, vol. 8, *Vietnam*. Retrieved from state.gov.

Uselding, Paul, ed. *Business and Economic History*. Urbana: University of Illinois Press, 1976.

US Holocaust Memorial Museum. "Warsaw." Retrieved from ushmm.org.

———. "World War I: Treaties and Reparations." Retrieved from ushmm.org.

US Postal Service. "Postage Rates for Periodicals: A Narrative History." Retrieved from about.usps.com.

Van der Plas, Rob, ed. *Cycle History 4: Proceedings of the 4th International Cycling History Conference*. San Francisco: Bicycle Books, 1994.

———, ed. *Cycle History [5]: Proceedings of the 5th International Cycle History Conference*. San Francisco: Bicycle Books, 1995.

———, ed. *Cycle History [7]: Proceedings of the 7th International Cycle History Conference*. San Francisco: Rob van der Plas, 1997.

———, ed. *Cycle History 15: Proceedings of the 15th International Cycling History Conference*. San Francisco: Van der Plas, 2005.

Vanderbilt, Tom. "The Best Bike-Sharing Program in the United States." Retrieved from slate.com.

———. "Cargo Bikes: The New Station Wagon." *Wall Street Journal*, July 5, 2013.

Veblen, Thorstein. *The Theory of the Leisure Class: An Economic Study of Institutions*. New York: Macmillan, 1915.

Velocipedist. "Cammeyer's Union Grounds, Velocipede Track." April 1869.

———. "The Future of the Bicycle." February 1869.

———. "The Jersey City Skating Rink." April 1869.

Viator. "Tricycling." *Wheelman*, December 1882.

Victoria Transport Policy Institute. *Transportation Cost and Benefit Analysis: Techniques, Estimates and Implications*. Retrieved from vtpi.org.

Vincent, Ted. *Mudville's Revenge: The Rise and Fall of American Sport*. Lincoln: University of Nebraska Press, 1994.

VonHerrlich, Phyllis. "Women's History Trail." Retrieved from dll.umaine.edu.

Waller, Julian A. "Bicycle Ownership, Use, and Injury Patterns among Elementary School Children." *Pediatrics* 47, no. 6 (June 1971): 1042–1050.

Wang, Dianhai, Tianjun Feng, and Chunyan Liang. "Research on Bicycle Conversion Factors." *Transportation Research Part A: Policy and Practice* 42, no. 8 (October 2008): 1129–1139.

Ward, David C. *Charles Willson Peale: Art and Selfhood in the Early Republic*. Berkeley: University of California Press, 2004.

Ward, Geoffrey C., and Ken Burns. *Baseball: An Illustrated History*. New York: Knopf, 1994.

War History Online. "Crafty Gadgets and Famous Spies of WWII." Retrieved from warhistoryonline.com.

Warner, Patricia Campbell. *When the Girls Came Out to Play: The Birth of American Sportswear*. Amherst, MA: University of Massachusetts Press, 2006.

Warner, Sam Bass, Jr. *Streetcar Suburbs: The Process of Growth in Boston, 1870–1900*. Cambridge, MA: Harvard University Press, 1962.

Wartella, Ellen, and Sharon Mazzarella. "A Historical Comparison of Children's Use of Leisure Time." In *For Fun and Profit: The Transformation of Leisure into Consumption*, edited by Richard Butsch, 173–194. Philadelphia: Temple University Press, 1990.

Washington Post. "Army Bicyclists in Wyoming." June 30, 1897.

———. "Bar Bows on Shorts Issue." May 11, 1991.

———. "Bike Riders Beware." April 20, 1974.

———. "The Cycle of Change." April 25, 1986.

———. "The Death of a Fad." December 16, 1906.

———. "Impress of Wheel on the Face." *Washington Post*, June 28, 1896.

———. "Ping-Pong Face the Latest." March 16, 1902.

———. "P. T. Barnum Under Arrest." April 3, 1883.
———. "Soldiers to Use Bicycles." September 20, 1891.
———. "Workers who Wheel and What They Gain." April 7, 1907.
Watson, John F. *Annals of Philadelphia*. Philadelphia: Carey and Hart, 1930.
Watts, Steven. *The People's Tycoon: Henry Ford and the American Century*. New York: Vintage, 2006.
Weber, Bruce. "Morton Gottlieb, a Broadway Producer, Dies at 88." *New York Times*, June 27, 2007.
Welter, Barbara. "The Cult of True Womanhood: 1820–1860." *American Quarterly* 18, no. 2 (Summer 1966): 151–174.
Westcott, Lucy. "More Americans Moving to Cities." Retrieved from thewire.com.
Western Spy, August 14, 1819.
Western Wheel Works. "Crescent Bicycles." *Youth's Companion*, March 22, 1894.
Westfield Manufacturing Company. *Westfield Columbia-Built Bicycles*. Catalogue, 1941.
Wheel and Cycling Trade Review. "The First 'Pneumatic' in America." June 20, 1890.
———. "When Flying Machines Replace Bicycles." April 29, 1892.
White, Paul Dudley. "Expert Cites Gains in Heart Studies." *Chicago Daily Tribune*, October 30, 1955.
Whitten, David O. "The Depression of 1893." Retrieved from eh.net.
Whorton, James C. "The Hygiene of the Wheel: An Episode in Victorian Sanitary Science." *Bulletin of the History of Medicine* 52, no. 1 (Spring 1978): 61–88.
Wilcox, Julius. "Ladies' Bicycles." *Bicycling World*, March 30, 1888.
Willard, Frances E. *A Wheel within a Wheel: How I Learned to Ride the Bicycle, with Some Reflections along the Way*. New York: Revell, 1895.
Williams, Henry Smith. "The Bicycle in Relation to Health." *Harper's Weekly*, April 11, 1896.
Wimshurst, Ed, and Clare Wimshurst. "16th–18th Feb—Vietnam—Phon Nha Ke Bang National Park." Retrieved from cledward.wordpress.com.
Wood, Daniel B. "U.S. Crime Rate at Lowest Point in Decades." *Christian Science Monitor*, January 9, 2012.
Woodland, Leo. "It's ALL About the Bike." Retrieved from crazyguyonabike.com.

Wright, Orville, and Wilbur Wright. "The Wright Brothers' Aëroplane." *Century*, September 1908.

Wright, Wilbur. "Otto Lilienthal." *Aero Club of America Bulletin*, September 1912.

———. "Some Aeronautical Experiments." *Journal of the Western Society of Engineers*, December 1901. In *Annual Report of the Board of Regents of the Smithsonian Institution*, 133–148. Washington, DC: Government Printing Office, 1903.

Young, Michael E. "Soldiers in the Shadows." *Fort Lauderdale Sun-Sentinel*, May 29, 1994.

Youth's Companion. "Lovell's Boys' or Girls' $35.00 Safety Bicycle." June 11, 1891.

Zeman, Theodore J., ed. *The Greenwood Encyclopedia of Daily Life in America*. Westport, CT: Greenwood, 2009.

INDEX